Fighting on the Home Front

Fighting on the Home Front

The Legacy of Women in World War One

Kate Adie

W F HOWES LTD

This large print edition published in 2014 by
W F Howes Ltd
Unit 4, Rearsby Business Park, Gaddesby Lane,
Rearsby, Leicester LE7 4YH

1 3 5 7 9 10 8 6 4 2

First published in the United Kingdom in 2013
by Hodder & Stoughton

A CIP catalogue record for this book is available
from the British Library

ISBN 978 1 47125 425 3

Typeset by Palimpsest Book Production Limited,
Falkirk, Stirlingshire
Printed and bound by
CPI Group (UK) Ltd, Croydon, CR0 4YY

CONTENTS

CHAPTER 1

THE HOME FRONT

In the days when much of the globe was coloured pink and Victoria was not only a queen but an empress, war happened far away: the British Empire's battles were distant. Men went off to fight in places with exotic names; news came back fitfully, often long after the last shot had been fired.

In 1914, war came to the Home Front. The conflict was unavoidable and dominated every aspect of life, from whole streets of men marching off to be soldiers to the local pub having its opening hours rudely curtailed. The sound of the artillery in France could be heard from across the Channel in the fields of Kent. The sky over England saw the new flying machines arrive carrying bombs. The war was immense, like no other in memory, and the country so tested, so stretched, that for once it needed the strengths and abilities of its women – otherwise there would be no victory. They rose to the challenge, proved themselves capable, and were partly granted the vote when peace returned. But they were then also expected to give up their new jobs, return to their second-class status and forget their endeavours and achievements. However, they had achieved so much and demonstrated that they could weld, deliver the post, saw off a leg, drive a tram, entertain troops to the sound of shell-fire, read the lesson in church and play decent football in front of twenty thousand people – all previously thought utterly, completely and absolutely beyond a woman – that they left indelible footprints of a giant stride on the way to fairness and equality for their sex.

The memory of that war, though hazy for many, still hovers over the nation and over families. Schoolchildren are taken to the Flanders cemeteries to see the unending rows of white headstones. No illness in my youth was without the words: 'Your grandmother died from that flu in the Great War – now take your medicine.' Flying enthusiasts still talk warmly about the Sopwith Camel and 'string-bags'. 'It's a Long Way to Tipperary' can be hummed by millions. Family history searches turn up great-grandfathers and great-great-uncles who died very young in some corner of a foreign field that is forever England: even the poetry has embedded itself in our collective consciousness. And the reasons for that whole terrible, relentless conflict which engulfed millions are still argued about. I have reported on wars which have been violent, grisly, destructive, heart-breaking – but seem small skirmishes in comparison with descriptions of World War I. Modern military operations attract keen attention and tend to dominate because of their brutal significance and their grim drama: bombing, shells, explosions, destruction, monstrous cavalcades of death-dealing machines and the endless curiosity with the willingness to fight and to kill.

I first learned of warfare through the entirely domestic prism of a splintered walnut sideboard embedded with iron fragments, courtesy of Hitler's Luftwaffe in 1943, some years before I was born. In the 1950s, I saw fear cross neighbours' faces when the air-raid siren was occasionally tested and there were bomb-sites full of rubble and buddleia to play in. My childhood was full of the echoes of World War II – and my family lived a long way from any battlefield. So I brought to my reporting a sense that war affected everyone, even if they were not in uniform and had never heard a shot fired. Looking at the Great War – as World War I was initially known – I was curious about what happened to all those who were enjoined to 'keep the home fires burning'. What did the war demand of women – and how did they respond? Maids and duchesses, housewives and young girls. The nurse, the student, the factory worker, the suffragette. How did the war change lives at home? If we remember the millions of men who sacrificed their lives, what should we remember about those who fought on the Home Front?

CHAPTER 2

DRUMBEATS AND FEATHERS

There is something about the human spirit which glows brighter in the face of adversity: in other words, there's nothing like going to a dance or watching a film while there's a war on – something that fundamentalist fighters like the Taliban have never grasped. They close places of entertainment and ban music: they'll never win.

Even so, it comes as something of a surprise how determinedly people enjoy themselves between bombing raids and queuing for scarce food. And the sound of a wartime popular song is possibly more evocative than the sound of gunfire or an air-raid siren.

A hundred years on from their composition, the strains of 'Keep the Home Fires Burning' and 'It's a Long Way to Tipperary' are still familiar. They are ghosts of wartime, able to summon up images and family stories. Few of the plays, comedies and films of the time have survived, and even the famous artistes who sang the songs have faded from memory. But the songs linger, perhaps because this was the first war which was entwined with popular culture. Ordinary people could afford a ticket to the music hall, and women went as enthusiastically as men to see and hear the risqué, the titillating, the saucy – it may not have been for the upper-class matrons, but it was a rich diet for those on tiny incomes who had a hard life. It was fun, sociable, sometimes thrilling – acrobats and magicians – and the big national stars were just across the footlights. The audience were encouraged to sing along with the orchestra, and it was a great night out.

Scan any newspaper from the days of World War I. On the front pages, solemn despatches about military setbacks and casualty lists sit side by side with columns of theatre, music hall and 'kinema' advertisements. In a single town, the sheer number of establishments operating is testimony to the part played by entertainers to sustain normality and bolster morale. It also represents the way propaganda got into bed with popular culture.

In November 1917 in Newcastle, the Tyne Theatre was trumpeting a New Musical Comedy – albeit with the rather unlikely title *My Uncle the JP* – and George Bernard Shaw's *Pygmalion* was on in the following week. As was the D'Oyly Carte Opera Company at the Theatre Royal, which was presently hosting 'Miss Violette Melmotte's Entire Company in a New Farcical Comedy entitled *What a Catch*'. The Palace Theatre had 'A New Drama of Industrial Life – *A Pitman's Daughter*'. Escapist dramas and musical revues dominated;

woven into the musical entertainment were popular songs such as ‘Keep the Home Fires Burning,’ Ivor Novello’s overnight hit of 1914 which never failed to stir civilian audiences. Although the theatre was regarded as generally out of reach of the poor, in the largest provincial playhouses a seat in the gods on a hard bench was cheap and the scarlet and gold decor gave everyone a sense of living it up and forgetting the hard slog of factory work. Additionally, the view that theatrical life in general was not particularly ‘respectable’ had begun to wane: spirits needed to be cheered and women were welcomed to occupy seats left empty by the men who were away. Theatre fliers promised ‘Tearooms and Popular Prices’.

Music hall had had a revival with the advent of war and touring companies of actors, musicians and dancers knew the railway timetables almost by heart, as they criss-crossed the country in order to appear ‘twice nightly with extra matinees’. In 1917, the ‘Great Character Actor’ Bransby Williams was appearing at the Newcastle Hippodrome and the Empire Theatre had an All-Star Programme including the Ten Tommies, though behind the bill-board posters the war was never far away. Bransby Williams had lost his son, a nineteen-year-old captain, only three months earlier and the Ten Tommies were a troupe of ex-soldiers, billed as having between them spent ‘100 weeks in hospital.’ The Sunderland Empire was bringing the war to its audiences by presenting a re-enactment of a

British submarine attacking a German dreadnought, with a full-size replica of the submarine on stage.

The cinema business was like a noisy teenager, the new kid on the block, full of extravagant claims and longing to be taken seriously. At the start of the war, with seats in the stalls at threepence or less, it was still regarded as the 'poor man's theatre', but it too was gaining respectability. Over the course of the war the middle classes had an excuse to head for the local 'flea-pit', as many a picture house was known: the new-fangled newsreels and the government's propaganda films were the seal of approval on a seat in the back stalls (or more likely the circle upstairs for the more prosperous), and by the end of the war 'going to the pictures' would dominate popular culture.

In November 1917, the five main cinemas in Newcastle reflected the mixture of fighting and frivolity: the Empire Cinema was showing Charlie Chaplin in *Behind the Screen*, while the Queen's Hall was screening an American propaganda epic: '*Womanhood, the Glory of the Nation* – a Militant Spectacle!' Down at the Westgate Picture House there was extravagant promotion for a fantasy film shot in Hawaii: '*The Bottle Imps* – a Wonderfully Exciting Tale of a Wishing-Bottle, Featuring the Eminent Japanese Actor Sessue Hayakawa: Thrilling Plot, Terrific Excitement'. 'A Magnificent Programme', enthused the billboards, 'with the Latest War and Topical Pictures'.

For those who still held to the Edwardian view

that the cinema was a suspiciously decadent place where lower-class men and women sat together in the dark, the turning point was the film *The Battle of the Somme*. Produced in 1916, it was a relatively straightforward account of trench warfare at its worst and most destructive of human life. Although filmed by officially sanctioned cinematographers, the censors removed some of the most horrific scenes; however, and despite being silent, it was a graphic record which did not dodge the realities of fighting. It was a huge success, with 20 million tickets sold in the first few weeks of distribution. It gave those women who flocked to picture houses, most of whom were not expected to enquire into the violent details of battlefield activity, a novel and shocking experience. The Prime Minister Lloyd George's secretary, Frances Stevenson, was one of them:

> We went on Wednesday night to a private view of the 'Somme films' i.e. the pictures taken during the recent fighting. To say that one enjoyed them would be untrue; but I am glad I went. I am glad I have seen the sort of thing our men have to go through, even to the sortie from the trench, and the falling in the barbed wire. There were pictures too of the battlefield after the fight, & of our gallant men lying all crumpled up & helpless. There were pictures of men mortally wounded being carried out of the

> communication trenches, with the look of agony on their faces . . . I shall never forget. It was like going through a tragedy.

But whatever the pull of the cinema and theatre, the music hall artistes were still the biggest stars, the celebrities of their day; they toured, attracting huge audiences who often joined them in song. They were able to connect very directly and personally with their admirers: just the people to help with the war effort, especially recruitment.

The standard methods – national appeals, posters and military bands outside recruiting offices – produced three hundred thousand men in the first month of the war. The recruits poured in, the length and breadth of the land, with thirty-three thousand enlisting on just a single day in September 1914. Local meetings, speeches by politicians and the iconic poster 'Your Country Needs You', featuring the Secretary of State for War, Lord Kitchener, pointing his finger, were aimed at recruiting able-bodied male volunteers. Very quickly, though, women were directly appealed to by the government: 'Women of Britain Say Go' was the blunt message plastered on walls, lamp-posts and public transport, with an elegant mother and her family proudly watching soldiers march away. 'Why is your Best Boy not in Khaki?' challenged young women to pressure their boyfriends and husbands, adding, 'If your young man neglects his King and Country, the time will come when he will neglect you.' Different areas of the country tailored the message: 'Women of Lancashire – do you realise if you keep back a son or sweetheart you are prolonging the war and adding to the peril of those who have gone?' It was relentless: 'To the Women of Britain – some of your menfolk are holding back on your account. Won't you prove your love for your Country by persuading them to go?' Posters reached a huge audience; the tone of many was not so much an order but a call to examine your conscience, to feel a moral obligation. As women were commonly considered to be the more moral and virtuous side of society, they were the target.

In earlier wars, women had stood by while their menfolk went off to war. Their almost immediate inclusion in the official recruiting campaigns was recognition (somewhat back-handed) that they had influence. It also implied that they bore responsibility. That their image was now appearing in official literature was another development. In newspapers and magazines of the time, their portrayal was mainly in fashion adverts, a singularly large number of which involved underwear. Society grandes dames, the royal family and well-known actresses were photographed at public events, but by today's standards there were few, if any, pictures of housewives, servants or ordinary women workers who were in news stories. Before the war, suffragettes in their campaign for the vote often got the sneering lens on them: much of the press portrayed them not as brave, but as badly behaved. In typical style, the *Morning Post* carried a story a couple of months before the outbreak of war, when a suffragette meeting at Streatham Common in London had been disrupted by three young men: 'There were ugly rushes to get at the women speakers . . . and an effort on the part of the young men of Streatham to put the militants in the pond.' In reporting the court hearing, the paper blithely emphasized the magistrate's view that 'it was impossible to shut one's eyes to the fact that the behaviour of these women had created a strong feeling of resentment and disgust'. The three defendants were discharged, and the story was headlined 'Public Indignation'. It did not need to add 'At the Women's Behaviour'.

Inevitably, when a government passed legislation or introduced social change, it addressed men. Women were seen as wives, daughters, mothers – not as individuals. The suffragettes' actions before the war highlighted the palpable dislike in some quarters of having to deal directly with women on serious matters. Some men felt uncomfortable doing so, others found it demeaning – attitudes which are still found today in societies in which women are second-class citizens. I've experienced it myself in front of Saudi minor royals, Afghan warlords and Iranian clerics: you are invisible, you don't matter, your voice doesn't count, it's embarrassing to treat you seriously. As one cameraman once observed: 'He's looking at you as if you were the cat – and he wouldn't be caught dead talking to his cat in public.'

In the first few weeks of the war, when public emotions were high and decisions taken abruptly, the involvement of women pushed open a door – a few inches – to greater acceptance. It was a door that the suffragettes had had to hammer on for years. But now the women were needed.

The nearest a woman got to being treated favourably if she dared emulate a man was on stage. Cross-dressing had a long tradition in the theatre, though it mainly involved men in women's clothes. But in 1914 a woman dressed in khaki evolved into a recruiting sergeant.

Vesta Tilley was the most famous and highest-paid music hall star of the day. Having first appeared on stage impersonating a well-known male opera singer in 1870 at the age of six, she was given full rein to her particular talents by the outbreak of war.

She came from a theatrical family, and early in her career decided to stick with male impersonation, saying, 'I felt I could express myself better if I were dressed as a boy.' As she grew older she refined her act, rehearsing meticulously and dressing with great care and attention. Indeed, she became something of a role model for men's fashions. In the music hall there had always been a tradition for tilting at convention and her fame grew at a time when women's clothes could not have been further from the male silhouette, sometimes with the aim of emphasizing the 'unbridgeable gulf' between the sexes. Even though simpler and more practical styles were being introduced at the turn of the twentieth century, corsets, long skirts and rigid dress codes persisted.

Not surprisingly, women liked Vesta as much as men when she strolled jauntily on stage in male evening dress – top hat, tails and cane. It was public knowledge that she pursued authenticity by wearing male undergarments. She was daring and she looked smart; she was famous and very well paid – the antithesis of the Victorian view that decent women should neither have nor desire a public life. She appeared in judge's robes, as a curate and a policeman, and created characters such as Burlington Bertie and Piccadilly Johnnie – men-about-town, stage-door johnnies, the metrosexuals of their age. She dressed in both a sailor's and a soldier's uniform long before the war started, and sang 'Jolly good luck to the girl who loves a soldier' as early as 1906 – always using her own soprano voice, never resorting to a 'false bass'. Off-stage, she was noted for dressing as 'a womanly woman', pretty and neat, described as always 'very tender to a loving husband', Walter de Frece, who wrote many of her songs.

Immediately the war began, the call went out for volunteers to enlist. Lord Kitchener announced that he wanted half a million men to join up – and soon doubled that figure; he then asked for more. Nearly two and a half million men were to take the King's Shilling in the next eighteen months.

Initial recruitment took place in a frenzy and the world of show business joined in, with the stars of the music hall including patriotic songs in their acts. Vesta Tilley went further: she actually recruited. And to counter the prevailing popularity of the navy, in a country where small boys were frequently dressed in sailor suits, she chose to emphasize the ordinary soldier. Khaki became her signature colour. And as thousands of young men were donning uniform she became a perfectionist, honing the details of her military appearance: 'When I sang "Six Days' Leave", I went to Victoria Station to watch troops come in – to see how they took their packs off. For this song I was kindly allowed by the War Office to have on the stage with me several huge Guardsmen.' She had a wooden gun as a prop which she complained wouldn't make the right noise when it was banged on the floor. The next evening, one of the Guardsmen presented her with a regulation service rifle – which she politely declined. 'Better have it, miss', he said, 'because I can't possibly put it back. . . . We couldn't bear to see you so upset about your little wooden gun.' She accepted it, only to hear a few months later that her 'gallant supplier of weapons' had been killed in France.

But this in no way affected her remarkable determination to make her act a tool of recruiting. She recalled later that she selected her 'war songs solely for their cheery nature' and was proud of her active role in getting men to volunteer by singing 'The Army of Today's All Right', saying that it was 'instrumental in obtaining many recruits before Conscription was enforced, and the War Office used the latter for a poster asking for volunteers – in Hackney, in one week, I enlisted a battalion'. She had invited all the eligible young men in the audience to come up to the stage and enlist, assisted by Horatio Bottomley, a colourful some-time MP, swindler, journalist, jail-bird and indefatigable recruiter. He duly carried the message to other actors and actresses at a meeting in the Savoy Hotel, where he stated that 'Miss Tilley obtained three hundred recruits – now called the Vesta Tilley Platoon.'

Other artistes had already taken up the military refrain: Marie Lloyd, famed for her earthy innuendo, was hugely popular among the working-class women about whose lives she sang. She was now touring the halls with:

> I didn't like you much before you joined
> the army, John,
> But I do like you now, cockie, now
> you've got your khaki on . . .

Florrie Forde, an ebullient Australian star and queen of the sing-along, had audiences in full voice with 'Pack Up Your Troubles in Your Old Kit Bag' and 'Tipperary'. Paul Ruben's rallying cry 'Your King and Country Want You' was sung by many. But Vesta Tilley added a dash of brio, belting out the lyrics while marching:

We've watched you playing cricket and
every kind of game,
At football, golf and polo you men have
made your name.
But now your country calls you to play
your part in war.
And no matter what befalls you
We shall love you all the more.
So come and join the forces
As your fathers did before.

Oh, we don't want to lose you but we
think you ought to go.
For your King and your country need
you so.
We shall want you and miss you
But with all our might and main
We shall cheer you, thank you, bless you
When you come home again.

She toured military hospitals in Britain and raised money for rehabilitation schemes; she performed at the Coliseum Theatre in London through a Zeppelin raid, describing this as a 'thrilling experience'. As the war progressed she projected the character of the soldier as someone who would be ready for what was wanted of him and would see the job through. She was not mawkish or sentimental and was known for her grace and charm, keeping her hold on audiences for the duration and never shy about her nickname of 'Britain's Best Recruiting Sergeant'.

Vesta retired after the war when her husband – knighted, most probably for *her* efforts – became an MP. She was remembered with affection and respect, in contrast to another enthusiastic recruiter and widely read writer, Jessie Pope. Where Tilley had flavoured her recruitment with humour and a touch of satire, Pope began an outpouring of poems which took patriotism up several notches. She was a pioneering journalist whose articles were eagerly consumed in the *Daily Mail*, the *Daily Express* and *Punch* magazine and her poems earned her both wartime praise and eventually the charge of jingoism:

> 'Who's for the trench—
> Are you, my laddie?
> Who'll follow French—
> Will you, my laddie?
> Who's fretting to begin,
> Who's going out to win?
> And who wants to save his skin—
> Do you, my laddie?

Pope now evokes little admiration; however, around the figure cut by Vesta Tilley there is still a warm glow. Her obituary in the *Times* recalled that 'her power of creating a character was such that no one who saw . . . her walk across the stage as the absurd little red-coated recruit with the large cigar, in her song about "the girl who loves a soldier", is ever likely to forget the picture.'

Whether she altered women's perceptions of themselves as she cleverly poked fun at men – while dressed as one – is difficult to judge. She pushed boundaries: in late Victorian times her audiences would probably never have seen a woman show her legs in public, and even during the war there were numerous complaints about the practical clothes that women were adopting for jobs such as shovelling coke and cleaning trains. She was a high-profile celebrity in today's terms and successfully managed to avoid the pitfalls of working-class girls making their way in what was still considered the sleazy, none too respectable 'life on the halls'. Her fans adored her, though she protested that she 'was puzzled' by the fascination she exerted. Whether they were inspired by her is hard to discern; she never suggested for a moment that women should be in uniform and heading for the trenches. Perhaps a kitchenmaid in the gallery impressed by her sheer glamour, talent and success went away with the thought that it was at least possible for a woman to achieve such heights.

One aspect of Tilley's performances reflected a wider campaign, carried out almost exclusively by women, to winkle out unwilling recruits. There are a number of reported instances of white feathers being handed out to men who failed to come forward and sign up at her performances.

The 'White Feather' campaign had quickly assumed a contentious place in the recruitment drive. Although its originator was a man, it was wholly associated with women. The idea of relying on volunteers instead of introducing conscription impelled a retired admiral, Charles Penrose Fitzgerald, to found an organization which would target men apparently reluctant to enlist. He chose women to undertake his mission, and within a couple of weeks of the start of the war, on 30 August 1914, thirty women went on to the streets of Folkestone in Kent armed with white feathers to give to able-bodied men not in uniform.

The driving force of the Order of the White Feather was shame: the feather stood for cowardice. In a society in which 'manliness' was the backbone of a boy's education and which accepted masculinity as a superior kind of behaviour, the very notion that a man might dodge his duty was a powerful insult. Manliness embodied not only physical strength and courage, but also honour and a sense of duty.

On 5 September, the *Chatham Times* reported excitedly that 'an amusing, novel and forceful method of obtaining recruits for Lord Kitchener's Army was demonstrated at Deal on Tuesday'. The town crier had been walking the streets and, 'crying with the dignity of his ancient calling, gave forth the startling announcement: "Oyez! Oyez!! Oyez!!! The White Feather Brigade! Ladies wanted to present the young men of Deal and Walmer . . .

the Order of the White Feather for shirking their duty in not coming forward to uphold the Union Jack of Old England! God save the King."'

The admiral was joined by another enthusiast, Baroness Orczy, already a well-known author due to the success of her Scarlet Pimpernel novels. A month into the war, her article in the *Daily Mail* was addressed to the 'Women and Girls of England'. Understatement was not her style:

> Your hour has come! The great hour when to the question which you yourselves have asked incessantly these few weeks past: 'I want to do something – what can I do?' your country has at last given answer. . . . Women and girls of England, you cannot shoulder a rifle, but you can actively serve your country all the same. You can serve her in the way she needs it most. Give her the men whom she wants! Give her your sweetheart, she wants him; your son, your brother, she wants them! Your friends, she wants them all!

And several more paragraphs before she reaches the key word: '. . . what English mother is there who would see her son called for ever after by that terrible name "Coward!"'

Her Women of England's Active Service League attracted twenty thousand members, who took a pledge not to be seen in the company of a man 'who had not answered his country's call'. Much was made of a small ad. which appeared in the *Times* on 8 July 1915: 'Jack F.G., if you are not in khaki by the 20th, I shall cut you dead – Ethel M.'

Stories abounded of men being cornered, confronted, stopped in the street and getting feathers tucked in their hatbands or their lapels by women who looked at them contemptuously. It is not possible to estimate how common the practice was; however, it is an image which caused considerable debate across the country. The idea had its roots in the increasing popularity of 'flag days', when respectable ladies with a tray of miniature flags or emblems politely stopped strangers in the street and asked for a donation in return for them pinning one to a jacket. Quite daring for Edwardian times, but it caught on as a very profitable way of raising funds. However, the white feather gesture was giving rise to reservations – particularly about its consequences. There is no doubt that some men who were not fit for active service felt themselves disgraced and quickly enlisted; others joined who should have remained in jobs which were deemed essential war work. But as the war turned out not to be short and 'over by Christmas', injured soldiers returning from the front found themselves horrified recipients of a feather; not the least of these was a young man who had changed into a suit having just returned from being decorated with the Victoria

Cross at Buckingham Palace by King George V. By 1916 the government was issuing badges to workers in state industries and the civil service and to honourably discharged wounded men: the campaign had caused unease.

At the time – and subsequently – arguments about the motivation of the women who took part in this activity were divided. Was it driven only by pure patriotism, or was it a chance to shame men? Was it an instinctive response to a situation where women were unable to have any part in the 'manly' and 'heroic' gestures open to men who wished to serve their country? Many of the women were described in articles as 'shrill' and 'cruel'. Others were dismissed as silly young girls. It was put about that some had been militant suffragettes, provoking more disapproval.

On the other hand, many women embraced the chance to participate in recruitment, whether or not it served government propaganda. The country was not about to be invaded: indeed, there was initially a sense that the Home Front would not be too directly involved in the conflict – it was a fight far away, to be fought only by men, and there was no suggestion that women should alter their feminine ways and perhaps gain opportunities because of it. Urging them to get involved in recruitment was highlighting their persuasive side and reinforcing their home-centred role: the government saw no reason to alter the status quo. But it was a novel appeal that they should personally do something for their country. As the reasons for the war were not universally clear to each citizen, the message had to be one with an emphasis on duty – to family, to country, to an all-embracing idea of a way of life that was under threat. Women responded – and the figures of Vesta Tilley in army uniform and a woman brandishing a white feather were just part of what was expected of women and what was acceptable to men.

CHAPTER 3

INTO THE LINE OF FIRE

'Don't put your hand down the back of the sofa.' It seemed to me, as a small child, yet another confusing remark about bad manners. Later came the equally baffling explanation that most of the living room window was down there. It took a careful description of a night in 1943, well before I was born, to bring a little sense to these remarks. During World War II the German Luftwaffe had dropped thousand-pound bombs just behind our back gate, and glass from every window had arrowed into the soft furnishings. In post-war Britain, sofas were expensive and hard to come by. The injured furniture had to be tolerated – but there was no hunting for anything that had slipped between the cushions. That Herr Hitler had had such a personal effect on our lifestyle was emphasized by my parents rather obtusely insisting that our greenhouse had been the Germans' objective. The pride and joy of Wilfrid, my adoptive father, and source of a few precious tomatoes during rationing, it had disintegrated completely.

Small children, even though playing in peacetime

among bomb-sites, get a curious view of war. It has obviously had a major impact on the lives of every parent you meet, but seems incomprehensible. However, the fact that you are led to believe your own greenhouse – a totally unwarlike object – was a prime target leaves you with a sense that war can come very close indeed, even when you are not a soldier and you are far from battlefields. I soon also learned that people had been killed just a few doors down. There were gaps in the row of semi-detached houses behind us. Our greenhouse was a minor casualty: other unwarlike buildings had been destroyed and non-soldiering people had been killed.

This may seem a trivial view of horrendous conflict, but all of us can read and learn of momentous events and yet, though moved by them, have no genuine understanding of the fear or shock involved until it comes to our own doorstep. Nor are we usually aware that society around us may change because of such an event.

In the nineteenth century, imperial Britain fought far from home. Soldiering was almost exclusively in foreign climes and news of conflict came back slowly, to be digested long after the battle was over. Unlike many European countries, the British had experienced no invasion of their soil since a French attempt was thwarted by the Welsh at Fishguard Bay in 1797. We sat on our island, maintained a large navy, and felt safe.

There had been conjecture among politicians and

military men about a new form of warfare, probably involving some kind of air attack, well before World War I began. But the general public was not looking to the skies and expecting trouble from that direction. And certainly not young Wilfrid Adie, who was one of the people who got the shock of their lives when the Germans paid a call on his home town of Sunderland – in a Zeppelin airship. As a schoolboy he witnessed one of the major instruments of social change in that war: the shocking impact of airborne violence and destruction visited on ordinary families and their homes.

Wilfrid's father, James, was the engineer in charge of sea-trials at Doxford's, one of Sunderland's large shipyards. He was fascinated by all things mechanical, and was hoping to own a car some day. He took pride in the great engines turned out by Doxford's, and assumed, like most of his generation, that as long as British seapower remained formidable our coasts would not be under threat. Towards the evening of Saturday, 1 April 1916, father and son went for a walk on the cliffs just south of the town. They wouldn't have been aware that an alert had been ordered by the police, as a result of which the electric lighting had been dimmed throughout the town. Standing in a quiet field, looking at the sea, they both heard the throb of the engines of *L11*. Wilfrid's shock was tempered by his father's gasped admiration for the huge grey Zeppelin. James had never seen a flying machine of any kind in the air before and was enraptured by the sight. Had he been a more imaginative man, he might have wondered where it was bound: nowhere specific, it turned out, as twenty-seven bombs rained down on the tram depot, a school, part of a train station and several houses. Twenty-two people were killed and twenty-five seriously injured, and over a hundred had minor injuries. Wilfrid remembered people describing the crew leaning out of the gondola and seeing them drop the bombs. The town was agog with tales of narrow escapes, including a bomb punching a hole in a wall, dropping on a bed and failing to explode, much to the relief of the woman in the bed.

The airship's captain, Viktor Schutze, was mightily pleased with the raid: 'The effect was grand; blocks of houses and rows of streets collapsed entirely; large fires broke out in places and a dense black cloud, from which sparks flew high, was caused by one bomb.' When the local gun battery south of Sunderland opened up he headed off to Middlesbrough to do some more damage. There, twenty-two people were killed and over a hundred injured. Women and children and a baby were among the victims. James Adie, like almost everyone else in Sunderland, was speechless and could find no way of explaining to his son what had happened. This was home, not the battlefield in France.

The local paper was nervously restrained in its coverage, heading its stories as 'passed by the censor', referring only to 'a north-east town' and minimizing the casualties. This contrasted with the reactions to German naval bombardments in the same area a year and a half earlier, which had been almost hysterical: no one knew quite how to cope with the extraordinary situation of ordinary citizens now appearing to be on the front line. Fury? Stoicism? Disgust at 'despicable behaviour by the Huns'? Anger at lack of defence by the Royal Navy? Invaluable propaganda against the Germans? What *was* agreed was that a new term was emerging: the Home Front. The kind of danger which soldiers were expected to face was now confronting their families at home. The government was meant to protect civilians: it found itself cornered by the frightening new situation, which was changing the nature of war.

In December 1914, the shelling of Old and West Hartlepool, Scarborough and Whitby had had an impact far further and greater than the high explosive which fell on the streets. 'Hartlepools, the Greatest Sufferers – Terrific Rain of Shells – Serious Loss of Life', reported the *Hartlepool Gazette.* Over a thousand shells had been fired at the town from three German warships creeping out of the early morning mist. A hundred and two people died, including fifteen children. The hour-long attack caused panic as no one knew whether it was safer to shelter indoors or to head for public parks. More than three hundred houses were damaged, along with seven churches and five hotels.

The first military casualty of the war to be killed on British soil was Private Theophilus Jones, a soldier in the Durham Light Infantry who was manning one of the town's gun batteries when it was hit. Shortly afterwards a seventeen-year-old tailoress, Hilda Horsley, who was on her way to work, may have been the first woman to die. Or perhaps it was one of two women, Annie and Florence Kay, who lived on the upper floor of a house near the battery which was hit: 'Two maiden ladies lived there. One of them was in the passage making for her sister's bedroom, possibly disturbed by the noise outside. The shot struck one sister, inflicting terrible wounds in the chest and killing her instantly. When neighbours went, after the bombardment, to search for the second sister, they did not find her. Careful exploration of the wreckage has showed later she had been literally blown to bits.'

Alongside fifty male civilians and some soldiers at the battery, the published list of casualties names fifty women including an eighty-six-year-old; also six-month-old Eleanor Necy and several schoolchildren. There was no argument that this was mere 'collateral damage', in today's terms. The Hartlepools would have achieved more fame had not further German battle cruisers been steaming towards the popular seaside resort of Scarborough – the 'Brighton of the North' – whose inhabitants were just sitting down to breakfast. Puzzled by the sounds 'cracking overhead', many ran into the streets; a good number headed for the station, while some, terrified and wanting to head out of town, made for open fields.

Other just sat at home, completely baffled as to what was happening. The fashionable Grand Hotel, high on the cliffs, was hit several times; the lighthouse, the coastguard station, the already ruined castle and numerous houses were shelled. Eighteen people were killed. The fishing port of Whitby was next: there were three casualties, and the ancient ruined abbey lost a bit more stonework.

Statistically, only a tiny number of people perished on home territory compared to the mass slaughter already evident in the trenches. However, the newspaper reports of the time could match today's in personal detail and outraged description. Babies who were killed in their mothers' arms while fleeing the shells, tragic discoveries of schoolboys beneath the ruins, young women horrifically injured. This was not how war should be fought. Civilians, women and children in particular, were not part of the conventional equation – the military at war, shielding civilians at home. However, if civilians became enemy casualties, they became muddled up in actual warfare.

In December 1914, censorship was not yet operating to curb information with the intention of keeping up morale. There were graphic descriptions of the damage and numerous photographs of wreckage and victims. The impact on the country was enormous: Hartlepool suffered more, but was an industrial centre and couldn't match the fame of the 'Queen of the North'. Scarborough was symbolic: a pleasant place associated with beaches and parks and holidays. It became a rallying cry: 'Remember Scarborough!' There were recriminations about the lack of naval defence, and demands that people remain calm and confident in the face of adversity, but Scarborough's suffering was proving to be a very fruitful piece of propaganda: the beastliness of the Germans, killing women and children; their lack of scruples.

The posters went up almost immediately. One depicted Britannia leading young men to defend a town in flames. Another demanded: 'Men of Britain will you stand this' above a pile of rubble – a photograph from the local paper. 'Enlist Now!' cried yet another, with the reminder that 'the Germans who brag of their "Culture" have shown what it is made of by murdering defenceless women and children at Scarborough. But this only strengthens Great Britain's resolve to crush the German Barbarians.' It had the desired effect, with worldwide publicity and increased recruitment nationwide. There were local appeals: 'Men of Yorkshire, Join the New Army and avenge the Murder of innocent women and children in Scarborough, Hartlepool and Whitby. Shew the enemy that Yorkshire will exact a full penalty for this Cowardly Slaughter.' (In the towns themselves, Hartlepool had an immense rush to the colours but Scarborough was somewhat less enthusiastic, over six thousand mainly wealthy people having departed after the raids.)

Realization slowly dawned that if the Germans

showed no sign of stopping, and if the British defences were unable to safeguard civilians, then everyone was at war. Part of the outrage had its roots in the international conventions about 'open towns': places with no military significance or defensive emplacements were considered out of bounds in combat. However, well before the war started there were good indications that newer forms of warfare might challenge such agreements. The submarine was already a new worry, and the arrival of the Zeppelins over Britain added to it. Your home wasn't safe. The people who were working to help keep the army supplied at the front line were now in danger themselves. Munitions plants were targets – and they had huge female workforces. Panic on the streets had to be controlled: women and children were going to have to become part of a national effort to defy the enemy in their own town centre or village. The women were needed to keep the country going in a huge range of jobs. And some of them were going to be killed. For the first time, women – even if only as victims – were involved in the same kind of violence as the men in uniform. This changed their status in war: it became just a little more obvious that they had no say in going to war, yet were dying in it.

CHAPTER 4

MAKE YOURSELF USEFUL

The beginning of the war saw an explosion of energy which was immediately channelled into thousands of volunteer projects. Women who had had time on their hands as frustrated non-working middle-class wives were ready to organize and fund-raise. There was an army of experienced charity workers, battalions of women who saw their duty as service to others, ranks of bazaar veterans and untold numbers of knitting and sewing experts. Added to this were the hardened warriors of the suffrage movement, skilled at publicity, public speaking and confronting prejudice. It was not a sudden awakening, but a loud call to arms.

It took a little time for the reasons for their energetic enthusiasm to be examined properly – nearly all of it was at first ascribed to patriotism. A good two years later the newspaper proprietor Lord Northcliffe, always keen to put his finger on the popular pulse, ventured to observe that 'the war has proved that woman has not been given her opportunity in most parts of the Empire. For some years, her cause was obscured by the hysteria of the Suffragettes. Today it begins to look as if the votes-for-women demonstrations were but manifestations of the tremendous pent-up energy of more than half the nation.'

Upper-class women seemed to dominate the first few months of frenzied activity: titles were sprayed across announcements of the formation of committees and leagues and societies; not surprisingly, considering that they had confidence, expected to be taken note of, and were used to being patrons, chairwomen and presidents of a raft of charities and welfare organizations. At the top of the social tree, a remarkable number were related: marriage and breeding was still a highly selective activity according to rank and lineage: the gene pool was pretty concentrated. Their husbands, fathers and brothers were active in politics, diplomacy and national institutions; business was still considered slightly unpleasant, though great inroads had been made into the House of Lords by successful Victorian entrepreneurs. The net result was that string-pulling took place across the dining table, at social soirées, in quiet words with in-laws and with friendly letters to a social circle which included very 'useful' people. What we would now call networking was already in place for these women: they were, of course, excluded from the male-only decision-making enclaves which dominated public life and private clubs, but they were able to use their family and social connections to such men to great advantage.

Lady Lugard had not led a conventionally sheltered life. In Victorian times, as Flora Shaw, she had travelled the world as the Colonial Editor of the *Times* newspaper, specialized in politics and economics, championed the cause of empire and invented the name of a country – Nigeria. She married Lord Lugard who became Governor of Hong Kong, and later Governor-General of Nigeria. Intelligent, opinionated and energetic, she embodied a can-do attitude which pushed against traditional barriers: she had proposed travelling through Africa from the Cape to Cairo in 1899, and informed her editor that 'I really have a practical gift for travelling without hurting myself. The reason is that I am able to make myself thoroughly comfortable everywhere. When I slept soundly on shingle in the Klondike, the men told me that I ought to try sand, which, they say, is the hardest thing there is. Obviously the desert is required to complete my experience.' Being fully aware – in a rather unorthodox manner – of the need to sleep soundly, she embraced the challenge of organizing accommodation for refugees in the war's first civilian emergency.

The outbreak of war brought an almost immediate flight of refugees from Belgium. No one had expected them – and certainly not a massive exodus – but the news from across the Channel was so shocking that the British immediately agreed to take people in. That news featured one of the major elements which caused feelings to run high:

atrocities. From the first week of the war, headlines screamed of terrible things done to the civilian population as the Germans invaded 'little Belgium'. The *Sunderland Daily News* printed a typical story: '"The Gaulois" states that the Chaplain of the 19th Army Corps, who visited a village near Roye, reports finding an eight-year-old girl nailed by the hand and the feet to the door of a house. The child was still breathing when found.' The stories grew in their gruesomeness and many were subsequently found to have no basis in truth. The atmosphere was fevered and the public both excited and scared, for demonization of an enemy is a common phenomenon in confused and frightening times. (In the first months of the Balkan War sixty years later, I listened to frequent tales of Serbian soldiers wearing 'necklaces of babies' fingers'.) Such stories serve the purpose of intensifying hatred and confirming the virtue of your own side.

Journalists based in France and those back in Britain were having immense difficulties gaining access to fighting areas in the first few weeks; standard war-reporting of military engagements was thwarted by chaotic conditions, so the vivid vignettes of brutality, which made good copy, multiplied:

> Proofs of German Barbarism: Mania of Destruction.
>
> Press Association War Special: Paris, Sunday.

A special representative of the Havas Agency, recording his impression of a tour along the front line in Lorraine, describes the irrefutable proofs of German barbarism that he saw in the hospital of Nancy.

It appears that the Germans are in the habit of mutilating defenceless wounded on the field of battle. He says that the troops are intensely anxious to march forward, notwithstanding their previous losses, because they now do what they like with the enemy.

At Berevillers he found heartrending testimony of the incomprehensible German mania of destruction. In this little town they shot 60 people, and outraged and murdered several women.

After having made themselves drunk they burnt everything down, including the Château of Lambertye, containing a collection worth several million francs.

Murder, mutilation, manic destruction and money. The press lapped it up. Nevertheless, there were undoubtedly many horrifying incidents in Belgium, and when the first refugees arrived from across the Channel the information came first-hand. People burned out of their homes brought eye-witness reports – it later transpired that around twenty-five thousand buildings had been destroyed not in fighting, but as a result of wanton arson.

However, no one was expecting the Belgians to come so quickly, nor in such numbers.

Lady Lugard had already decided that 'something must be done' on 17 August. Considering it was a Monday and communications with chaotic Belgium were difficult, she began to consider her options; and was somewhat taken aback to hear that at the end of the week there were apparently thousands of homeless people all over the port of Ostend, desperate to cross the Channel. The Royal Navy informed her that a 'shipload' was expected on Monday, 24 August. Most people would probably have felt like disappearing to a pleasant country house for the weekend, but luckily Flora was made of sterner stuff and set about acquiring an office, a committee and staff, and the means to house several hundred refugees. She was joined by Edith Lyttleton, widow of an MP, indefatigable and literally well-connected – her memoirs begin: 'I was at my home in the country when war was declared, in August 1914. We had been on the end of the telephone wires most of Sunday the 3rd having a round-about connection with the Downing Street telephone, where the cabinet was deliberating far into the night. . . .' She realized the war had actually begun when the local shepherd arrived the next morning saying that his sheep had not been allowed on the train.

Edith headed for London and 'cast about feverishly to find useful work'. Then she ran into Lady Lugard who was wondering what to do about boatloads of refugees. '"Good Heavens", I said, "There isn't a moment to lose."' Edith started pulling strings: in one afternoon she'd contacted the Duke of Norfolk, the Comte de Lalaing, Lady Gladstone, Lord Hugh Cecil and sundry others.

By Monday morning, Flora had persuaded an insurance firm to lend office premises, and the War Refugees Committee was moving in. Edith surveyed the premises in Aldwych in central London in some alarm: 'We had three small rooms, a male secretary, and a typist. The place was besieged at once; not by refugees but by volunteers. There was no order, no place, nothing had been thought out or organised, for everyone was submerged by the huge piles of letters and queues of people offering their services.'

The previous day, the ladies had sent a letter to the press announcing a Refugee Appeal. On Monday evening, the postman must have been somewhat surprised to find himself delivering a thousand letters to a near-empty office containing some rather determined women. They tore open the letters to find every kind of help on offer: homes to go to, meals, clothes, money and transport. On the Tuesday, two thousand more letters arrived. Having hardly had time to sort the mail, on Wednesday they received a telegram from Belgium which read: 'One thousand arriving Folkestone tonight, can you take five hundred tomorrow?' The rest of the week saw four thousand, then five thousand, letters, along with twelve hundred callers at the office.

Even to the most organized of welfare-experienced ladies, the scene must have been frantic. They had an offer of two buildings: the Army and Navy Stores had some space and there was an old shirt factory in Victoria Street. Beds and bed linen, plates, cutlery and spare clothes were bought or borrowed, and more appeals went out. That evening, hundreds of Belgians arrived from Folkestone and all were fed a hot meal and accommodated. This was only the beginning: twelve thousand were soon crammed into the store and two exhibition centres. Like refugees anywhere, most had very few belongings with them and many were in shock.

On 9 September, the government announced that it would offer 'victims of war the hospitality of the British nation'. Flora Lugard, Edith Lyttleton and thousands of other British women were already working flat out trying to house and feed tens of thousands. They were faced with rich and poor, displaced gentry, homeless shopkeepers and uprooted farm labourers. True to the *mores* of the time, people were placed as much as possible into the kind of accommodation and society they had been used to: large villas were lent to the upper class while the less well-off were initially accommodated in halls and hostels before a more systematic distribution could begin. Other women's voluntary organizations were drafted in to help with cleaning, cooking and, as Edith noted, meeting people at stations:

> Station work thrilled everyone. It was extraordinary to go to the station, to find rows of nurses, V.A.Ds [Volunteer nurses], Women's Service Corps women, officials etc etc. All waiting for the trains which never arrived when expected, and never held the numbers they were reported to hold, but almost always many more . . . and out of them would pour streams of refugees of all classes – just a sample of the whole population of a country; city folk, village folk, country folk, old and young, healthy and ill, some truculent, and some frightened. . . . Some of the sights were very pitiful. People would arrive who had lost their children in the crush getting on to the boats; women alone whose husbands had been taken by the Germans, or had already joined the army; old women carrying butter and cheese, sometimes a mattress rolled up; mad people, ill people; all hurrying and miserable, and with only the clothes they stood up in. We did what we could, but it was a rough business.

There was no time for sentimentality – especially as the entire contents of the prisons of Antwerp were mixed in with the desperate families. The committee ladies and their volunteers met, registered, reassured and made time to listen to individual stories from people who had lost everything.

By early October, two hundred thousand refugees were in Britain. The offers of help still poured in, though there were endless complications as no one seemed to want male refugees, and letters were often specific about what kind of refugee they would like: 'would take a child if it had lost its parents' or 'would like to have a child who has been ill treated by the Germans'. The organizing committee had to rebuff those seeking cheap labour from 'a strong healthy girl', and found itself scrutinizing offers of marriage 'for a widow, or a woman who had been outraged by Germans'. Overall, the most generous offers came from working-class families to take in people like themselves, and from entire villages providing food and a cottage. The Belgians were dispersed to homes across the country, welcomed in the wave of sympathy for the 'little nation' which was suffering.

In Torquay, a young women who had initially volunteered as a nurse and was now working in a dispensary noted that 'quite a colony of Belgian refugees' had come to live in one parish, a good number of them 'suspicious peasants who wanted to be left alone, to be able to keep themselves to themselves'. Dispensing was much less pressurized than work on the wards, so a rather bored Agatha Christie fell to musing about writing a detective story – surrounded as she was by lots of poisons, an ideal method of murder. She needed a different kind of detective from Sherlock Holmes and his kind: why not a Belgian? A very brainy one, with the 'little grey cells of the mind. . . .' Thus Hercule Poirot was born, the product of a refugee crisis.

Christie later recalled that local people became irritated when the refugees did not seem to be sufficiently grateful for what was done for them. Elsewhere, the capacity to receive a crowd of 'foreigners' was severely tested, none more so than in Birtley, just south of Newcastle.

In 1915 this village acquired a new neighbour in the form of a complete Belgian town, due to a dearth of British women workers. Elisabethville was built to house over six thousand men, women and children who arrived as the result of a deal between the Munitions Ministry and the Tyneside firm of Armstrong Whitworth. The ever-expanding need for shells demanded more workers, and just about every able-bodied local woman was already at work in the immense network of armaments and engineering plants in the north-east.

So three and a half thousand Belgian men, injured but deemed fit to work, were withdrawn from military hospitals in France, the Netherlands and England and sent to the new Birtley shell factory. There was a degree of nervousness about their arrival – especially as they wore uniform, lived in their own enclave and were under Belgian supervision. They had their own school, church, market, laundry, police station and prison. They also had their own disagreements – most of the supervisors were French-speaking Walloons, but the workers were Flemish. They worked hard, well exceeding the expected output, putting in twelve-hour shifts in their heavy serge clothes which were not exactly suitable for the sweaty, filthy conditions. The locals initially tended to think that they were soldiers skiving off from war service. Their purpose-built prefabs, with indoor lavatories, electric lights and hot and cold running water, were also the subject of much envy – Birtley was a classic example of terraced Victorian industrial dwelling, with the 'nettie' down the back yard. The two communities lived separately to start with, partially because of language difficulties, but in time culture brought them together with the locals, many of the Belgians with musical talent raising money for war charities.

Occasionally, the old suspicions about local girls (weak and susceptible) and foreigners (wily ways with women) got an airing via the courts. New laws were enacted requiring all aliens to be registered at a specific address: if found elsewhere, the worst was usually thought and the law stepped in. Nearby Chester-le-Street police court saw several cases, for instance:

> Auguste H. Frederick, 28, a Belgian, was charged with having failed to notify the authorities in Birtley of his change of address. Sergt Dixon said he found the man in the house of a Mrs Bennet, the wife of a soldier at the Front. He admitted that he

> had lived there four months, and had given the woman money, boots, a gold watch and other things. There was only one bedroom.
>
> Defendant said he knew the woman was married, but did not know where her husband was. He was committed to prison for four months' hard labour.

Mrs Bennet, who said she wouldn't have done this if her husband hadn't treated her badly, was fined twenty shillings. Mr Bolam, the magistrate, barked at her that 'there was a condition of affairs existing in Birtley which would have to be stamped out'.

Today there is almost nothing left of Elisabethville – the Belgians were repatriated amid happy scenes in 1918, though a couple of dozen men remained and married local girls. Birtley must have been one of the very few places, if not the only one, during World War I where men were substituted at work for women.

With over a quarter of a million refugees eventually in Britain, a large number of other voluntary organizations had to intervene to support them. Considering that the kind of national charities which operate today would be more than stretched to cope with such numbers, it is a testament to the doughty actions of 'organizing ladies' that a welfare disaster did not occur. There were inevitably a lot of hiccups, but the extraordinary set of emotions which gripped people in the first few months somehow kept the machine going. New societies were formed, committees sprang up, an alphabet soup of organizations: WFL, WVR, WEC, WAF, WFGU, WTS. . . . 'W' for 'women' began to form a gigantic web of energized, purposeful females, taking the initiative and shouldering responsibility in a way never seen before across the nation. They were not a unified 'movement', since they differed widely in class background and activities, but represented a distinctive throb of activity – entwined with the drumbeat of war.

Those with automatic expectations of leadership because of their lineage were already in action in the first days of the war, one duchess crossing the Channel with a medical unit in the first week. Nor did the Refugees' Committee have a monopoly of the titled brigade, for scores of grand ladies were running their own show.

There was a marked inclination among some to don military-style uniform: it would signify a commitment and fulfil the desire to 'defend the nation' on home ground – something which had been much discussed by women in the decade leading up to the war. The Women's Volunteer Reserve was soon into khaki, wearing longish skirts and military-style jackets with lots of useful pockets: 'serviceable and sensible, and could be worn at any time'. The newspapers spotted small groups marching up and down and were mightily excited and amused; the term 'Amazons' came readily to hand. The organization's stated aim, 'to provide a trained and efficient body of women whose service could be offered to the country at any time', was a tad vague.

These were early days, and the concept of women imitating or operating in parallel with the male military was disturbing for many. Despite this, hundreds of recruits were taken on, and there was warm praise from seasoned observers such as Jennie Jerome, Winston Churchill's American mother:

> The immediate object of the Reserve was to train a body of girls who, expert, disciplined, and efficient, could do much to stem panic in the event of a German raid by sky or sea. In the same way as the Boy Scouts, in time of need these feminine recruits agreed to act as messengers, despatch riders, signallers, first-aid workers, and generally make the old and helpless of any attacked locality their particular care.

So far, not particularly militaristic, though the training emphasized discipline:

> For responsible work of this sort it was evident that severe and systematic training was needed, and this was afforded to the members of the Volunteer Reserve by a series of evening classes and drills arranged at various local centres in London and provincial towns.

The organisation was planned on a strictly military basis, with the Marchioness of Londonderry as colonel-in-chief, and the Hon. Evelina Haverfield, daughter of Lord Abinger, as honorary colonel. Regular drill practice, insisting that 'ordinary women' salute their 'officers' and parading for inspection by the real military brought rumblings of concern and provided a field day for cartoonists. However, from Birmingham to Brighton, Gateshead to Guildford, young women were learning to wrap puttees round their legs and to do fencing and signalling. (Healthy activity was much encouraged – not entirely in keeping with conventional views of how young girls should behave.)

Following the bombardment of Scarborough and Hartlepool in 1914, and the resultant swarms of people who besieged the local railway stations and streamed out on to the main road, the mayor of Gateshead was moved to hand responsibility for the civilian population to the WVR should his town be attacked. In Wolverhampton, recruits were promised an 'opportunity for Women and Girls over 18 years of age to prepare themselves by Drill and other Training, viz.:- Signalling, First-Aid, Camp Cooking, etc., to render efficient service to the State in case of NATIONAL EMERGENCY'. The local *Express and Star* went along to the first drill session and delightedly reported that 'several hundred ladies pirouetted into the Brickkiln-street Schoolyard. Some who did not intend becoming members of the Reserve shyly agreed to fall in at the behest of one or two recruiting ladies.' Not all were very young – the paper noted that 'few women admit to being over fifty . . .'

The 'officers' were suitably grand and the middle classes were over-represented, probably in part due to the uniform which cost what would have been several weeks' wages for working-class women. Evelina Haverfield, born in a Scottish castle, had gained some idea of military operations when she accompanied her first husband to the Boer War, herself organizing remount horses for the army. She had subsequently become a prominent suffragette and had been briefly in prison for 'rushing the Houses of Parliament'. Smartly turned out in khaki, with a short skirt over tailored riding breeches and topped with a felt hat, Evelina knew how to use a rifle and had to counter public suspicions of the spectre of armed women organizing themselves to fight.

Their uniforms and association with the military image were a bone of contention, particularly in the fevered atmosphere at the start of the war. MPs such as Henry Chaplin was reported that 'he would like to see rifle shooting included in the training, and he would especially like to see practice in pistol shooting. It must be remembered that what they had in contemplation was the invasion of this country by hordes of German barbarians.' But his remarks had to be quickly tempered by reassurance that 'It was not intended to create a force either militant or of military character or anything in the nature of a body of Amazons fighting side by side with men. . . .'

With the exception of a very few instances where weapons training was suggested, the idea of arming women was not something which ever warranted serious general discussion: a bridge too far, even for those drilling and parading. Women could – just – be allowed to wear uniform (Queen Victoria had reviewed her troops in a dashing military tunic), though it was not at all popular with a large number of people. But that women should be soldierly and have a weapon was out of the question. And as more men died in the fighting, the gap grew between the image of the soldier and these women who had no intention of taking up arms. With tens of thousands of women in various uniforms as the war gathered pace, the country as a whole was circumspect about entertaining the idea of them as any kind of army. There was still a conventional gap to be maintained between what the men were doing, and what women were supposed to do.

Even so, for all the emphasis on soldier-like qualities, the reality of the WVR's work turned out to be very similar to that of many other emerging organizations: they cooked for the army, they cleaned, they learned first aid, they ran canteens. They did not take aim at anything other than bluebottles on food. Typically, in Wolverhampton they packed Christmas parcels for troops overseas and in 1916 volunteered to clear snow from the town's streets – 'they cheerfully braved the elements, and, energetically working, often in four or five inches of slush, attracted no small amount of attention, particularly from members of the "stronger sex", who, however, showed no great inclination to assist'.

In the event the WVR took up useful work for soldiers, not as soldiers. They cooked, they washed up, they worked as drivers and motor-cycle messengers, much as their sister organization, the Women's Legion. This group was also in uniform, but was a much milder version which from the start announced that it intended to act as substitutes for men needed for the front.

The over-arching body for the myriad emerging volunteer groups was the Women's Emergency Corps, formed the day after war began by suffrage campaigners, including Evelina Haverfield. From the outset they were adamant that women's work was to be seen as no less vital for victory than the contribution of the fighting man. They aimed to act as a central hub for volunteers, a clearing house for paid and unpaid labour, matching skills to tasks, giving training and liaising with local and regional organizations. They became an immense but co-ordinated octopus, involved in a vast array of activities and spawning other groups for specific needs. Some of their first volunteers acted as interpreters for the thousands of Belgian refugees arriving in Britain, while others scoured Smithfield and Covent Garden markets for surplus food to feed them. They drew in hundreds of existing charities and welfare societies, ranging from the Actresses' Franchise

League to the British Women's Temperance Society, the Irish Suffragists' Emergency Council to the Women Golfers' War Fund.

The WEC possessed a phenomenal amount of administrative zeal and the ability not to be overwhelmed by dealing with nationwide contacts, uniforms, paperwork, committee meetings, fund-raising, transport, public speaking, articles for the press and the ability to wear hat or cap with elan. The WEC was non-political, non-sectarian and infused with a strong sense that they were on essential work, and not stuck in women's traditional role of being given 'something to do'. They set up a toy factory, taught young soldiers basic French and German, oversaw the inception of the quaintly named Lady Instructors, Signals Company which trained army recruits at Aldershot, and organized women doctors and nurses.

The Edinburgh branch opened workrooms for sewing and tailoring, gave French classes for nurses, set up an artificial flower-making industry, ran coffee rooms for 'uncared-for women' and found jobs for several hundred unemployed women. In Bournemouth the WEC sent parcels to prisoners of war abroad, ran a library and a bandage-making room – completing 33,925 in one year – and had a workroom making kit-bags, mosquito nets, satchels for gas masks and vermin vests. Their sandbag room expanded into a 'Thrift Room', from which emanated in 1916 almost twenty-five thousand articles made from 'odds and ends': bags for moss dressings, pincushions, bath gloves and limb cushions. Into the sphagnum room came 'the most excellent Sphagnum Moss' from the New Forest to be made into highly absorbent moss swabs. The Bournemouth branch aimed 'to utilize the energies of every capable woman who has, or who can "make", spare time, so even those women who have never trained for special work can find opportunity for "doing their bit"'.

The explosion of activity drew mostly admiring comment – as long as the work kept within the frame of traditional welfare and caring. What had not been foreseen was that the tentacles of the voluntary groups would spread far beyond the Home Front. Nor that their efforts would begin to change patterns of life, especially for middle-class girls. There was now an excuse to go out on your own, to avoid being chaperoned, to try new skills – even if it was pouring tea in a canteen, when you had previously only ever been served tea by your maid.

Life speeded up in many provincial towns, with voluntary work replacing enforced leisure: local newspapers were full of details of bazaars, lectures, meetings, first-aid classes, appeals for ladies to 'receive, sort, and pack' gifts for soldiers: the 'comforts' industry grew to a mammoth size. Lord Northcliffe's assertion about 'tremendous pent-up energy' was not entirely accurate. There were opportunities to be seized and also a great deal of frustration to be sublimated in war work.

No one announced this: the official view was that women were intensifying their usual roles, with a few novel – wartime – innovations: trousers had already made their appearance in the munitions plants and the voluntary organizations thought lady motor-cyclists were just the thing for speedy communication. On the other hand, women such as Evelina Haverfield and many of her acquaintances had their roots in the suffrage struggle – and had learned a great deal about pushing the boundaries.

Evelina and her upper-class friends with their easy connectedness and committee experience found it natural to organize and delegate. In some cases, they just tweaked well-established charity committees or raised a suggestion with a powerful dinner guest. Outside the gilded circles there were many more who built on municipal traditions and fired up local enthusiasm, giving the lie to the cosy picture of passive, knitting people, bereft of initiative. What had been hitherto lacking was opportunity, and Miss Gladys Storey was someone who seized her chance with a simple idea. She wrote a forty-one-page record of her activity during the war, which centred on a small jar in her store cupboard.

> I commenced my fund on my own initiative without a Committee of well-known and titled people and without capital. In December 1914 every woman was busy sending socks and comforters and other necessary garments

> out to the front. It seemed to me very evident that during the winter months some nourishing and practical comfort for the inner man would be very welcome to our soldiers in the trenches, and more particularly for those in the actual firing line, where they are unable to obtain the hot meals otherwise provided for them.

Miss Storey was a moderately successful actress in her twenties, the daughter of a painter. She had lighted upon a jar of Bovril. Meat extract was to consume her energies for the rest of the war. She got official approval, and to fund her activities began selling memorial postcards of army hero Field Marshal Lord Roberts at sixpence each. Newspapers carried the story and she found herself in a never-ending Bovril supply chain. Though she had donations from the firm itself, she strenuously had to deny any promotional link.

The first consignment was despatched in December 1914 and letters began to pour in from happy Bovril-drinkers be they generals or private soldiers. Up to her neck in tins of meat extract she forged ahead, gathering prominent supporters, press coverage and donations from the public and wealthy benefactors. Letters full of gratitude came back from France. Queen Mary wrote to say how interested she was in Bovril and congratulated Miss Storey on initiating 'such a useful project'. Cases were heading not only for France, but for regiments in Salonika, Mesopotamia and Gallipoli and the military hospital in Mombasa. The advertisements in the press reflected the spread of her personal campaign – with almost every regiment in the army supplied, and a delivery area stretching to Africa and the Middle East. In the first six months she happily recorded that her charity was operating at expenses of half of one per cent.

Almost every letter she received could stand as the ultimately desired endorsement for a product: 'a Godsend', 'most comforting for the inner man', 'it brings not only comfort and strength to the wounded, but strength to those who work'. By 1917 she must have had one of the most impressive collections of personal letters from every general of note and lots of approving noises from the Army Board.

It is curious to read the soldiers' words to her, the earnest warmth in reply to the gift of a crate of Bovril:

> It was a cold dark night and the snow lay thick on the ground – when the message comes through 'Forty men will report to you; they must have a bath, clean change, and a feed, to go off early. Well, of course I only get one ration for each man, and before I received this message their rations had left. What was to be done? There were no shops and all the canteens were closed. We must look round the stores – these men

> must be fed and with something hot. 'Any ration soup?' 'No, sir, but I've a dozen tins of Bovril left, sir, that you said I was not to let go without an order from you.' 'Splendid – that lady's Fund turns up every time as our guiding star. Now, then, get a move on.' At last the forty loom in sight, cold and weary. 'Come along, boys, get in here by the fire and have a drink of this.' They exchange glances, and one says: 'I see that Fund is still true to us, sir. God bless the folks in Blighty. Here's to them.' These are not gifts of the imagination but hard facts and you may feel assured that those who survive will always remember with feelings of gratitude the many kindnesses received from your Fund. A. Ridley, Captain and Quartermaster, Kensington Battalion, London Regiment, France 1918.

The men in the trenches sent her notes and little sketches and perhaps what strikes a resonant chord – and belies the modern feeling that this is promotional gold – is that the men all mention the cold, the damp, the watery dug-outs, the muddy sentry positions; even in brief letters the sheer monotonous, chilly and uncomfortable life comes to the fore. And they thank her personally – it's that important link to home: this little gift has come from a woman – the person who knows that you need a hot drink when you are worn out and your feet are wet. As a single-minded venture, it was an extraordinary success. There was sniping in some quarters that 'Miss Storey' was something of a mystery and was surely a front for the Bovril company. Awarded the OBE after the war, she left the stage and turned to a life of writing, publishing a biography of Charles Dickens's daughter Katey – before starting all over again with another Bovril Fund in World War II.

CHAPTER 5

A WOMAN CAN DO THAT!

One of the effects of war is to boost smoking. Even in these days when the ill-effects are well known, and when many countries hound the furtive smoker out of the office and restaurant and pub, there is still one group of people who ignore the general trend. Soldiers smoke in war zones – many who have never smoked at home suddenly find themselves lighting up. It's communal, comforting, calming.

Before 1914, most working men would own a pipe or roll loose tobacco. The richer men favoured cigars. Ladies did not smoke in public: Queen Mary in particular, and her mother-in-law Alexandra, were immensely discreet about their habit. Other society ladies were considered daring if they accepted a cigarette at a social occasion. Middle-class women never smoked in public until the 1920s. Poorer women usually regarded it as an expense too far, when every penny counted.

Any pub was a thick, foggy place. Tobacco was relatively cheap and a pipe was regarded as part of a man's character. No one thought it dangerous; in fact it was often seen as a very benevolent, soothing habit. Just right for the tensions of war – and the tobacco companies went into overdrive from the very first moment. Very soon they discovered that men carrying kit and rifles, endlessly on the move in dreadful wet conditions, did not have time to fiddle about with loose tobacco. The cigarette came into its own, smaller than today's, fitting neatly into packs or tins which could be stowed safely in uniform pockets.

As the tobacco barons took note of the vast numbers of men heading for France, they upped production and also added their names to the war effort: millions of cigarettes were produced for the War Office to add to basic supplies and many more millions were freely donated. The public was encouraged to fund the habit, and Lady Denman's Smokes for Soldiers Fund was wildly successful; private clubs and societies cajoled their members with leaflets and posters: 'They are hungry for Smokes – give them tobacco and there is no hardship they will not cheerfully suffer,' announced the Overseas Club Tobacco Fund. Local newspapers such as the *Derbyshire Times* bolstered the cigarette's virtues: 'There are many reasons why our Soldiers should be kept supplied with smokes. The first thing is because nothing comforts them so, nothing soothes their nerves in the same way, and nothing they enjoy so much. There are, however, other reasons that could be given such as from a hygienic point of view. A trench cannot be the sweetest place imaginable, even with the greatest care for cleanliness, and the smell of tobacco helps.' For a shilling, the readers could provide a parcel of seventy Wills' Woodbines.

In a highly competitive market, the Carreras firm had a marketing brainwave: cigarette cards could be allied to the patriotic spirit. These cards had been used to promote sales for many years, and the mania for collecting, swapping and trading them was well established. They were issued in sets and covered an enormous range of subjects, from popular sportsmen, military uniforms, birds, fish and animals to glamorous actresses and new-fangled automobiles. Some of them were highly informative, with snippets of history and information alongside the attractive coloured images. In 1916 Carreras included on its cards a set of cartoons which it had obtained from a famous Dutchman, Louis Raemaekers. His work was widely admired in Europe and he caught the popular mood of the times with his powerful anti-German drawings. Reproduced to a high standard on the little cardboard squares, tucked snugly into the cigarette packet, they gave the Carreras Black Cat brand a terrific boost.

Looking for their next set of images, the company realized that they, like so many other industries, now had an increasingly female factory workforce. They commissioned a set of fifty drawings of pretty – but not outrageously glamorous – young women wearing the clothes or uniforms of their work. The series covered almost every kind of job: tram conductor, gamekeeper, electric train cleaner, potato shoveller, leather dipper, steam roller driver, pork butcher, refuse collector and many others. The pictures, detailed and warmly coloured, were despatched in their millions.

On the back of each numbered card was a short description which in many ways encapsulated contemporary attitudes, with a little added glow of approval for what the women were doing. A very fetching outfit accompanied No. 25, Gardening, in which a girl in a cute hat and a knee-length skirt (!) pushed a wheelbarrow, with the acknowledgement that there had been few lady gardeners before the war, but that 'this is work which is very suitable for women'. Whereas No. 47, the Brewery Worker, pointed out that 'this is work which requires a good deal of muscular strength, consequently only really strong women are able to do it. Still, there are plenty of fine, strong, able women who are willing to turn their hands to this, as to many other equally strenuous tasks.' No. 11 was the inevitable munitionette in a mob cap, titled Making Shells: 'The women can't go to the front, but they can help to keep the men in the trenches supplied with ammunition. They have done splendid work in the factories, helping in the most dangerous as well as the more simple processes.' For No. 32, the Red Cross Nurse in her long white apron and long-tailed cap, 'Hospital nursing is of course essentially women's work; but the conditions today are entirely without parallel.

Hospitals, hospital ships and trains are frequently under deliberate enemy fire, but these fine women have shewn themselves utterly indifferent to danger, and quite devoted to their duty.'

It's evident that there was no glossing over what women were facing at this stage of the war: nurses under shellfire, munitionettes vulnerable to explosions. The impact of these cards, which must have been seen by thousands upon thousands of men, spread the news of what was happening at home. The Home Front was changing, and the upbeat message of the cards was that women were doing well, and should be admired in their new roles. Part propaganda, part sales gimmick, but also straightforwardly informative: the tone on the back of the cards has just a touch of condescension, but that was seen as the natural order of things by the men for whom they were intended. Women were seen as the weaker sex, but more caring, adaptable, and suited only to certain work. There are the feminine touches – frilly caps, nice hairstyles, slim waists, shy smiles, no dirt to be seen even with Coal Workers or those Barrowing Coke – and there was always an emphasis on 'womanliness' when presenting these new roles to the public; it has to be remembered that smoking was very much associated with the image of manliness. For all the commissioned artwork and official photographs of the war, these little vignettes stand as masterly images of women at work – at that time.

On the Home Front, reactions to women taking over 'men's work' were varied: encouragement, outrage, anxiety, amusement. Whatever the response, it was tempered by the public acknowledgement that it was only 'for the duration'. The extraordinary demands made on the country in order to fight a massive war justified women stepping into new, sometimes alien territory because it was both necessary and sensible – and officially blessed. Much of the comment directed publicly at women was framed in the comforting idea that the moment war was over, women would return to their pre-war occupations and status. And indeed many of the jobs, as in munitions, would automatically disappear.

In the meantime, the novelty effect never seemed to wear off. The press, fascinated by the idea of female workers, carried articles, letters and cartoons month after month. Most ignored the fact that women had been a sizeable part of the workforce before the war, and that a good deal of that work had been hard and necessary in order for them to survive, especially in industry. However, except for a few notable individuals who thought it exciting or interesting to join shift workers on the factory floor, the upper classes stayed away from industry. Nor was there a rush by middle-class women to get covered in oil and dirt in grimy workshops – they would supervise others, but were not motivated to break down class barriers and announce that all were equal, particularly amid noise and squalor.

Even in the less well-off parts of the middle class, there was no desire among wives and daughters to leave domestic security in order to clean floors or toil on a production line, especially when career opportunities were so few and far between. I remember an elderly Nonconformist minister's wife – who had managed on a very modest income in 1914 – shuddering in horror, well into her eighties, at the memory of work in the Sunderland shipyards: not that she did any. 'My dears,' she said to us children, 'all those rough girls in dirty clothes having to work in the rain and cold – it was terrible.' She came from a working-class background in a Yorkshire mill town, and like so many of her peer group, feared slipping back into the grind of Victorian industrial labour. To have her own little household and the status of a wife who did not need to work – and whose husband thought it his duty to support – was to be in seventh heaven.

Living in a shipbuilding town, I grew up fully aware that the yards were still a place for men: full of tradition, not to say ingrained attitudes, and a slightly mysterious business. The clanging of steel and iron, the thump-thump of a massive engine running on a test-bed, all took place behind high brick walls and was shrouded in steam and smoke on the riverside. At a minute or two before four o'clock in the afternoon, the huge gates were pulled open to reveal hundreds of men jostling across the entrance, like marathon runners about to set off. Look closely, and you could see the thick line of paint across the road, marking the boundary that the men might not cross until the hooter blasted, on the hour. As the men burst over the line and half-trotted home I used to think it curious that, forty years after the end of World War I, they were still dressed much as the men in the newspaper pictures of King George and Queen Mary visiting the yards in 1917. Shabby, thin suits and white mufflers were the norm, with flat caps and hefty boots. Most worked in the open air in all weathers, small, wiry, lean men in a man's world. Their tea would be ready on the table the moment they reached home, the women's world. If I had left school and asked to be apprenticed as a riveter, plater or carpenter, there would probably have been a nonplussed silence, followed by laughter.

The fact that women had gone through the gates and worked in both world wars had faded into history and failed to influence the present. Heavy industry involving skilled teamwork and physical effort was still reluctant to entertain change. Men defined themselves by skill, hardship and physical endurance. Remembering those attitudes in my youth makes one wonder how much tougher things were for those women who were sent into the yards forty years earlier, in World War I. Just over five hundred women went into the Wearside yards – those 'girls in dirty clothes'. As unskilled workers they were set to cleaning and carrying; they wore long skirts and black shawls and clogs – the innovative trousers and shorter skirts which were making their appearance belonged to a softer, trendier world which held little sway in these communities. Although there are compelling images of Clydeside and Tyneside and Wearside women hefting hammers and welding, there's anecdotal evidence that within the yards they rarely worked on the actual ships, though a few got limited training. As in coal-mining, there were all kinds of superstitious ideas which were useful to deploy whenever women got too near the heart of the job. Steelworks were equally a male bastion: forge and galvanizing work was bound up with the notion that a woman would be trespassing on forbidden territory. The complete lack of lavatory facilities also served as a useful deterrent.

In a much-publicized case in 1915, a woman was discovered working in a timber yard which supplied the naval shipbuilders in Barrow. She was desperate for well-paid work, having a family to support, but had been turned away from other jobs just because she was a woman. The newspaper stories of the day were not in the least interested in her situation but they delighted in her method. Under headlines such as: 'Weak Points in a Woman's Disguise as a Man', they went into great detail about her attempt to disguise herself with a moustache. She managed to fool both the military and police guard and her fellow workers for three days of physically heavy work, and her colleagues all attested that 'she was a splendid worker and was equal to the best man in the gang'. One of the soldiers eventually rumbled her, saying that she 'had a very narrow waist and small hands and feet . . .'. She herself ruefully protested that 'if she had added side whiskers to her face she would never have been found out'. The story was syndicated nationally, but without mention of her need for work or the fact that she had proved she could do it.

There were many who could not envisage a different world where women might have broader horizons and greater opportunities. There was plenty in the newspapers to reassure them that working men in particular agreed, according to the *Sunderland Daily Echo*: 'The subject of the introduction of female labour on to the pit heads of the county of Durham in order to relieve the work for men underground came before the Council of Durham Miners' Association at a special meeting in Durham . . . the press were informed that the delegates were practically unanimously against female labour.'

The coal mines were – and remained until their near-disappearance – unwaveringly all-male. With the exception of the Lancashire 'pit-lasses' who had always done surface work and jealously guarded their right to it, the very thought of a woman at the coal face prompted all kinds of objections, not the least of which was a fanciful clutch of superstitions. There was also the practical problem of hygiene, but no one thought this worth discussing, such was the refusal to consider the matter. Decades later, in the 1970s, having negotiated a visit to one of the deeper pits in the county, I was forcefully informed that one of the inconveniences of dealing with women was the lack of trousers worn down the 'hot pits'. Why should the men have to put their clothes on, just to accommodate females?

As the war grew to a monstrous-sized operation, and more men left their jobs to enlist, many employers were wary of upsetting their remaining male workers: the trades unions were convulsed with arguments about how to protect the difference in earning power between the sexes – a reinforcement of the view that a man should be able to support a wife and family. He was the breadwinner; he should have the right to be able to keep his wife in the same state of idle domesticity as his employers' wives. There was also the insistence that 'skilled men' should always earn more than 'unskilled' – which is how many jobs taken by women were reclassified; and there was also the problem that if women were paid too little they would become a more attractive, cheaper alternative to men, therefore undermining the chaps. And 'it stands to reason' was the view that women could never, ever earn as much as men, so were completely unable to support others.

Not that campaigning for equal pay for equal work was a forgotten issue: women trades unionists, former suffrage activists and many public figures kept up the demand. But they faced both a government and captains of industry absolutely determined not to upset the wages' applecart – even if only 'for the duration'. They were terrified that the idea would take hold and that post-war bargaining would see a completely new world in which traditional pay rates had disappeared. At the core of this lay the simple conviction that people should be paid not for what they did, but for who they were.

For decades before the war, women had generally been paid at less than half the going rate for men's work. In many instances, it was nearer to a third. Women responding to be part of the war effort knew that they would be paid less than men, whatever they were doing. A situation which continues, usually covertly, for quite a number in the workforce today.

The miners could always make a major issue out of wash room and lavatory arrangements – in 1914 they had hardly any for themselves. However, the rest of heavy industry and a great number of workshops also had to grapple with 'ladies' facilities'. Offices were still used to gentlemen clerks and often retained a 'men-only atmosphere', even though lady typists had been tolerated for some years. With relentless recruitment emptying the desks and enabling women to be 'lady clerks', the war saw a change in the layout and welfare provision of the workplace and highlighted the divisions which existed in daily work. Should ladies use the same entrance? Should they be called by their surname, like the men? And what about lunchtime? They could not possibly go to the pub for a pie and a pint. Getting used to having more lady typists and filing clerks caused eyebrows to be raised and teeth to be gritted: the 'business girls' were now earning slightly higher wages than before. Any slight change in their behaviour was pounced on, always with a hint that things were 'getting out of hand'. The *Daily Mail* kept a watchful eye on these developments: 'The wartime business girl is to be seen any night dining out alone or with a friend in the moderate-priced restaurants in London. Formerly she would never have had her evening meal in town unless in the company of a man friend. But now with money and without men she is more and more beginning to dine out.' The paper added knowingly that there was also the public smoking of 'the customary cigarette'.

Essential to the smooth running of industry were the railways, with a spider's web of lines that is only discernible today in a few grassy cuttings and forgotten station names. You could hop about the country, from small village and country town, to all the main cities with comparative ease. There was style in first class, and third was affordable. Not only work, but much leisure, was reliant on the trains. Special excursions were immensely popular, and thousands got their first glimpse of the seaside via the railways. This was the era of competitive companies, with smart livery and frequent services. All of this was abruptly interrupted by the government who in 1914 took over the entire network and every bit of rolling stock. There were troops to be moved, and munitions, then every piece of kit that was wanted abroad, some of it loaded on to special ships which took the goods – and the train as well.

Men in the almost exclusively male world of the railways volunteered in droves: they were eagerly accepted, for the war in France was going to be fought with the help of railways as close to the front line as track could be laid. To construct and run this network, forty thousand experienced men were eventually serving in the Royal Engineers Railway Unit. The vacancies at home caused unease: railway world was male. There were a few areas where women might work – some of the larger companies owned hotels and restaurants where women had the usual cooking and cleaning jobs, but as at the Great Western Railway Company, there was deep suspicion. A few lady typists and telephonists had arrived in the office in the 1870s, and when women upholsterers and French polishers were taken on, the company had intentionally built a separate women-only workshop. Initially they were 'provided with a separate entrance and leave at somewhat different hours from the men'.

Come the war, and more office workers were hired not just to type and take shorthand but to do accounts and financial paperwork. Across the country, the civil service and the banks were facing up to employing women as 'clerks' – a major shift in their employment procedures. The title 'clerk' was old-established, carried a certain gravitas – and was held by a man. That these women should qualify to be called 'female clerks' or 'lady clerks' undermined the men in these huge establishments steeped in bureaucracy and a rigid sense of hierarchy. However, no one seemed to find an acceptable alternative, so women stepped on to the career ladder in a small way.

At the GWR there was a great deal of foot-dragging when it came to replacing the departed men – young boys and older men were considered more appropriate, and at least half the railway industry was still putting up resistance even in the second year of the war. By this time, the government felt it needed to push the matter, as enormous demands were being made on track, trains and staff: three hundred thousand men eventually left the railways to serve in the forces, the rolling stock was being over-used and maintenance was difficult. Reluctantly, the GWR agreed to hire female ticket collectors and dining-car attendants, knowing that the industry's men had deep-seated reservations about women's 'limitedness', as they put it. The *Railway Gazette* conveyed their feelings in 1915: 'That the employment of women on the railways of this country has contributed in no small degree to the maintenance of an efficient transport system cannot be gainsaid. Female labour, however, is limited to those grades in which experience is not of the essence . . . and the vocations must not entail contact with train movement.'

Although the press featured female train guards and crossing keepers in their company's livery – looking every inch as if running the trains was now the responsibility of women – the majority were in clerical jobs, earning half of the male clerks' weekly wage. When they were introduced into signal boxes there was friction because of the small spaces and often isolated locations, and official complaints were received from the men: 'Women will not accept responsibility.' There were reservations about women's intellectual abilities: one management superintendent calculated that it took three women to undertake two trained men's duties. There was also a suspicion that the insistence on jobs being given back to men when they returned from the war – many of those hired were told they were replacing specific individuals – might detract from a wholesale commitment to work efficiently; and this was an argument that was used *against* evaluating women's ability, rather than for it. Indeed, some single women had a desire to 'do their bit' for the war effort but no intention of continuing in peacetime – especially if it interfered with the traditional goal of marriage and a family. The great watchword for girls was 'security', and their low wages would not support the marginally more comfortable role underpinned by a man's higher earnings. But no one was quite sure, for enquiry into motivation was not part of the hiring business and no one ever thought to give women equal pay to see if they might have greater commitment. Nor was a great deal of attention paid to the age-old and continuing argument about doing a job *and* running a home. The Sunderland Suffrage Society noted that the women on the Great Western Railway had been on strike; their reasons are still rehearsed today:

> . . . the women carriage-cleaners protested against the heaviness of and the length of the hours. On inquiry being made as to the conditions it appeared that most of the women were widows and had homes to keep in order. It was therefore not to be wondered at that they found it impossible to work for longer than nine hours a day. As somebody remarked: 'It is not fair to argue that a woman cannot do as much work as a man from the fact that she cannot do twice as much.' And as far as these women are concerned, the solution seems to be that more women should be employed, shorter hours required and pay in proportion. The incident serves to illustrate a general truth concerning women-workers, viz., that the average girl and woman wage-earner has generally other responsibilities and duties. The woman 'mill-hand' often not only works all day in the mill but slaves in the evening and on Saturdays and Sundays in her home; and in all classes, even where the woman is comparatively free from such obligations, it is the general rule

> that a thousand and one duties fall to her which are not expected from the man wage-earner. There can be but one alternative in such cases: either the work is not well done, or the worker breaks down, and it will have to be recognised in the home in particular and by society in general that girls no more than boys, and women no more than men, can burn the candle at both ends.

The view in 1916 has not changed that much. On the railways, ticket collectors and porters were highly visible to the general public, but there were fewer of them compared to those washing down train carriages, oiling machinery and cleaning engines – 'an occupation well-suited to those belonging to the working-classes'. The publicity photographs of the cleaning gangs, often perched on the huge steam engines, must have all been taken prior to their shifts – it was a filthy job, where grit and soot clung to everything and got in your lungs as well. There was no doubting that women could do the work, though no one ever discussed whether they could do the most significant job of all. Nowhere in all the different work categories filled by women is there the slightest suggestion of 'train movement': not a hint that a woman should drive one. That took another six decades.

The railwaywomen were given uniforms, usually a version of the male outfit but with a long skirt instead of trousers; the carriage cleaners were in skirts, but the engine cleaners wore overalls. Going up ladders seemed to be the clincher: letters to newspapers were full of male discomfiture about ladies up ladders with ankles – or more – on view; all of them written from the angle of 'protecting' women from lewdness. There do not appear to be many letters on the subject which came from women. Indeed, looking at the immense number of photographs taken at cokeworks, steel furnaces, coal yards, gas companies, power stations, glass manufacturers, shipyards, timber merchants, flour mills, chemical factories, engineering workshops and other industrial premises, there are far more trousers than skirts. For reasons of practicality, would be the obvious retort today. However, there's enough evidence from reaction to the munitionettes' uniforms very early in the war to emphasize that it was a hard battle to overcome employers' and public prejudice. The munitions plants were among the first to engage women on heavy work in often filthy and dangerous conditions, and even they compromised initially by having the women wear tunics over their trousers.

Uniforms acted as a visible sign of change – the Edwardian world of ladies' fashions had rarely attracted regular comment from men, unless to complain about extravagance or to be amused about women on bicycles. Uniform was a signal, invested with hierarchy and significance. Even the most non-military 'uniform' outfit could catch the male eye:

> Looking in for dinner at the Reform Club last night, I happened upon a novel scene. Gone from the dining-room were the waiters in knee britches, silken stockings, silver-buckled shoes, some of whom I have known for more than a quarter of a century. In their place tripped about waitresses in neat costumes of black frocks, white aprons and coquettish caps. This was a development of the scheme of substituting wherever possible the service of women to the displacement of the more highly-paid men. I hear that the system has been adopted by the neighbouring Athenaeum Club, where aprons have hitherto been in evidence only when worn by such members as are bishops.

Sir Henry Lucy, a journalist who wrote for *Punch* magazine, noted the wind of change blowing through even the cosseted lives of the wealthy in 1915. Heading for London's fashionable Army and Navy Stores, he found women instead of men operating the lifts 'attired in a neat, becoming uniform which, whilst distinctive, does not clash with the femininity of their ordinary attire'. It's a *tide* of women: 'She is everywhere superseding men, notably in shops. At the big stores, women are found behind the counters, where they certainly seem more at home than did the strapping young men they replace. . . . Formerly boys were engaged at the pay desks. Today girls fill their places, and, as far as observation goes, are equally efficient.' He has also just learned that 'in many City offices women are taking the place of men acting as clerks. I hear that the Bank of England have within the last few months engaged no less than 350 women in that capacity.'

The home was no defence against this rising tide, as he quoted from a 'Livery Outfitter' that so many footmen had enlisted there is 'difficulty of procuring this class of servants – many of the nobility and gentry are temporarily replacing them with parlourmaids'. The outfitter was coping by designing a uniform that he hoped would will prevent a shock when the front door was opened: 'a narrow skirt, surmounted by a striped waistcoat under a jacket with stand-up collar and tie'. Sir Henry's views reflected the sheer numbers involved, the fact that formal traditions were crumbling, and the desperate need to couch women's advancement in terms of 'womanliness' and light approval. 'Temporarily' was the comforting word: however well the women performed, this was just for the duration of the war, surely? For not everyone was entirely happy with the situation. As the enormities of warfare savaged the population, the Chancellor of the Exchequer, Lloyd George, was moving to become Minister of Munitions. This was to have a profound impact on the war effort, but Sir Henry was busy noting that his exit from his official London residence had been received in some quarters with specific relief: 'Lloyd George's trim housemaids will no longer flout what has hitherto been regarded as a fundamental principle of the British constitution by opening the door to callers at No.11, Downing Street, in place of a butler or footman!'

Punch may have been a moderately satirical magazine, but throughout the war it slyly reflected many of its readers' anxieties about change. Sir Henry might probably use a taxi for his journeys – even there, he could have found himself with a lady driver, the first of whom on the streets of London was greeted by the *Times* with a warning to people of a nervous disposition: a female Jehu was at large (though the taxis of World War I could probably not keep pace with the speed of an ancient Israeli war chariot). The men of London Transport had been particularly quick off the mark to enlist – three and half thousand in two days. The immediate response to the vacancies on trams, buses and the Tube was to employ 'men unsuitable for war work'. Within months, enlistment took even more men – three hundred of them – to France, with their buses too. The London General Omnibus Company started a recruitment campaign aimed at women – with the help of Scotland Yard. 'They were ever so strict. We had to have three references, there was a medical check-up and our photographs and fingerprints were taken by Scotland Yard. I felt sorry for one girl who didn't get a job because she hadn't paid her dog licence.'

Twenty-three-year-old Lesley Davis was excited

by the prospect of being 'on the buses' and went along to the bus school in Chelsea to be trained. Sixty years later she recalled just how you got through the course:

> When it actually came to learning to do the job, I found it was very much the practice to give the Instructor a good cash tip! I think the uniforms were free, but we were sent up to Manor House offices for a 'passing-out parade' in our new uniforms before the bus chiefs. The high-legged boots, long skirts and jackets may have looked smart, but they were very uncomfortable to wear all day long. But when I felt miserable about the job, all I had to do was think about our boys in the trenches, and I soon pulled my shoulders back.

This kind of sentiment was heard all the time during the war, and today it sounds to some as if it used to come out parrot-fashion. Lesley Davis was eighty-five when she was interviewed, and it was deeply felt.

The job wasn't a cushy number: crews were paid for a nine-hour shift, but usually found themselves working near eleven or twelve, due to their responsibilities for checking the vehicles and cash collected – never mind the long walk home. Even so, there were many keen applicants and of the seventeen hundred who presented themselves in London in

November 1916, over seven hundred had been in domestic service. Anything was better than 'below stairs' and Miss Davis was thrilled at the weekly pay of £2 10*s* (£2.50) – it was twice what most girls earned 'in service'. Most weeks the conductresses reported at 6 a.m., six days a week and throughout their time on duty they had to stand. The war years were by no means without industrial disputes, and one of the conductresses' gripes was the standing – so they decided to strike for a platform seat. They soon discovered that although they paid their union subscription of 4*d* a week, only the men decided if a strike should go ahead – and then only the men got strike pay. Somewhere in the negotiations a pay rise for the women had been agreed, to bring them a little closer to the men who did identical hours and shifts. It never appeared.

More stoppages occurred later in the war, with women bus and Tube staff demanding they be paid a bonus that was on offer to the men who did the same work. The phrase 'Equal Pay for Equal Work' was becoming more than a suffrage slogan: the women had shown they could do the work, so why should they not get the bonus? The strike spread to transport depots well beyond London and the government feared it might catch on in munitions factories and elsewhere, so coughed up the bonus. It arbitrarily batted Equal Pay etc. not so much into the long grass as totally out of the grounds.

On the buses the skirt question occasionally arose,

with objections to conductresses going on to the top deck; however, this seems to have been combined with the pre-war convention that 'ladies rode inside' and therefore things were a bit rowdier upstairs. The buses were crowded at all times – the small number of private motorists, combined with a shortage of petrol, meant that bus and Tube travel was democratized. The prevalence of shift-work, the curtailed shop opening hours and the number of soldiers passing though London on leave disrupted the more rigid patterns of travel before the war: ladies who had the leisure to shop mid-mornings found themselves squashed alongside factory girls and troops. Several conductresses found themselves getting a hard time from such ladies, and agreed among themselves that they were getting a dose of resentment from women who had lost their maids.

Crowds of passengers, London fogs and then Zeppelin raids were not, however, Lesley Davis's main preoccupation. As the war dragged on, food shortages affected everyone; she thought about dinner constantly: 'Most of our working hours seemed to be concerned with getting enough to eat – although for 3*d* you could get a huge helping of faggots and pease pudding!' She was working alongside a driver with similar thoughts, and on the day their No. 21 bus was due to head for Sidcup in Kent he told her to bring a bag to work: he'd had a promise from a local farmer. 'He stopped the bus and went off to collect the potatoes, leaving me with a busload of angry passengers. When he eventually came back, a few of them complained. He told them where he had been and said "The trouble with you lot from Sidcup is you don't even know there's a war on. My family of four have not had a potato for two months, and I would do it again!"' He got his potatoes, but both he and Lesley were suspended and lost three days' pay.

Before the war a small number of women had qualified as carriage drivers; they perched on top, guiding fidgety horses though London's increasingly motorized traffic. When these swaying contraptions were finally ousted by the motor omnibus, the drivers were all men. Come wartime, only a few women omnibus drivers appeared – and then just in the provinces. Driving was still a very privileged accomplishment and only the rich rode in motor cars, so inevitably the lady driver was a rarity – on the Home Front. Across the Channel, unwieldy ambulances carrying wounded men were being driven through shocking conditions close to the front line by women; apparently an omnibus – laden with healthy passengers and not able to exceed the twelve-mile-per-hour speed limit at home – was considered a step too far. It was a step that London Transport finally took in 1974, trailing in the wake of England's first woman bus driver in Bristol three years earlier. Similar nervousness was to be found on the Underground: 'electric train ladies' were to be seen in the ticket offices and as cleaners, but were not in the driving seat of a Tube train: that came in 1978.

The tramcar world, in contrast, was progressive-minded. Glasgow had a large network, with a thousand electric tramcars. Less than a month after war was declared, an entire battalion of the Highland Light Infantry was recruited in one day from its men. Women were immediately hired to replace them, both as conductors and as drivers. They wore smart long tartan skirts and were the subject of press fascination. Wielding the long poles needed to switch the overhead wires above the trams, looking like deep sea anglers with a very recalcitrant shark on the end of the hook, they were filmed, photographed and gawped at.

Trams were more glamorous than omnibuses, cleaner and quieter, and they were soon used in numerous cities as part of the recruitment campaign. Rochdale trams bore posters asking 'Are you fighting for Rule Britannia – or only singing?' Southampton and Leeds went one better and dressed their vehicles overall with coloured lightbulbs. They looked magnificent, clanging over the rails with 'God Save the King' illuminated in huge letters.

Southampton used the word 'conductorettes'; in Bristol they were 'clippies.' Annie Goodall was a driver in Sunderland, alongside eighty-five 'lady conductors', including Sally Holmes. The trams were immensely popular – the town had a pit almost at the end of the main street and belching shipyards covered the riverbanks – but you could head away to the beach along the whole seafront for a few pence. The ladies were not immediately popular with everyone – local lads appeared in court for 'throwing stones, street refuse, etc. at female conductors and cars'. On the evening of 1 April 1916, the Zeppelin seen by Wilfrid Adie and his father scattered its load over several buildings, including the tramway offices, killing an inspector. Sally Holmes was collecting fares on tram No. 10 nearby as another bomb went off, shattering the vehicle, blowing her off the platform and leaving her with a badly injured leg.

The atmosphere in which outrage was engendered by civilian deaths, particularly of women, goes some way towards explaining the popularity of Jessie Pope's poetry, and in particular a poem she published some months later with the title 'War Girls':

> There's the girl who clips your ticket for
>   the train,
> And the girl who speeds the lift from floor
>   to floor,
> There's the girl who does a milk-round in
>   the rain,
> And the girl who calls for orders at
>   your door.
> Strong, sensible, and fit,
> They're out to show their grit,
> And tackle jobs with energy and knack,
> No longer caged and penned up,
> They're going to keep their end up,
> Till the khaki boys come marching back.

There's the motor girl who drives a
heavy van,
There's the butcher girl who brings your
joint of meat,
There's the girl who cries 'All fares please!'
like a man,
And the girl who whistles taxis up
the street.
Beneath each uniform
Beats a heart that's soft and warm,
Though of canny mother-wit they show
no lack;
But a solemn statement this is,
They've no time for love and kisses
Till the khaki soldier boys come
marching home.

At least Pope was celebrating their work – few butcher girls and clippies had ever featured in published verse before. There was also a nod to their earlier, restricted existence, along with the likelihood of domesticity when the boys came home. Whatever the tone, this was realism, 1916-style.

CHAPTER 6

KNITTING ROYALLY

Ethel Maud Hedinburgh had a difficult war. With two small children and her husband likely to be called up, she also had to contend with the neighbours' whispering campaign. 'A Hun!' shouted the neighbours' children, as the Sunderland police dropped by yet again to question this God-fearing Methodist and pillar of the local amateur operatic society.

Vainly protesting that her father had been Austrian and lived in England for decades, my maternal grandmother in my adoptive family was no isolated case. Aliens were suspect, and one of the first services patriotic British citizens felt they could perform was to deliver anyone remotely German to the authorities. Laws had been swiftly brought in to restrict the activities of 'enemy aliens', and in many instances intern them. The papers were full of information about how to spot these newly dangerous people: opening her local paper, Ethel Maud could read in just one edition that 'eleven German residents of Jarrow, who are mostly pork butchers, have been placed under arrest by the Jarrow police, and at Wallsend five are in custody'.

In Tynemouth a German seaman in the Workhouse Hospital had been placed under arrest, while along the Tyne in Dunston 'Inspector Rispin and Sergt. Whaley arrested thirteen Germans early this morning. They were taken from their respective homes and detained at the police station.'

Spy fever gripped the public's imagination. 'Possible foreign persons' loitering near any kind of military depot or significant locations such as canals, bridges or ports were likely to be collared, either by special constables or by enthusiastic spy-hunters. Women were often hauled before the courts because they had married a foreigner, therefore acquiring his nationality; there was a lurking suspicion that women would be more vulnerable to coercion and thus betray the country of their birth.

Once spotted by the authorities and officially classified, aliens faced restrictions. The *Newcastle Chronicle* excitedly reported that 'Louis Feldman, being an alien enemy, namely an Austrian subject, did travel more than five miles from 34 Edwards Road, Whitley Bay, his registered place of residence, contrary to the Order.' The bench had no time for the young barber's protestations that he had no idea he needed a permit to go a mile or two. They thought this 'a very important case . . . Mr Feldman had betrayed the lenient code imposed by the authorities . . . a leniency which was feared was not shown in Germany! Accused would be fined £5 and costs, or one month's imprisonment.' The same day, more pork butchers were being arrested in Chester-le-Street in County Durham and the police in Durham City were having trouble controlling 'huge crowds of people gathered round the Shire Hall' where two men were being questioned. One was a German brewer's travelling rep and the other 'had a foreign accent'. The *Chronicle* intoned that 'In Durham, a sharp look-out is being kept for spies.' And nationally the *Daily Mail* had advice for all its readers: 'Refuse to be served by an Austrian or German waiter. If your waiter says he is Swiss ask to see his passport.'

Waves of anti-German feeling regularly rolled around the nation throughout the war, sometimes provoked by news of enemy atrocities, both real and apocryphal, and dreadful events such as the loss of civilian life when the liner *Lusitania* was torpedoed on her way to Liverpool from New York – over eleven hundred were lost. The atmosphere of suspicion and hostility towards 'Huns' produced serious rioting several times in the East End of London, the internment of many butchers and tailors, and the occasional victimization of blameless dachshunds. The intelligence services expanded massively, though actual proven espionage continued to be difficult to pin down and resulted in only a small number of convictions.

The headline 'Woman Spy' appeared frequently; women were thought to be unreliable, faced with conflicting allegiance: one wonders what exactly Mathilde Smith had done to harm the nation as she faced sentencing at the Old Bailey for ‘unauthorised communication of information with intent to assist the enemy’. Tried behind closed doors, the forty-four-year-old widow with that suspect German first name was given ten years’ penal servitude. The sensation-filled story of the Dutch dancer Mata Hari, accused of being a German agent and executed in Paris in 1917, reinforced the popular view that as well as ‘weak’ women, those who were ‘wayward’ were not to be trusted. Having lived as a circus performer, artist’s model and exotic dancer, and flouted convention with many lovers, she was on shaky ground when the charge of espionage was brought. The hysteria which drove much of the spy fever encouraged crude judgements about loyalty. For a woman, live a less than blameless life and your protestations when faced with a firing squad would be less likely to be believed.

Well into 1915 the papers were still obsessed with aliens and the *Daily Mirror* gleefully reported on ‘rounding-up day’, adding that in London alone there were still between twenty and thirty thousand Germans who had to be ‘dealt with’. Despite that, ‘there was a renewal of rioting in North London last night: many German shops which had hitherto escaped were attacked and the windows smashed, and in some cases there was a good deal of pilfering by the crowd’. The inhabitants of Hull were subject to many Zeppelin attacks and the *Hull Daily Mail* stoked the anti-German sentiments: ‘Why is it that in all the Zeppelin raids over England we have not heard of the least damage being done to the life and property of the naturalised alien living in sublime contentment among us. Is it possible they have a secret code of signals indicating where they lie fermenting their hate, or is it that, since we have proved they are in league with the evil one, he insures them as a reward for their cooperation?' A novel kind of protest had also occurred in Birmingham, where 'anti-German feeling was openly expressed for the first time, when a restaurant in High Street was damaged by customers, who seized jars of salad dressing and other articles and threw them though the windows'.

The courts were swamped with both suspect foreigners and aggrieved patriots. On one May Saturday in 1915, West Ham police court in London was dealing with rioters in batches, sending fifty-two people to prison in one sitting, while Thames police court was hearing cases in groups of thirty. Mob rule was clearly evident in some parts of the capital, with the police admitting that it was dangerous for foreigners to present themselves at stations for fear of demonstrations, and meanwhile they were having to deal with German and Austrian women who were in fear of their lives. The *Mirror* reported an encounter near Charlotte Street in London's West End – where many German businesses were located: ' "If you please, I'm a German", said a middle-aged, tearful, frightened woman at one police station to an officer. "Will they be unkind to me if they put me in a camp or send me away?" "Don't you worry, ma'am," said the policeman, in a kindly voice. "You will be all right. It will be for your own good if you do go away." '

One family with close German connections and a German name did not have the option of 'going away'. When Prince Albert married Queen Victoria, he introduced the distinctly non-English Saxe-Coburg-Gothas into the British royal family and all their descendants were members of that House. In 1914 King George V possibly had more German relatives than almost any of his subjects. The enemy was led by his first cousin, Kaiser Wilhelm II. He was connected to a horde of Württembergs, Hohenzollerns and Schleswig-Holsteins and many, many more scattered throughout Europe. His own Royal Navy's First Sea Lord was Prince Louis of Battenberg. His wife, Queen Mary, had a Princess of Hesse-Kassel for a grandmother. And although the King felt himself to be irrefutably British and his wife had announced at the age of nine that she was very definitely a true little English girl, there was no denying their interwoven relationship with Germans and Germany. However, the Queen did not particularly even like Germans and within days of the outbreak of war set about showing her patriotic fervour.

What was expected of her? She was the King's wife, brought up partly under the eye of Queen Victoria, and hedged around with all the formalities of the court. Her husband was a rather rigid, unimaginative and none-too-bright man (with all the intellectual capacities of a railway porter, according to his biographer Harold Nicolson), who ran his household and family like a ship's captain on the quarter-deck: in command, fond of routine and punctuality and not expecting anyone to veer off course. He had two passions: shooting and stamp-collecting; his wife stood around while her husband blasted at anything which flew and then sat sewing while her husband pored over rare colonial issues. The general public did not expect from him much more than assiduous attention to formal duties.

His wife was a royal wife, a role that was – and continues to be – hedged around with convention and vulnerable to suggestions of change. Mary was not without strength of character, but had been brought up in royal circles. She summed up her view of suffragettes in a letter to her Aunt Augusta (a Mecklenburg-Strelitz) in 1913: 'Those horrid suffragettes burnt down the little tea house close to the Pagoda in Kew Gardens yesterday morning at 3 a.m. There seems no end to their iniquities.' Her views would always be confined to family letters because discretion was bred into her; nor were they different from those held by most of the women who shared her background. Not that she was without sympathy and concern for the poor, having had to act, for many years before her marriage, as her mother's secretary and companion in a constant round of charitable activities. She had the sympathy and concern for the poor and disadvantaged, without curiosity as to the cause of their problems.

In this, she was again in the company of upper-class women who saw it as no business of theirs to interfere with what might be deemed the 'natural order of things'. Lady Bountifuls were still regarded without cynicism: they raised money, visited the poor, distributed food and clothing, and wrote generous cheques. Mary's mother, the Duchess of Teck, had been a popular figure, known for her complete inability to sort out her finances and for ignoring the royal family's concern about her public appearance: she weighed in at almost twenty stone and was fully aware that the public called her Fat Mary. She was particularly fond of the work of the Needlework Guild, a network of ladies' groups which for many years had made and distributed clothing to the needy. Her home was White Lodge in Richmond Park where journalist Sir Henry Lucy recalled dropping in one day and finding 'the Duchess of Teck in an underground apartment busily engaged, with the assistance of the daughter who is now Queen of England, in superintending the making up of parcels of suitable clothing for deserving recipients . . . "a class of the community gently reared who had fallen upon evil times . . .".'

Queen Mary now had a great determination to carry out charitable duties specifically aimed at alleviating the 'evil times' the war would bring.

Knitting might not be seen as a heroic act, but the statistics attached to the upsurge in clicking needles in the first few months of conflict attained heroic heights. Indeed, knitting became a kind of moral duty, with mutterings that no woman should be seen just sitting, she should be sitting knitting. Even the single knitter found herself part of the national effort, spearheaded by needles wielded by Queen Mary. The Queen had re-energized the Needlework Guild and appealed for comforts for the troops and also clothes for families and civilians 'who will feel the sharp pinch of war'. Cardigans, socks, sweaters, mittens, scarves and anything else that could be knitted began to be produced in enormous amounts, and knitting became a common sight on the London Tube, on trains, and in the theatre and cinema.

Then needlewomen and seamstresses received the royal call. Initially the Guild focussed on clothing for the troops and the sick and wounded in hospital and their families. The Queen's appeal, printed in the papers, went into detail with Her Majesty personally advising that 'all flannel garments should be made in a large size, and suitable patterns can be obtained from Butterick, 179 Regent Street'. The Queen was careful to stress that work should not be taken away from those who already worked in the garment industry; and that those with the means to do so should 'employ needlewomen and "little" dressmakers, whom the privations of such a time as this must be overshadowing, and by paying them for their aid as cutters-out, machinists, and so forth, help them to make both ends meet'.

Notwithstanding hand-outs to 'little' dressmakers, within days it dawned on people that volunteer knitters and needlewomen might put ordinary women workers out of a job. The Queen found herself targeted by one of the most redoubtable campaigners for improving women's wages, Mary Macarthur. The Queen may have had a vague idea of how much went into the wage-packet of the average seamstress, but even considering what she'd learnt from her own mother's pile of debts and the problems it brought, she was unlikely to have dealt with the penny-counting hardship experienced by large numbers of poor women. When the first financial contributions were publicized for the Guild and the Red Cross, members of the royal family wrote cheques for hundreds, and at times thousands, of pounds. Mary Macarthur, on the other hand, led the National Union of Women Workers and was an expert on the desperate position of 'sweated labour'. She'd campaigned for piece-workers who found it difficult to make even £20 in a year. Hearing about the Queen's Guild busily knitting and sewing for nothing, she was widely quoted as praying for someone 'to stop these women knitting'. A swift shift was made to reposition the Guild as a source of extra supplies and comforts, delivering those items which the government was not ordering from factories.

Mitts and mufflers, jerseys and blankets started

to arrive in enormous quantities, and all had to be coordinated and collected, sorted and sent. After five months of war, 175,000 articles had arrived. By the end of hostilities, over a million women would have been knitting and sewing and coordinating over 15½ million garments. Dressing-gowns, pyjamas, bandages, pillows, women's underclothing, wader stockings, hot-water bottle covers, pneumonia jackets – a seemingly endless list was publicized regularly. Guild groups were at work from Banbury to Bulawayo, Rhodesia, from Torquay to Toorak, Australia.

In London, sorting and repacking took place in Friary Court in St James's Palace; the Queen insisted on almost daily reports and turned up frequently to inspect the work. An elegant badge was produced that could be purchased for a shilling and worn by ordinary knitters and sewers. The *Evening News* offered a badge to members who joined its own Guild branch and soon announced that fifty thousand women were wearing one, even in Hong Kong, India and New Zealand; it could not resist printing a letter from a very young member, 'Little Winifred Morris', of Medusa Road, Catford in South London:

A Letter to the Queen:

Dear Queen Mary,

I have made a pair of mittens for your Guild, and granny sends a pair, too. I have made mine all myself. Daddy sent me 6*d* for a Christmas present, and I have sent that with the mittens for one of your brooches. If you will please let me have one. Lots of love. Winifred Morris.

The Guild expanded and sent parcels to the Red Cross, to prisoners of war, to widows and orphans and refugees, and to the unemployed; to sailors and soldiers in every theatre of war. Military hospitals appealed for specific items from cardigans to shrouds. The Queen lent her name to a range of charities and soon found herself in political waters. Having had her attention drawn to the ease with which women could lose their jobs, she inaugurated the Queen's Work for Women Fund as part of the National Relief Fund. It was aimed at raising money to retrain and employ those thrown out of work by the initial 'general dislocation' in industry. This time she was accused of starting 'Queen Mary's sweat-shops' by the suffrage campaigner Sylvia Pankhurst. A not very princely 3*d* an hour was to be paid, well below even the general low wages for women. Despite this, there were plentiful applicants wanting the meagre earnings.

One consequence of these charitable hiccups was that Mary Macarthur received an invitation to see the Queen, whose views on anything with an aroma of 'Socialism' were private but it was known to leave her feeling unsettled. To everyone's astonishment they hit it off, though there were many who wondered at Macarthur's happy assertion that she 'positively lectured the Queen on the inequality of the classes, the injustice of it'. Apparently the Queen did not interrupt and asked to be sent suitable reading matter on the subject. The desire to further the war effort produced curious alliances. Miss Macarthur was asked to advise the Work for Women Fund's committee and a year later a report was published on its activities, which illustrates the accepted chasm which existed between educated women and their poorer sisters: 'It was characteristic of the Queen that she thought at once of the women workers in the shadow and the silence. These poor women, upon whom not one single ray of limelight fell, were to matter much to England's future. Her warm sympathy prompted her to help them on the instant; the ordinary workaday world, she saw, must be quickly and skilfully readjusted. Women must be taught new trades.'

Written in glowing terms by Jennie Jerome, Winston Churchill's American-born mother, the report was the result of a lecture tour of the country. Judged by today's standards, its enthusiasm is wrapped around a patronizing attitude, but it would not have seemed so to the contemporary audience. Taking an interest in the problems of the poor was part of philanthropy; charitable concern rather than social awareness. Noblesse oblige. Jennie had spent some time observing the stream of women who turned up at the Fund's London headquarters asking for help:

> No woman is turned away unheard, unhelped or unfed. To the seamstress and milliner, sewing is handed to be done at Trade Union Rates [the minimum, and much lower than men's]. Typists, actresses, tea-shop girls, and any other worker who has lost her occupation through the war, can apply and be sure of help:
>
> 'I 'ardly 'ad the nerve to go,' said a young girl who had been on the variety stage in a troupe of acrobats, 'for I couldn't do anything useful. But they smiled at me ever so kind, and one lady in furs sez, "Oh, we wants such as you to learn." So I felt all right after that.'
>
> The directors asked her in which direction her fancies lay, and she chose to be taught the mysteries of toy-making with excellent results . . . but wherever the occupation is new, the women and girls are 'paid to learn.' Three pence an hour is given with good meals and expert tuition! It reads like a fairy tale to the woman at close grips with real poverty, but it is sound common sense and national economy.

One cannot help suspecting that Jennie had been to see the production of George Bernard Shaw's play *Pygmalion* in London two years earlier. Eliza Doolittle had made a strong impression on the audience.

At court, duties proliferated as the war gathered pace. The rest of the royal ladies were all expected to pull their weight, and there was a good swathe of aunts and cousins and in-laws, most of them Highnesses, to grace committees, write cheques, open bazaars and knit. The Queen was said to have a piece of needlework in every one of the royal apartments, 'so she may take up her work anywhere she finds herself with an odd minute of leisure'. Meanwhile, there was committee work, letter-writing, inspecting packing depots and consulting with the stream of society women who were all busy setting up their own welfare schemes and volunteer societies and keen to get a royal name as patron. It did not take long before an endless round of hospital visiting began: the war-wounded were returning in droves and the Queen duly headed for ward after ward, looked at work in prosthetics departments, toured kitchens, peered into vats in soup kitchens, went to orphanages and children's homes, met recuperating soldiers and talked to bereaved families. She always seemed eager to talk, full of questions: the newsreels show her among nurses and patients and officials, chatting and animated. She was by nature shy, the role demanded engagement and enthusiasm, tempered with dignity; and she duly played it. Film and photographs show her wasp-waisted – she was a true believer in corsetry – in hats piled with feathers and flowers, always prodding the ground with an elegant parasol. Her husband's views on dress were well known: he was a nit-picking stickler for detail and propriety, and the Queen would never, ever have defied him when it came to public behaviour or appearance. She always deferred to him.

George V's views on legs (female, never to be seen in public) induced her to keep hers (shapely, by all accounts) hidden and to pass on the prohibition. Just before the war she had sat in the circle at the Palace Theatre for the first Royal Command performance by the stars of the day. The music hall world was thrilled – it was the ultimate sign that respectability had been achieved. Vesta Tilley appeared in one of her famous male costumes, as Algy, the Piccadilly Johnnie. At the first sight of the trousers, Queen Mary turned regally to the ladies in the royal party and they all buried their heads in their programmes.

Unlike those of other British women, the Queen's floor-skimming skirts never rose an inch throughout the conflict: when inspecting wartime allotments she swished happily through the cabbages. After food shortages beset the nation she was pictured digging her potato plot at Windsor, somehow coordinating spade and trailing skirt. However, pictures of her planting vegetables or picking apples only appeared in her private photograph album and comments were confined to her diary: 'Worked from 3 to 5 planting potatoes. Got very hot and tired.' The royal family stuck rigorously to the idea that public relations was confined to public duties. The rather monotonous life in Buckingham Palace, with a king who decidedly disliked socializing, meant fewer servants and some nods towards economizing were mentioned in the newspapers, but these reports were devoid of any personal details. The press avoided printing gossip, though the public were suitably impressed by the virtuous decision to have no alcohol in royal palaces while the war lasted, a suggestion from Lloyd George. However, they were not informed that this was neatly bypassed 'under doctor's orders', the King having realized that no one else had decided to follow his example. Years later, courtiers recalled the Queen's determined assault on the royal breakfast menu, which had hitherto involved eight courses – porridge, kippers, kedgeree, cold meats, bacon, etc. She decreed that no one should have more than two courses: her son, Prince Henry mounted a rearguard action and won a small victory for an extra fried egg 'for health reasons,' but no one gossiped about the Queen presiding over a table of slightly hungry people. Nor did anyone know the Queen's view of breeches-clad Land Girls, whom she met on several occasions; unfailingly polite and gracious, she smiled, nodded and kept her personal opinion to herself. However, by 1916 she was writing to a friend: 'The length of this war is most depressing. I really think it gets worse the longer it lasts.' Meeting so many wounded men and bereaved families, she called on her upbringing to curb any display of sentiment. Lady Airlie was often by her side: 'She had always been so affected at the sight of suffering that even as a child she once fainted when a footman at White Lodge cut his finger badly, But . . . she trained herself to talk calmly to frightfully mutilated and disfigured men. Her habit of discipline gave her complete physical control.' The Queen was dutiful, and so was her daughter. Princess Mary, seventeen when the war began, was a permanently attached accessory on public occasions. Dressed like an Edwardian schoolgirl, with a smaller hat and a fractionally shorter skirt than her mother, she looked serious or seriously glum in most locations. As the only daughter and a royal princess, she had no choice but to follow mama and occasionally make polite conversation. She was reported to have knitted 'yards and yards of mufflers'. At least her own charitable initiative was wildly popular: Princess Mary's Christmas Gift was a small brass tin, elaborately embossed, to be given to everyone wearing the King's uniform and serving overseas on Christmas Day 1914: nearly half a million were immediately ordered.

The Princess's appeal appeared in November: 'I want you all to help me send a Christmas present from the whole nation to every sailor afloat and every soldier at the Front' – and a staggering amount of money rolled in. Inside each tin was a picture of the princess and a Christmas card, with twenty cigarettes, a pipe, lighter and tobacco; non-smokers received a pencil and khaki writing case; there was a pencil made from a bullet and sweets for young boys, and chocolates for nurses.

The quantities involved proved a challenge,

especially as most of the brass in the country was heading for the munitions plants. Over 13 million cigarettes had to be sorted and packed, and the delivery of the tins presented a logistical nightmare. Even so, a third of a million arrived for Christmas, while others had to wait as the massive production and distribution operation struggled to honour the royal gesture. The money made it possible to supply the gifts to *all* those in uniform, British, Indian and colonial, prisoners of war and also to bereaved relatives . . . eventually over 2½ million people.

Such gestures caught the public imagination, but didn't prevent regular murmurings that the family were still very entangled with their German relations; one of them was First Sea Lord at the Admiralty. Despite forty years as a career officer in the Royal Navy, two months after the war began Prince Louis of Battenberg was forced out purely because of his name, which was subsequently anglicized to Mountbatten. There were outbursts of intolerance of all things German – as well as the dachshunds having a hard time, bottles of hock were smashed alongside splintering Bechstein pianos – and rioting recurred frequently. The violence after the sinking of the *Lusitania* had disturbed everyone: it took place not only in London, where mobs had gone on the rampage, but in Liverpool where two hundred shops, businesses and houses had been gutted. Trouble was reported also from Bradford, Nottingham, Newcastle, Southend, South Shields and many other towns. But none of this included any overt demonstrations against the royal family. Respect and deference were very strong within all sections of society. However, the fact that George V belonged to a royal house with the name of Saxe-Coburg-Gotha, and that he had fifty-odd first cousins bearing very non-English names, was unavoidable. So was the cousins' fall from grandeur: royal houses in Europe, some of them but tiny statelets, were not only wobbling but disappearing. Another cousin, Tsar Nicholas II, had abdicated from the Russian throne. To have shown any trace of nervousness or worry in public was not the royal way; even so, there's no doubt that the royal family privately pondered their own future, just as the Germans launched their long-range bombers towards London. Faster craft than the lumbering Zeppelins, reaching a top speed of 87 mph, they first raided London in brilliant sunshine on a June morning in 1917.

They were watched by large crowds, amazed at this first daylight attack, who seemed oblivious of the damage about to be inflicted. By today's standards these fourteen rather fragile-looking bi-planes would probably not make much impression, but they were then at the cutting edge of aerial warfare and proceeded to drop bombs randomly. Eighteen children died in a primary school in Poplar in London's East End; buildings in the City were reduced to rubble. Altogether, 162 people died and 432 were injured.

The nation was outraged and the funeral of the young pupils was headlined: 'London's Massacred Innocents Laid to Rest'. It continued: 'There were pathetic scenes in Poplar on June 20th, when 15 children (all but three aged five years) were buried in the East London Cemetery. A sixteenth coffin contained fragments of little bodies unidentified. A great number of wreaths – over 500 – had been sent from all parts of the country, schools, hospitals, factories and official bodies.' The pictures showed immense crowds watching the procession and a vast carpet of flowers outside the cemetery. The Bishop of London read a message from the King and Queen and demanded action against 'the places from which the air-raiders came, and the strongest punishment for the perpetrators and designers of these raids'. The 'air-raiders' from Germany were flying aircraft called Gothas. Just like the royal family. It took less than a month for the King to be persuaded, the formalities to be completed and the royal proclamation issued: Saxe-Coburg-Gotha was to be replaced by Windsor.

Meanwhile the royal family were redoubling their patriotic efforts: the King and his wife headed for France and the war zone. While he met military leaders and inspected fortifications, the Queen spent hours in hospitals, hostels, workshops, garages, canteens and laundries. She was confronted by the novelty of uniformed ambulance drivers curtseying to her. These were some of the hundreds of women who were living a life a world away from her experience: unchaperoned, independent, in breeches, heavy boots, overalls or practical (shorter) skirts, and working in hard conditions. The nurses and VADs and ambulance drivers were inured to the horrors of the front: many worked to the sound of gunfire and some had come under shellfire. The Queen – huge hat and parasol perfectly in place – was polite and interested, encouraging and concerned. The press were reporting her every moment, and royalty always remained calm and unemotional. She went to see the deserted battlefield of the Somme and listened to descriptions of the fighting. She stood with her Lady-in-Waiting, the Countess of Airlie who wrote in her memoirs that 'We climbed over a mound composed of German dead, buried by their comrades – all that was left of a whole regiment who had died wresting this strip of land from our troops, only to lose it again . . . scattered everywhere in the ineffable desolation were the pathetic reminders of human life – rifles fallen from dead hands, old water bottles, iron helmets, and in the distance, the guns boomed relentlessly, making new sites of destruction like this one. We stood there speechless. It was impossible to find words. The Queen's face was ashen and her lips were tightly compressed. I felt that like me she was afraid of breaking down.' She went walkabout, stopping her car when she spotted large contingents of soldiers, watched tank and aircraft displays, received countless bouquets from French mayors and even managed a bit of sight-seeing in Amiens cathedral.

Eleven days on tour, every detail in the press back home, and five days later a new family name. The Windsors were being changed by the war, and ensuring that their own royal house would qualify for survival. (Might it be suggested that longevity was on their minds when King George inaugurated the first regular congratulatory telegram to a centenarian that year?) Not that the Queen saw herself as an arbiter of change. Royal women were not revolutionary: stability and consistency were all. Certain rituals were tweaked, slight concessions made to fashion and interests, but the Queen knew what she could do – and was more certain than most women what she *should* do.

At the end of the war, the royal family emerged with a reputation as dignified, diligent, slightly boring public figures – just as they would have liked: burying the excesses and mistresses of the Edwardian age and now striving to appear more of a virtuous and less distant monarchy. They had dug potatoes, visited the wounded and set an example. They had also seen much of the immense intermarried network of European royalty – their cousins and in-laws – shunted off thrones by disgruntled subjects. The very idea of royalty was in question, and the Grand Dukes and Serene Highnesses were being declared redundant. Another cousin, Tsar Nicholas II, and his family had been murdered. Their only daughter, Princess Mary, who before the war would have been expected to marry a prince, very probably German, was now in her twenties. Towards the end of the war she had trained at Great Ormond Street Hospital as a children's nurse; she worked for a while as a probationer, but never took up a full-time job. That would probably have been too much of a break with tradition, but it did suggest that royal princesses should perhaps step outside the palace and not have to follow mama until they married. The Earl of Harewood was now deemed to be a suitable match: that he was a none too youthful-looking, rather dull man some fifteen years older than his bride was irrelevant: he was very definitely English.

The royal house was now Windsor, and the change of name was popular. Back in Sunderland, Ethel Maud Hedinburgh had survived the war, only to succumb to the worldwide flu epidemic of 1918. However, when the relatives gathered for the funeral they were introducing themselves as 'Hedinburgh, rhyming with Edinburgh . . .'.

CHAPTER 7

SKIVVIES AND STUDENTS

'The servant problem' was a squawk of angst from the Victorian age to the mid-twentieth century, rising to a wail of protest during World War I when each class – and class mattered – felt the ground shifting. Today, the word 'servant' is avoided. It has gone out of fashion, even if the basic concept is still alive and well, if a little mutated: the daily, the au pair, the nanny, the cleaning lady, the help (the char and the treasure have been retired).

In modern terms, it is almost impossible to consider equality for women and also accept the idea of a servant. Feminism has wrestled with the question of working women whose doorway to freedom and independence also seems to admit a casually employed woman entering the house armed with a mop, or in charge of the children. Dual careers, parenting, affordable childcare and active shunning of the word 'housewife' all illuminate the large gap in lifestyle planning which used to be filled by the 'below stairs' army, even if that army only consisted of a parlour-maid. The washing machine, the dishwasher and all the other labour-saving devices which are no longer luxuries have failed to morph into the robotic cleaner or MopBot which was once predicted to transform housework. Dust, untidiness, laundry and washing-up all refuse to disappear. Despite years of shaming/persuasion/coercion – both public and private – husbands, partners and others in the household have, on the whole, declined to seize the vacuum cleaner with the enthusiasm reserved for football matches or pottering in the shed. A single-person household contemplates living a minimalist life rich in take-away food and dry-cleaning bills, but still cannot find a way of ordering the rubbish to take itself out.

Guilt attaches to most discussions on the subject, with perhaps a secret wistfulness for that pool of plentiful, cheap, compliant labour 'like back in the old days'. All of which ignores the tide, rather than pool, of foreign labour which has flowed in during the past few years. Linger in the office, and the clank of bucket and hum of vacuum will be mixed with a Babel of languages. Unconnected to your office hierarchy, outsourced and probably underpaid, the anonymous office cleaner is regarded in many ways like the below-stairs staff of yesteryear: useful, unseen and unlikely to complain.

At home, though, there's a constant fret about how to get the housework done: and in parallel to a hundred years ago, there's horror at the thought of regularizing domestic employment. Just as both mistresses and maids erupted with indignation when they were asked to contribute weekly to

Lloyd George's 'stamp' in 1911, which gave free medical treatment and sickness benefit to manual workers, no modern politician has managed to insert PAYE and National Insurance contributions into the modern dailies' financial transactions in the kitchen. And only a small part of that foreign influx has reached the home hearth: for whatever reason, there are few foreign accents heard cleaning in the suburbs.

What has genuinely disappeared is the huge country house which acted as sole local employer for the nearby village and many surrounding hamlets and farms. Sometimes benevolent and giving life-long security to several generations of servants – and sometimes a hard and unsympathetic employer – the great estates were the centre of life in rural areas. They were already beginning to decline in Edwardian times – not that the pampered and carefree house guests ever had an inkling as they shot and rode and ate and drank in splendour and comfort. Group photographs of the score of staff who made this possible often resemble those of an outing for an entire small school: everyone in a row, in uniform, looking serious.

However, in areas where farming was hard and industrial employment too distant, the needs of the landed gentry offered the only opportunity for security. For many cottage-dwellers, work 'up at the big house' was often much sought after rather than despised. Draughty rooms and long gloomy corridors with tiny bare bedrooms in the attic might be your surroundings, with the occasional foray to lay the fires in the grand drawing room, but there was a small army of retainers to meet and talk to, which compensated for the imperious behaviour of the frequent and demanding guests. And there was food. A member of one ancient county family reminisced to me that 'three meals a day was something you could only dream about in a damp cottage. Regular food, your own clean bed – it was the height of ambition in the villages round here to get into the servants' hall.'

From the housekeepers' book-keeping, the elaborate menus and the letters and diaries of Edwardian hostesses come the staggering statistics of entertaining in style: an array of dishes at every meal – particularly breakfast; home-baked bread and pastries, a pile of slaughtered game, a well-stocked cellar and hampers of delicacies from smart stores in London. In retrospect, the years just before World War I began to look like a golden sunset in the pleasure gardens of the rich and titled.

Despite the image of these magnificent country piles, across the country the largest number of servants overall was employed in town house terraces and suburban villas: a maid, a cook, perhaps a tweenie (a 'between stairs' maid) – or just one of these. No servants' hall with its own social dynamic – just a small room, meagre wages and frequently a difficult relationship with the mistress. Life in one such nit-picking household was summed up by Maud Truphet, from a large family in East London, who donned the obligatory cap and apron and became a housemaid before the war.

> My mother put us all into service when I left school at 14.
>
> My employer was very old and crotchety and always moaning that I didn't do this, didn't do that. And when I did all the vacuuming, we had old bellows – like a big box – and we pulled the handle backwards and forwards and with the other hand, pushed it round the room. When I was finished in each room, she used to weigh the dust to see if I'd done the right amount of work – about a cup and a half of dirt for each room! So I used to save a little bit of dirt, 'cos one carpet was red and one was green, so in the pothouse I had three or four bags of different colours so I could make up the weight. She thought it was wonderful!
>
> 'You've worked well, brought all that dirt up, the carpet looks lovely. . . .'
>
> I used to wash their stockings and towels and had ten rooms to keep clean, for 5 shillings a week. I did all the vegetables, cleaned the kitchen pots, and when chaps came to the door, like the milkman and the greengrocer and we went to give them a cup of tea, she'd run down the stairs and

> listen to what we were doing, and we'd get into a row.
>
> I had one day a month off, and one evening a week – so I didn't have a lot of friends – didn't get out much. . . .

Maud recorded her memories nearly forty years ago, indignant in her seventies about the way girls like her were treated but absolutely accepting that no other opportunities were ever considered by herself, her sisters or her parents. Marriage was seen as the goal – an escape from drudgery and often loneliness. All these girls could read and write. Their lessons had been dinned into them. The Sunday school introduced them to story-telling and a wider vocabulary, but the school-leaving age had only just been raised from twelve to fourteen, and the possibility of more education was beyond the reach of poorer families. If there was any money, it would be spent on the boys – there was still public adherence to the view that education was generally 'wasted on women'. In 1913 a domestic servant had no reason to imagine that the coming war would reach into every scullery in the land.

In Edwardian times my adoptive father's father, James Adie, had a cook, a housemaid and two tweenies, which was not deemed extravagant in a prosperous middle-class household in a thriving northern industrial town like Sunderland. They were always remembered as 'scurrying about', cleaning and mopping and scrubbing, heaving buckets of coal up four flights of stairs from the cellar to the top bedroom fireplaces before breakfast was prepared. Since this was a Baptist household of the bleaker kind, young men were not tolerated to hang around the backyard door; anyway, the maids were expected to attend the Bethesda Chapel in their 'free time' on Sundays. Not unsurprisingly, they too scrubbed their last step in 1914 and headed for pastures new.

Being in service was a 'respectable' job. To be candid, for most working-class women in Sunderland it was the only employment available in a town where shipbuilding and coal pits dominated: exclusively male and with few ancillary industries (boilermakers, galvanizers, ropemakers) needing – or wanting – women in their workforce. The surrounding pit villages in County Durham traditionally expected women to stay at home; there were few 'big houses' offering jobs, due to much of the land having been owned by the bishop, who made do with a modest palace and ensured that gracious country estates didn't spoil the view for many miles and several centuries. The villages were often isolated and self-contained: a Miners' Institute, a pub, a chapel, a Co-op, all institutions which preferred men.

Rural Durham was notable, like industrial Yorkshire and Lancashire (where women headed for the mills), in having many fewer women in domestic service, mainly due to poverty. There was, however, a hefty tradition of washerwomen in the north-east, who'd be found in every street and 'took in': they were not spoken of kindly, having somehow failed the test of keeping up with the other poor Joneses and having to resort to hours of boiling oily and coaly clothes. In other parts of the country even working-class families managed sometimes to employ a needy teenager from the workhouse or orphanage. As one travelled south the number of servants employed steadily increased until, in London and the leafy south-east counties and on the south coast, the middle classes would not wish to be caught without a parlourmaid to open the front door. The records of the Foundling Hospital in London show that for almost two centuries domestic service was the only future for a girl who'd been brought up in the huge building at Coram Fields. And as in many other Poor Law and religious institutions, from an early age the dress and training of the girls heralded their future: caps and aprons, scrubbing and polishing and sewing, and a sense of gratitude towards those who took them in.

When the twentieth century began, the decline in servant numbers started to accelerate as more opportunities opened up for women in clerical and factory work. Statistically, before World War I more women were working in industry than in domestic service. However, there were still over 1½ million women mainly in mob cap and apron. The statistics are somewhat blurred, for women's work was not always recorded in official and census reports.

Heads of household – always male – were well documented, but wives and daughters who worked often slipped from view. Laundry work, helping on the farm, being part of a family business, outworkers for the clothing and accessory industry, and many other types of work did not claim official attention. In many instances, it was assumed that a married woman could not be classified as a worker: there was a fixed view, often enshrined in employment regulations, that employment ended with marriage. Women became invisible working wives – and they also had to face housework, which was not the irritating chore of today but a relentless grind.

Even though we grumble today about washing machines that break down, boilers that give up the ghost when cold weather starts and dog hairs that are resistant to an industrial-strength vacuum cleaner, housework does not have the same meaning as it did a hundred years ago. 'Elbow grease' was needed then, along with stout knees to get down and scrub. Coal dust from open fires, windows smeared with sooty grime from industrial chimneys, water that always needed boiling, outside lavatories, freezing inside bathrooms, laundry that involved brute strength with a tub and a mangle, irons heated on the stove, and gaslights and oil lamps to clean; candle-wax would also have to be scraped off in many humbler homes. A woman's work was never done. Some labour-saving appliances were appearing, but they were only for the well-off and most households presented a daily physical challenge to keep clean and warm. No wonder women deprived of servants saw it as a problem. But was there no way out of this? Did poor women inevitably have to contemplate service? Did middle-class women have to devote a large part of the day to keep dust at a respectable level? Could they perhaps not better themselves?

These days we see life in terms of choice, sometimes hard, sometimes bewildering, sometimes an exciting pick'n'mix of opportunities. Women still have to consider their priorities when looking at career, family and lifestyle, for society has still to deliver full equality and adjustments to rights and responsibilities. But there is the great springboard of education – lots of it, with girls encouraged and enticed into higher education, training, university. Not so for those a hundred years ago. Even though most women across all classes could read and write at the beginning of the twentieth century, there was entrenched suspicion of the 'bluestocking'.

If you had been brought up in late Victorian times, it was far from unusual to hear that too much learning would spoil a girl. Never mind making her an unsuitably opinionated wife, there were endless spurious claims that women's brains would be injured if too immersed in study. All kinds of rubbish was spouted about 'smaller brains in females' being unable to function to the same degree as the male brain; that rational thinking was not possible for women; that menstruation sapped women of life-blood, therefore made them weaker – and with continued intellectual activity would shrivel their wombs. The line from one of the Victorian writer Charles Kingsley's poems, 'Be good, sweet maid, and let who will be clever', is open to interpretation, but it has been used down the years to squash smart girls and remind them of their destiny as non-thinking angels. The very notion of choice was missing from the upbringing of working-class girls: if there was a tiny amount of money to spare to spend on the children's education, it was the sons who were favoured. There was still residual prejudice that education for such girls should involve nothing more than very basic literacy, some Bible knowledge, the ability to sew and perhaps rudimentary cooking. It needed a combination of unusual vision, encouraging parents and money to change their lives and acquire more education beyond this basic schooling. Government saw no great benefit in a better-educated female. Parents ruled the roost: even if they had dreams, few girls would dare challenge their father's authority – and the same went for those higher up the social ladder.

Middle-class girls had mothers frantic that their 'educated' daughters would become dowdy and spectacle-wearing and ruin their marriage chances. What was the point of more education? Especially as there were severe limits to where a woman might apply her talents: most of the professions were closed to them. Upper-class girls were more likely than not to have a governess. Some girls were lucky and benefited from well-read, intellectually broad-minded women. Others got endless lessons in deportment, French conversation, dancing, drawing and needlework. Their brothers went to school.

By the beginning of the twentieth century, a determined, hard-working handful of females had made it to university – and they were a small minority among a tiny elite band of students. At Oxford and Cambridge they were subject to chaperones and countless rules and regulations: there were still some professors who could not face addressing women without distaste. There were subjects thought 'unsuitable' for them to take: degrees in theology, divinity, medicine and law were 'men only' courses in many universities. And medical teaching was occasionally bedevilled by crusty professors insisting that anatomy be taught in segregated rooms. As the war approached, the Oxford colleges were still arguing about women's status and their eligibility to graduate – to receive a degree rather than just 'attend' the university – and male lecturers could still object to the presence of women. There was always the usual background of muttered disapproval about women in the examination rooms, and despite very gentle steps towards acceptance, the female students still represented a disturbing species to some, resulting in careful reminders from the Principal, Mrs Bertha Johnson, to one of her students:

Dear Bernice,

We have had a very tiresome complaint that the men examinees are disturbed by the way our students sit in their tight skirts and show their legs. We do not know who are at fault, but we are bound to warn all.

Yours ever B.J.J.

However, only weeks into the war it was clear that patriotism had produced empty lecture rooms: young men abandoned their studies and universities faced the possibility of filling their place with women – however, colleges had been requisitioned by the War Office and hospital beds were crammed into ancient buildings. Eventually, the immense pressure on young men to show their willingness to fight, culminating in conscription in early 1916, emptied the university towns. The women who were left found themselves in an unsettling atmosphere. Vera Brittain, having won a coveted place at Oxford in 1914, saw a drastic change come over the city. Her later book, *Testament of Youth*, is seen by many as the classic description of the impact of war on middle-class women like her: she saw a university drained of its life blood, two thousand of three thousand young students had joined up, and her fellow students and friends were becoming casualties:

Everywhere their invisible presence was inescapable. As the Roll of Honour lengthened,

> their ghosts seemed to linger in the colleges where they had looked forward to the future, confidently and gaily, only a few months ago. Most pathetic of all, perhaps, was the generation of boys who had left school in July 1914, and had been about to come up to college. Occasionally they appeared in the city for a few weeks as cadets, but a large proportion of them died before the War ended without enjoying even one term of Oxford life.

For the women, student life soon lost its glitter; the young men were away, the teaching staff were from an older generation, and austerity reigned in the none-too-luxurious college accommodation. Food was stodgy and plain, coal was to be rationed and there were hardly any maids to bring it. At least the women – and the money they brought in – kept the universities going, though they found themselves constantly exposed to competing loyalties. The government wanted them to join the national effort – every able-bodied young woman was needed to make shells and tend the land, not to read books; the college dons, on the other hand, were desperate to persuade them not only that their education was worthwhile but that their enhanced skills would be needed when the conflict was over. Even so, several of the women dons felt they should direct their energies to war work, heading for France and the Balkans with voluntary aid groups and organizing the new women's military units.

The pressure to 'do one's bit' was ever-present. The result was often young women studying at all hours (sometimes by candlelight) after putting in time with local voluntary organizations. Their situation was always made more difficult because there was still not enough public support for them: pioneering and clever, they still had to prove themselves. 'Role models' had yet to be invented and those Oxford-educated women like Gertrude Bell, who had been a student in Victorian days, gained little recognition in their own time. She had been a brilliant history student, and became a formidable linguist, explorer, archaeologist and expert on Arab affairs; by 1916, after working with the Red Cross in France, she was head of the London Office for the Wounded and Missing, and subsequently she headed for the Middle East where, with T.E. Lawrence – 'Lawrence of Arabia' – her knowledge and influence shaped much of the area's future. Today she would have been a shining star for young students to follow: Oxford remembered her as intellectually formidable, but tempered by the domestic reservation: 'Would she be the sort of person to have in one's bedroom when one was ill?'

Of those who finished their courses during the war, some, armed with their education, were able to gain better positions in wartime organisations. They headed for supervisory roles in the Land Army, the women's services and government departments, though the usual caveat applied: only 'for the duration'. Others could not bear to sit quietly and study while their world tore itself apart: Vera Brittain left to work as a VAD in France.

CHAPTER 8

WE NEED VOLUNTEERS – YOU, YOU AND YOU

'I'm off to the pub. . . . I shall be at my club. . . . Rotary meeting . . . the Masons . . . a round of golf. . . .'

There were places where women could not tread; places where men socialized, discussed important matters, often decided public business. For young working women, there were few welcoming premises. For married women, it was acceptable to meet on parish business or do charitable work.

Across society in 1914 there were women who had been involved in the Mothers' Union, the Sunday school movement, the temperance movement, parish and social activities – unpaid work which was usually taken for granted. The middle classes were municipally minded and also had time on their hands. They expected their daughters to follow suit and to socialize with 'suitable' friends – though there were few opportunities to break out of restricted circles. For some years, the popular and acceptable diversion from endless tea and tennis parties had been the Red Cross and St John courses in first aid; and alongside, the recently formed girl guides had been determined to attract a wider cross-section of young recruits than was traditional. The Chief Commissioner, Lady Baden-Powell, prided herself that they 'are drawn from all social classes of society, from the peer's daughter to the daughter of the poorest citizen; all are bound together in this one big sisterhood'.

The guides acquired practical skills – along traditional lines, admittedly, and rather different from the boy scouts. However, you could earn badges as a cyclist, electrician, photographer and air mechanic. At the beginning of the war girls too young to join the workforce or the women's voluntary organizations had flocked to the guides, and at first found themselves knitting warm clothes for the boy scouts on coast-watching duty. They progressed to scullery maids, laundresses, waitresses, canteen workers and orderlies, and also to spinning, weaving and sandbag making. They taught English to refugees and in London worked as messengers in government departments. The guides were considered to be 'particularly conscientious.' Usefully, there was no question that they should be paid.

In just a few years the scout and guide movement had spread internationally, and in 1915 the British press carried a story about a French girl guide whose family found themselves under German occupation near the town of Loos. Emilienne Moreau was a seventeen-year-old miner's daughter who alerted the British to the enemy's positions and then sheltered wounded

British troops during heavy fighting. The details of what happened next are slightly blurred by the fog of war, but there is no doubt that she was extremely courageous. The *Evening News* had a particularly vivid account: 'In a hidden corner, five Germans kept firing on our troops unseen, until this girl discovered their position. She obtained some hand grenades and threw them in amongst them, killing three of them. The two survivors rushed out at her with their bayonets fixed, but she had armed herself with a revolver, belonging to a dead British officer, and with steady aim she fired, killing them both.' The French version has her shooting four Germans, but her Croix de Guerre decoration is indisputable, along with the British Military Medal. *The Evening News* ends with a flourish: 'It was the training this girl had received as a Girl Guide which enabled her to keep cool in the hour of danger.'

Lady Baden-Powell must have mulled over what her own guides were training for, but was at least immensely proud that her senior guides were asked to work as messengers at the Paris Peace Conference in 1919. She would be well aware that her guides were being given confidence, even though there was still great emphasis on their being good home-keepers and mothers as well as citizens. The guide movement was formed at a time when change was already in the air. In the two decades before the war, bubbling under the suffrage campaign had been a gradual acceleration in efforts to change women's status. The figure of 'The New Woman', first described by the writer Sarah Grand in 1894, was educated, independent and self-supporting. The image was popularized in the works of Ibsen, Henry James and George Bernard Shaw, who presented a more emancipated and intelligent female compared to the fainting heroines of Victorian literature; one who questioned convention and thought seriously about her role in society. This was not, however, something which spread like wildfire through all classes in society: The New Woman was firmly in the upper echelons.

Further education and the money to support yourself were available only to a limited circle. Nevertheless, better education for middle-class girls was giving more scope for employment opportunities to those of limited means and for a very few there was the excitement of entry into university and the professions. Business and industry were seeing lady clerks and secretaries, and office managers and supervisors were moving into jobs hitherto the preserve of men. The negative publicity given to the more sensational activities of the militant suffragettes, and the fierce backlash from those who saw the family and moral values under threat, obscured real progress: the New Woman, though not effecting any change to economic or legal status, could be *seen* to be different by all classes. She rode a bicycle. She wore practical clothes. Though she was lampooned in the press, you could goggle at her first and then perhaps think: *why not*?

The independent and organizing women who seized their chance to do something in 1914 did not appear out of nowhere. They had skills which previously had been seen as merely 'helpful' – unpaid, charitable, voluntary work which did not register as part of the nation's economy nor get counted in statistics. It was a netherworld compared to the serious business of politics, trade and industry.

Many women had been schooled in the suffrage movement and had acquired a fair idea of how politics, the police and the press shaped their lives. The idea of the New Woman had publicized the possibilities of a freer existence – more sensible clothes, driving and cycling *by yourself*. When hostilities started these women were already well versed in knitting, sewing, first aid, fund-raising, charitable work, gardening, tea-making, organizing and setting a good example. What the war brought was public recognition that they were wanted, and had moved from 'helpful' to essential. Even if they were still not wanted on the front line, there were ever-increasing opportunities on the Home Front.

Since the Boer War of 1899–1902, the Young Men's Christian Association had looked after soldiers returning from the battlefield as well as setting up canteens in the field. It could call on a large number of volunteers who helped at annual summer camps for the home defence reservists, the Territorial Army, and knew about organizing tented accommodation and canteens. In 1914 they were quick off the mark to France, and within the first ten days set up 250 'huts' attached to army camps. Women were permitted to work in them, in fact were frequently in the majority, but there were soon rumblings that they had no part in decision-making and seemed assigned only to domestic chores in the canteens. On the Home Front, the well-connected and formidable women who were throwing themselves into welfare work spotted a gap in the provisions being made. There was a world outside the army camps, and Lady Rodney, who had already been to France, reported that she was 'greatly struck by the sad condition of the British Soldier, who had no place to which he could go for wholesome amusement and recreation for his leisure moments. The towns were full of temptation, and it was not advisable that men should be left to the tender mercies of the various Cafés and Estaminets.' So in December 1914 the Women's Auxiliary Committee (WAC) was born, acquired a member of the royal family as president, and set about 'providing voluntary lady workers to staff the Huts at the Base Camps in France, and at the same time provide games and comforts for the men frequenting these huts'.

As in many other women's voluntary organizations, there was a hands-on approach at head office. A clutch of titled ladies, confident and able to pull strings, interviewed every single woman who applied to be sent overseas. If you survived the encounter with the Countess of Wimborne, the Countess of Bessborough, Lady Rodney, Lady Malcolm – and the frequent presence of Queen Victoria's granddaughter Princess Helena Victoria – you were clearly made of the right stuff. And you were going to need it. This was a foray into foreign fields, literally, with the excuse that you were taking the Home Front to them – reminding men of home and giving them the little luxuries and comforts which they associated with their families. A welcome. A cup of tea. A chat. Some chocolate to munch back in the trench.

Since the work was unpaid and volunteers had to cover their own expenses, the initial 'lady workers' came mainly from the middle and upper classes. However, as the war progressed there was a stream of applicants who had lost family members and then decided to provide 'a home from home' for soldiers in France rather than endure their own empty house. (Many wondered at these widows and bereaved mothers and daughters, not grasping that they felt the need to get to the country from which a man's body had not been returned. It was their own way of dealing with grief, intensified for everyone who never witnessed a funeral or burial because of the government decision not to repatriate the dead.)

Recreation huts were the priority, a friendly place where men could just sit, write letters home on the notepaper provided and buy hot drinks, biscuits and cigarettes. Later there were hostels for relatives of wounded men, dockside canteens, convalescent centres, teachers and educational books, and all manner of 'soldiers' comforts' provided by a small army of women who had adopted a smart grey uniform with a straw hat for summer and a black velour one for winter. A small grant was available to subsidize the uniform, but most wearers seem to have been able to afford it. Another indication of the volunteers' background was the number able to take their own car abroad at a time when lady drivers were something of a rarity. A YMCA 1916 Gift Book noted that 'At the Grosvenor Gardens Hut one evening a man in khaki was heard to ask one of the workers the name of the lady who had just served him with food. On being told it was Lady Ponsonby he replied "I thought as much. Before the war I was a servant in her house, waiting at the table. Now things are reversed, and her ladyship waits on me."'

No one whinged about the conditions they experienced: cheerfulness and a can-do attitude prevailed. Nor were the 'lady workers' shielded from the awfulness of the war: it was unavoidable, with injured men, bereaved relatives, exhausted soldiers, mud and mangled countryside all around. Betty Stevenson was an enthusiastic nineteen-year-old from Harrogate, whose mother Catherine was a YMCA supporter very much in favour of improving women's position in the organization. In 1916, Betty joined her aunt who was already in a canteen on the outskirts of Paris. A year later her mother replaced her aunt, with Betty advising, 'Don't imagine you won't want pretty clothes; you will, so bring all you've got. . . . Life isn't all composed of blue overalls and brown boots. Bring lots of overalls for the work, but not ugly ones. You've no idea how "they" love to see something pretty. They're dead sick of uniforms, I can tell you. . . .' For two and a half years she worked in canteens and later as a driver, often for Lena Ashwell's concert parties which provided entertainment for the troops. It was not an easy life, but both the excitement and the independence more than compensated for the hard conditions. Like many of the young middle-class women involved in these activities, she was living very differently from what was expected for the typical privately educated Edwardian girl. Writing from Etaples, she described going to see football and other sports at a park which happened to be next to a cemetery:

> Next door to Canada Park, in fact touching it, is the cemetery – acres and acres of little brown wooden crosses, They are burying at the rate of 40 a day and the systematic digging is awful. Three times during the afternoon the Last Post was sounded over some grave, and I shall never forget the impression I got each time all the games stopped, and all the thousands of men sitting on the slopes stood up in dead silence while the Last Post was sounded, and then sat down again and continued their ragging. It made the most enormous impression on

> me. During the afternoon a huge long Red Cross train passed. They come every day, hundreds of carriages, and crawling along at snail's pace.

In 1918, aerial bombing was becoming more frequent over areas some distance from the front lines. Betty drove through air raids in Etaples, slept in a bedroom with a hole blown in the ceiling and was sheltering under a roadside bank in the countryside when a German plane shed its bomb-load and she was killed instantly. She was given a military funeral, and the French awarded her the Croix de Guerre *avec palme* for courage and devotion to duty.

From today's perspective, little prominence was given to the dangers to be encountered in a war zone. The casualty figures said it all, from the very beginning. Few of the letters from young women dwell on risks, and there was much greater parental fuss about the propriety (especially for middle-class girls) of working unchaperoned among men than about the possibilities of being injured. Sterling qualities desired by welfare committees in their potential workers were honesty, enthusiasm, integrity and good manners. Questions were rarely raised about their attitude to danger, perhaps partly because women ordinarily were not expected to have encountered great threat or peril, so why discuss the hypothetical? Being of 'good character' encompassed the potential to deal with whatever they might encounter. Frequently the most frightening moments described in diaries and letters home involved men's injuries, which had to be faced and coped with. Again and again there were descriptions of grim sights and heartbreaking stories. The boom of guns and whistle of shells which could be heard, even at a great distance, were often brushed off as a kind of inconvenience to getting on with their work. Admittedly, the static nature of much of the war meant that huge areas behind the lines were well away from immediate attack; aerial bombardment only came later and was not widespread or constant. But modern attitudes to 'war zones' and 'risk assessment' would not have been understood.

Nor was the 'war zone' out of bounds to visitors. The front line trenches were under military command, but everywhere else received a stream of royalty, welfare organizers, politicians, writers, military observers and the well-connected curious who made their way across the Channel. Visits were more a bureaucratic hurdle for civilians than an emotional obstacle or military inconvenience, and produced endless complaints about paperwork, passes and permissions.

The Women's Auxiliary Committee members made frequent forays to France; they needed more funds to operate both at home and abroad and there was considerable publicity to be gained by delivering an eyewitness account. Princess Helena Victoria garnered lots of column inches when she toured numerous bases in August 1915; ten days were crammed with visits to YMCA huts and military bases, inspecting hospitals, bakeries, stores and a veterinary hospital, meeting nurses and generals, going to a hut concert and seeing a demonstration of how to throw a hand grenade. Royal visits don't change much, but here was a forty-five-year-old female member of the royal family gamely trotting around the theatre of war – just after the first German gas attack – as if it were just another official engagement.

The Countess of Bessborough was on tour too, and had praise for the women in the recreation huts as 'helpful and energetic', full of 'tact and devotion'. The 'sympathy and encouragement' for the men struck her deeply and nowhere is there mention of fear or danger, just that their work was 'fatiguing'.

What shines through today is the extraordinary contribution made by these women in psychological terms. In an era when scant attention was paid to mental health, when cowardice often meant the firing squad, and when shell-shock was only beginning to be recognised – they were responsible for a continuous theme of care and kindness. They listened to the men. They were sympathetic, helpful, polite, all of which mattered hugely in an atmosphere of army discipline, violence and staggering slaughter.

Such behaviour was seen as 'incidental' by the authorities, a little luxury, provided by these volunteers who were not part of the war machine. Even the nursing staff in the hospitals did not automatically include empathy in their work. In many descriptions of the canteens and recreation rooms, there is often an underlying note of slight surprise that small kindnesses could have such a beneficial effect, especially among 'the men'. The realization that ordinary soldiers had a sensitive side, the 'delicacy of emotions' expected only of the well-educated, fascinated many, who noted the cheers and thanks showered on these women. In the course of the war nearly two thousand women staffed the huts, in most cases running all-women units. As well as bringing comfort, throughout their efforts ran a thread of high-minded concern for soldiers' moral conduct:

> the men have been regularly supplied with socks and woollen comforts throughout the winter, with games and magazines, Christmas presents and free food. Voluntary lady workers have done invaluable work in the labour camps, making the huts comfortable and homelike for the men, and keeping them free from drunkenness by supplying wholesome recreation and music as a counter-attraction to the numerous estaminets within reach of the camps.

Such sentiments were not intended as condescending – heavy drinking, poverty and squalor were the background from which a large percentage of the army took its men, and back in Britain the WAC had very early turned its attention to the upheaval caused by refugees, troops coming home on leave and the thousands of munitionettes working away from home. The YMCA and the YWCA were providing a raft of welfare services across Britain, but Lena Ashwell, who, unusually for a woman in those days, worked in theatre management and was sharpened by prejudice to 'painted actresses', observed that neither organization could shake off what she called 'the spell of the early Victorian ideal of the fitness of things . . .'. With an entirely modern view of the relationship between the sexes, she despaired that 'they were bound down with the idea of keeping the sexes gracefully apart lest in any way they should influence each other on the downward path to ruin. The idea of companionship, friendship, equality of status and interest was undreamt of.'

As a result the YMCA in Britain was running clubs in which no woman – wife, daughter, mother, anyone – could cross the threshold for a cup of tea (even though women were employed to serve it). This, thought Ashwell, was the consequence of the antiquated education young people still received:

> When properly educated you entered a world where a member of the other sex was not referred to except as a strange and dangerous being who apparently made rare visits from a distant planet to spread havoc and

> destruction. There was every effort at first to follow this strange prejudice which strove to separate the two halves of the human race. There was much talk of the fearsome fact that the men who had come from the Colonies had, no doubt, wives and sweethearts who they had left behind, and the men must be saved from the intriguing women who waited for them in every street, behind every lamp-post.

Such fears ran through many a well-meaning charity and voluntary group trying to improve conditions for ordinary working women and girls across the country. Thousands were being moved into the munitions industry, others were getting jobs far from home or were without family support as the war created unprecedented conditions. There was quite a lot of hand-wringing – not everyone had Ashwell's 'New Woman' progressive views. As a result the WAC was patrolling the streets in several towns in an effort to control 'vice', which had become a burning issue with local moralists. But their main efforts were centred on opening canteens in munitions factories (serving over two hundred thousand workers daily by 1917) and running rest rooms and recreation huts for women.

In this they were joined by a myriad of voluntary organizations, both local and national, who achieved a degree of coordination often missing in charitable ventures. There were innumerable girls' clubs, set up to counter the problem of most women feeling unable, and certainly not expected, to go into pubs. Tea rooms tended to be too expensive for working girls, and in any case closed early. There was a general unease among even the most progressive and broad-minded voluntary organizers that the streets of many towns were not suitable places to wander in the evenings. Though licensing hours had been curtailed by the government, drunkenness was the norm in many areas: James Adie in Sunderland always remarked on the number of men prone in the gutter in his town's East End, even in wartime, with no one taking any particular notice. Girls' clubs sprang up to offer a safe and welcoming haven to women; many of them would today sound a bit starchy in their approach, but they were hugely appreciated by both women working away from home and by locals. The Sunderland Social Club stated that it provided 'a healthy amusement and bright social life and companionship under good conditions, in short, the raising of the standard of recreation and the setting of a higher ideal of life.' Its opening was praised by the local representative of the Ministry of Munitions and its high moral tone would undoubtedly have been set by committee member Miss Edith Ironside, a former headmistress of my old school, remembered as formidable Old Tinribs.

The Girls' Friendly Society offered to provide for 'the great Sisterhood of Labour . . . brighter hours untrammelled by the cares and worries of their positions . . . shelter, comfort and healthy recreation, and to see that they are given every opportunity of keeping clear of the temptations that beset them in their daily lives'. Admittedly they operated under the banner of Church and Empire, but that note of prim protectiveness was common to most of these clubs as a result not so much of religious views but of the influence of the lady welfare workers who were in the workplace. They were more worldly women who knew that many girls came from very old-fashioned homes and were not streetwise at all. Sex education was nil and such matters were *never* mentioned in most families. As a child, I remember an elderly family friend who had worked for the local Methodist girls' club during World War I recalling the problems for girls who were 'so'. This was her only permitted word to describe girls who were pregnant. The press and politicians (male) were beginning to observe what the *Times* nervously called 'the growing liberty of girls'. However, most of the voluntary societies were well ahead of them, aware that the war was nudging women into uncharted territory not only in work but at play too: uncounted numbers from poor working-class homes had hardly had the chance for any kind of leisure before the war, for they had no money to spare, and no time between the household chores. Sport, concerts, going dancing were nearly all out of bounds.

Three years into the war, even the Ministry of

Labour had worked out that it wasn't enough to get women working and perhaps give them a meal – they needed what we now call 'leisure activities' and the officials then called 'ordered play'. What was wanted in every hostel and club was a piano. The *Daily Telegraph* sounded as if it had discovered the philosopher's stone:

> The piano is the first essential! And dancing then was the natural sequence! No matter how tired the girls might have been, from their work with the machine tools, in the handling of high explosives, with all the precautions involved, or in putting the finishing touches to a heavy shell, dancing was always the first form of recreation. Indeed, when in the tremendous pressure of the winter of 1916–17 night work had to be done, the girls coming off at, say, seven a.m. demanded their dance before going to spend the best part of their day in bed.

Entertaining the men came under the umbrella of the YMCA, although, with few active men left after enlistment, another group of women formed the Soldiers' Entertainment Fund. It aimed to send musicians and entertainments to the 'five hundred camps which have been established throughout the country for the training of the gallant lads who are being prepared to fight the Teutonic foe'. They thought the concerts put on by the 'Tommies' themselves were all very well, but they deserved professional entertainment which could be provided in the YMCA huts, particularly in 'lonely country districts'. They also had over two hundred artistes on their books, many of whom had been 'hard hit by the war . . . professional people of proven qualifications, and naturally they are not asked to give their services gratuitously'.

The fund-raisers were hard at work and, as with so many other appeals, combined both patriotism and welfare concerns with strong cultural intentions. Those sitting on the committees had imbibed the Victorian virtue of 'improvement'; thus the ladies running the War Emergency Entertainments (which operated out of Claridge's Hotel in London) stressed that they aimed to give 'Free Concerts to Wounded Soldiers in Hospital and engagements for Artists suffering from the War' – and they also intended to 'Foster British Music'. They were particularly concerned about unemployed women musicians: 'We have cases of girls, who, through the loss at the Front of their brothers or fathers, are compelled to support a large family by their voice, violin or piano. The pianists, 'cellists, and violinists cannot do any kind of manual labour, as their hands would be spoiled, and after the War they would be thus deprived of their only means of earning a livelihood.'

Much of this activity was absorbed into the life of towns and villages across the land – hardly the stuff of headlines and official reports, but essential to daily life in extraordinary circumstances. Societies, fund-raisers, groups – many thousands of women were all unknowingly combating loneliness and often grief. The Home Front was being decimated; households were without men, young women were away working in engineering and munitions, death isolated many families. Packing parcels, serving tea, going to a girls' club, sitting on a committee, rolling bandages and making clothes at a sewing bee gave them an excuse to be together. As in many wars, there was an energy and an urgency which kept life moving along at an intense rate, though well before 1918 it was painfully clear that the scale of this conflict was causing exhaustion to creep into daily lives.

CHAPTER 9

BEDPANS AND SCALPELS

There's an angel in our ward as keeps
a-flittin' to and fro
With fifty eyes upon 'er wherever she
may go;
She's pretty as a picture and bright
as mercury,
And she wears the cap and apron of
a V.A.D.

The one single job which all agreed a woman should do, never mind could, was nurse. Tradition, convention, popular sentiment and necessity all combined to approve the work. But underneath lurked the worm of ambivalence. Angel or floor-scrubber? Cool fingers soothing the brow or hand on the bed-pan?

Half a century previously, Florence Nightingale had dragged nursing into relative respectability. She herself had initially despaired of the 'drunken old crones' who turned up at the Crimean War. The word 'nurse' then had implications well beyond the bedside manner, and after decades of effort there was still a view that 'nice' young women should really not be involved in tending men's bodies. The idea is not yet dead: it was voiced to me several times in Libya, southern Iraq and the Gulf States by indignant hospital doctors who said that only 'immoral Europeans' were suited to the work. At the start of the twentieth century, professional training was available in Britain and there was an understanding that nurses were an essential part of efficient treatment. Even so, it was still very much a working-class job, in part due to the thought that paying someone to be caring diluted the nurse's dedication. Nuns and charitable organizations did such work for free – it was a vocation, surely, a word which contained so much more virtue than 'job'. Caring was perceived as the core characteristic of being a woman. Why should you pay them to do what came naturally? So not surprisingly, the professional and the volunteer occupied very different spheres in the public mind when the war began.

The volunteer brigades were well established. In Edwardian times, the Red Cross and the Order of St John and their first aid courses had attracted the attention of many bored, frustrated upper– and middle-class women. It was something useful which didn't frighten the horses – you learned bandage-rolling and useful tips which added to a wife's or mother's accomplishments. There was also a uniform which was a touch romantic with a hint of the military, a hint of the religious: long blue dress, starched collars and cuffs, a cap with frilly tails;

and, immediately the war began, someone managed to authorize that the skirts be shortened to a full six inches above the ground! Initially there was a charge for taking the courses – and for the uniform – which restricted the applicants to those of independent means and set the tone of 'well-brought-up young ladies' well into the war years.

In 1909, there was some government prescience in the decision to include cooks, laundresses, clerks and drivers in these Voluntary Aid Detachments: moving the wounded, feeding them, administration – the army was not in any way organized for this. The military nurses, serving in the grandly titled Queen Alexandra's Imperial Military Nursing Service, were a tiny number: under three hundred on the day war broke out, with a reserve of just two hundred on call and another six hundred civilian nurses available.

The QAs saw themselves as very much part of the military machine, though they had no official status within the armed forces and fruitlessly manoeuvred for years to shift from civilian ranks to recognized military terms – something that time and again has been used to keep women in uniform in an unequal position. They were disciplined and trained and had to be twenty-five before joining, indicating that they were serious about their profession and expected respect. The first week of fighting saw them heading for France with little idea of the mammoth task ahead of them. The initial preparations involved setting up military hospitals well behind the lines: within weeks the scale of the operation exploded, with casualty clearing stations, plans for huge ambulance trains, massive dockside facilities to accommodate injured men to be shipped home, and hospital ships – never mind the demands of military hospitals on the Home Front. Suddenly, the VADs were indispensable.

There were nine thousand of them in August 1914 and they scrambled into formation: in every county, large houses were offered as temporary hospitals, recuperation homes and medical centres. Some VADs volunteered for work overseas, but the majority were based at home. Any thought that they might spend the time patting a fevered brow was instantly dispelled as the rail system shunted wounded men across Britain towards their local region. The war arrived home in the shape of hundreds of men filling up country manors, smart London houses, requisitioned schools and local hospitals. They had appalling injuries. No one had experienced this kind of medical emergency on home soil – the Boer War, and before that countless military operations in India and the rest of the Empire, had been a distant story, with no immediate experience of broken bodies and men in pain.

County Red Cross organizations began to build an immense network of twenty-four-hour, seven-days–a-week volunteers, often on shift work. In County Durham alone twenty-seven hospitals were set up, including ones at Brancepeth Castle and several stately homes, in a drill hall and in the private house next door to my old school. Not only local men were arriving: the country town of Hexham in Northumberland was not a little surprised to receive Belgian and French soldiers as well as English.

The age limit of twenty-one for UK-based VADs, twenty-three for those posted abroad, was quickly ignored. Keen teenagers were quick off the mark, with encouragement such as this from the *Lady* magazine: 'The fact one cannot bear arms does not excuse any one from helping their country's cause by fighting such foes as misery, pain and poverty.' Young women discovered that this was war work which their parents could hardly object to: a caring, traditional role, carried out locally. Even so, the arrival of these youthful eager beavers on the wards was not without problems. The professional nursing staff were unimpressed. First aid courses and a squeak of patriotic enthusiasm did not constitute proper training, in their opinion. To add insult to injury, their objections were further quashed by the Joint War Committee – which ran the volunteer system – publishing its decision on the correct way to address the young VAD: 'Nurse.' No one ever resolved the tension which existed in many wards over the years: dedicated VADs found themselves given most of the dirty work and at the sharp end of many a professional nursing sister's tongue.

It wasn't surprising that the influx of 'gently-bred young ladies' was more than irritating to the trained nurses, many of whom came from much humbler backgrounds and had often found themselves working in hospitals where poverty and Victorian conditions made their lives – and their patients' lives – extremely hard. Maggie Fancy from Dorset was sixteen at the start of the war and beginning her nursing training in London. She was paid ten shillings a month 'with money taken out for broken thermometers, bent needles (used repeatedly) and soiled uniforms'. Collars were so stiff that you couldn't move your head from side to side and there were no protective gloves – just nail brushes and carbolic soap. Nurse Fancy recalled that babies born at home were bathed in a saucepan or frying-pan – whatever was to hand: the average new-born in a poor family weighed in at only five or six pounds. The girls were discouraged from turning mattresses (horsehair or straw) and fluffing up pillows, due to the fleas and bedbugs snuggled underneath. Even so, hygiene and cleanliness were drilled into the trainees.

In the voluntary hospitals, professional nurses found themselves among confident middle-class girls who happily used their social skills to cajole and entertain and amuse the patients. Class differences were not merely assumptions of difference: they were barriers which were nearly insurmountable. Bringing flowers from home, offering to write letters, being able to call on a circle of friends with time and money to provide sweets and cigarettes, soap and bedsocks, the VADs were a constant reminder to the paid professionals that there was a vast army of women who did not work and who now beamed with excitement at being called 'Nurse'. They also got photographed – a lot. Again, they were a blessing for the magazines and illustrated papers which were printing bleak landscapes and the machinery of fighting: here were young ladies in attractive caps helping men on crutches, lighting cigarettes for bandaged patients, strolling in gardens, kicking a ball about.

What was also true was the sheer drudgery of hospital work, which no VAD was allowed to avoid: scrubbing, cleaning, emptying slops, laundry and often compulsory attendance at prayers. There was a lengthy list of Official Instructions to Members: uniforms were to 'be worn smartly and in a uniform way and not to suit the taste of each individual. . . . No additions or alterations, such as furs, veils, bowties, or shirt collars worn over the coat, are permissible.' Your uniform was inspected daily and you were told off for any minor infringement or imperfection. Heaven help the VAD who wanted a little beauty routine: 'all powder, paint, scent, earrings or jewellery, etc., should be avoided'. Doing what you were told was axiomatic, as you had to 'give a ready and willing obedience to the orders of all superior officers and never question or hesitate to obey an order'. Being a minute late occasioned more sharp words. Soiled dressings, bed-pans and sputum jars came your way every hour. And as wave upon wave of men were conveyed back from France, the terribly maimed, the seriously disturbed and the desperate wreckage of those who had been gassed became your daily responsibility. For many of the 'nicely brought up', this was not what they had been expecting. Although much of the major surgery was performed before a patient was sent back to England, there were still buckets of limbs for the VADs to lug down the corridors, while they were under instruction to 'perform all duties cheerfully and thoroughly . . . be patient, willing and attentive and to avoid all gossip . . .'.

Nevertheless, there was the undoubted kudos of doing the one job that the public had decided was the female equivalent of soldiering: these women were volunteers, they didn't get paid. They weren't challenging the established order, for they were merely continuing the tradition of 'social work' among the less fortunate. They weren't like the women who had headed for the munitions plants or were 'doing a man's job' in engineering or transport. They were in the same mould as the soldier: following the path expected of their sex, and urged by their commandant, Katharine Furse, to give 'an example of discipline and perfect steadiness of character'. No wonder the VAD assumed an almost mythic position by the end of the war. She wasn't demanding wages or a new kind of job. She was the one who didn't threaten society with change. There were also a very large number of them – possibly more than seventy thousand. They were spread throughout the land, and were encountered by all levels of society, in big cities and small villages. In a world with limited means of spreading an image, mainly by news magazines and posters, their smart little outfits were ubiquitous, proving what a young woman *could* do. Though whether she *should* be doing it hinged entirely on the circumstances provided by war.

The main body of VADs served at home – slogging away for years, scrubbing and washing, changing dressings and cooking. The experience in many cases was life-changing. It was manual work, full of petty restrictions and a hierarchy in which they were fairly low down the pecking order, despite being addressed as 'Nurse'. Many encountered working-class men in a way that would have been unthinkable before the war. Many relished the feeling of being wanted, of doing something useful, however menial: it was a far cry from tennis parties and chaperoned social life and 'mother needing you at home'. The VADs found themselves admired, but every one of them knew how much hard work lurked behind the image. They also knew that the professional nurses had training and that this gave them an edge over the middle-class volunteers – even if they were socially not as 'refined'. The reality of the working world had come a little closer, a major lesson for young women who before the war had never considered that real 'work' might be part of their lives.

When Vera Brittain's *Testament of Youth* was dramatized on television in 1979, the most talked-about moment was her father's letter insisting that she return home from France to look after him because her mother had had a breakdown and was in a nursing home. Vera was working amid desperate scenes in Etaples, within shelling distance of the front line and dealing with the victims of gas attacks. Her father wrote that it was her duty to return and look after the house: 'As your mother and I can no longer manage without you, it is now your duty to leave France immediately.' That her father thought it his right to order his twenty-four-year-old daughter home, and that she complied, produced quite a reaction in a TV audience which had just seen a decade of legislation improving women's legal and economic status. There was amazement in some quarters at such behaviour, underlining the speed with which rigid codes of social convention are soon forgotten – and difficult to comprehend or even imagine.

Those who volunteered to serve abroad encountered the same friction with professional nursing staff, both military and civilian. Vera Brittain, whose book delivers one of the most unforgettable accounts of serving in France, was no stranger to the hostility, but like her fellow VADs abroad she experienced the full blast of working in a war zone. At home, there was sometimes more fretting – for obvious reasons – about those who found themselves near the fighting than about the fighting itself. Newspapers carried lengthy articles written by women working in tented hospitals, draughty religious buildings and laden hospital trains – mainly reassuring descriptions of the contribution they were attempting to make to the war effort. They avoided or made light of the dangers. And so they escaped being seen as 'adventuresses', their volunteer status giving them a virtuous defence. The press liked the word 'heroine' – which in many cases was well deserved.

But what caught the headlines was a particularly grand form of volunteer: the titled ladies who decided that they could single-handedly run their own medical show. Duchesses and countesses used clout and formidable fund-raising skills to make a considerable impact on the medical front. Wealthy individuals started their own establishments: Lady Carnarvon immediately converted Highclere Castle in Hampshire and wondered if the dozens of beds would be filled: by Christmas, the vast house (the setting for TV's *Downton Abbey*) was full to bursting. This wasn't surprising, as in the next few months the casualties from across the Channel reached a rate of twenty-four thousand a week. The Duchess of Sutherland took her own band of doctors and nurses to France, barged through enemy lines, talked her way back to England and set off again to organize a hospital at Calais; the Duchess of Westminster set up a hospital at Le Touquet, complete with her wolfhound and a group of her friends who graced the wards every night in full evening dress and tiaras to cheer everyone up. Lady Paget made it to Serbia, set up a six hundred-bed medical unit in Skopje, ignored the enemy

Bulgarian troops descending on the town, and with her staff continued to nurse as a prisoner of war. The Dowager Countess of Carnarvon was busy organizing nurses to be sent to her in Egypt, and during the Gallipoli campaign held possibly one of the more exotic posts of any woman in the war: Coordinator of Hospital Ships, Alexandria – where Lady Howard de Walden was supervising her own convalescent hospital, despite hostility from the army's medical service. Lady Dorothy Feilding, daughter of the Earl of Denbigh, went with the Munro Ambulance Corps to France one month into the war and spent nearly four years driving the wounded under fire; for her bravery, she became the first woman to be awarded the Military Medal.

These women's exploits gained admiration, though there is no mistaking the classic words which attend the commendations from press and public: they were all 'splendid' and they showed 'pluck'. The imagination, the determination, the sheer bloody-mindedness and courage which all their exploits demanded were not to the fore in published comment. Organizational ability, allied with financial skills and vast reserves of energy, seemed to be taken for granted; and it was too much to mention courage – that was a soldierly attribute. The language had yet to absorb terms which could be used of women when describing the customary preserve of men. These were early days. And after a century there are still skirmishes in the linguistic field: men are ambitious, women are pushy; men are forthright, women are strident; and so on, through a very long list . . . though at least 'plucky' seems to have lost ground.

During World War I, there was little sense that the very description of what women were doing and could achieve was in itself constricting and patronizing: rather than professional, successful, courageous, competent and stalwart they were magnificent, splendid, heart-warming, astonishing and spirited. Reading the reports, diaries and memoirs of women who took charge of large numbers of volunteers, often in horrendous conditions, commandeered buildings, acquired equipment and stores, set up administrative systems, ran their own transport, delivered food, treatment, and above all care, it does not take any stretch of the imagination to see that large parts of the British war machine would have been as well, if not better, run if these women had been in charge. They could do it.

In a daughter's letter to her mother just a few weeks into the war, in September 1914, those sentiments were eloquently expressed. Seventy-eight-year-old Elizabeth Garrett Anderson probably knew more about prejudice against professional working women than anyone else, having overcome an entire steeplechase of obstacles to qualify and work as a doctor, the first woman to do so in Britain. Her daughter Louisa had followed her into the profession, and was also an ardent suffragette – her mother's sister, Millicent Garrett Fawcett, was the leader of the National Union of Women's Suffrage Societies. Clever, campaigning and capable, these women knew how to seize opportunities, and the French Embassy in London found Louisa and another doctor and suffragette, Flora Murray, on the doorstep immediately war broke out. They were all too aware that the British military were set against women doctors; indeed, the medical profession generally was still none too welcoming. The women believed the French might be more receptive to their offers of help, for their army medical service was known to be in dire straits. The conversation in the embassy proceeded rather haphazardly, due to much enthusiasm and poor French, but somewhere along the line the right signals seem to have been exchanged. On 15 September Elizabeth waved off her daughter and a small group of volunteers at Victoria Station, saying, 'I would be going with you if I was twenty years younger.' When Louisa reached Paris later that day, she sent a brief note home: 'This is just what you would have done at my age. I hope that I shall be able to do it half as well as you would have done.'

Three days later Louisa and her Women's Hospital Corps team were still trying to juggle turning the newly built, empty Hotel Claridge in Paris into something resembling a medical facility, while already performing operations in the part-converted ladies' cloakroom, using fish kettles to sterilize instruments. She was in her element, already with sixty-eight patients:

> We have a lot of surgery: sometimes I am in theatre from 2–9 or 10 at night and have eight or more operations. The cases come to us very septic and the wounds are terrible. . . .
>
> I wish the whole organisation for the wounded – their transport, the disposition of base and field hospitals and their clothing and feeding could be put in the hands of women. This is not military work. It is merely a matter of organisation, common sense, attention to detail and determination to avoid unnecessary suffering and loss of life. Medical women could do it so much better than it is done – especially if the right medical women were chosen for the job – ahem!! We have a scheme already and are gradually breaking it to the old officers who come round to see us. We are having a wonderful time. I hope we will be able to do the job really well. Very much love dearest mother, yours LGA.

The wounded from the first battle of the Marne were the initial challenge: the women rose to it, even though the kind of surgery they were performing wasn't anything they had experienced. Until then gynaecological cases and children's ailments had been considered their area of expertise; there were many fusty professors in the medical schools who believed that women should not look closely upon men's bodies, never mind interfere with them medically. When they qualified, it was rare that women even got to treat a man. It offended propriety, authority and the entire administrative structure of medicine. Such views were not confined to the professionals: there were just over five hundred qualified women doctors in the whole of the country in 1914, and many people had never encountered one. The army, living in its monastic world, was even less familiar with the female medic of the species.

The general public was not even 100 per cent happy about professional nurses, but at least they were in a traditional, conventional role for a woman – who always obeyed the doctor. Having a woman usurp that senior role, which involved personal questions, peering under the bedclothes, decision-making and prescribing treatment was not to be contemplated, particularly if you were feeling terrible. Such attitudes did not disappear in a trice merely because there was a war on. However, as an injured soldier you didn't have any choice: you were lucky to get away from the battlefield and this was not the time to be picky. The new and unavoidable factor was that the injuries were horrendous. The combatants were literally blasting each other to smithereens. Added to which, in the early days of the war it took time to get casualties to relative safety. Roads and transport behind the front line were in chaos. No one had ever had to cope with such numbers of badly wounded men. There was dirt everywhere, wounds turned septic, and first aid was rudimentary or non-existent. Amputation was still often the only way of saving life. Surgery, by anyone's standards, was a brutal job. That women should be doing it was nothing less than a sensation. The activities in the Hotel Claridge were lapped up by the French press, who memorably sent a journalist to see for himself the lady surgeon in the operating theatre. He was reported to have exited shouting that it was all true – he'd seen the knife in her hand!

In early 1915 the WHC shifted to a château at Wimereux, near Boulogne, and achieved a subtle development – the RAMC had gritted its teeth and made overtures to the women. Wimereux became the first women's hospital recognized by the British army. It was a victory, but one that had depended on the Surgeon General himself, who had become aware of the Paris hospital's excellent reputation. The rest of his vast staff were yet to be won over, and a considerable number of them never budged in their attitudes. This became abundantly clear as the biggest challenge yet was put before the WHC: would they run a large hospital, over five hundred beds, in London – for the military? The doctors, as elegantly as they could, grabbed with both hands.

There were other hospitals run by women in Britain – the first being the New Hospital for Women in London's Euston Road, founded by Louisa's mother Elizabeth. But she herself was to run a *military* establishment – which meant that acceptance had been achieved on a different level. Not that the building resembled a step up in the world. Returning from France, Flora Murray found herself inspecting a ghastly old workhouse in Endell Street, Bloomsbury, said to have been the model for the workhouse in Dickens's *Oliver Twist*:

> A glass-covered passage ran down the centre of the square and across to either block. It was fenced in with high iron railings, and the free space on either side was divided by more railings into little pens. The little pens had padlocked gates and were labelled: 'Old Males,' 'Young Males,' 'Old Females,' 'Young Females;' and it was in these cages that the inmates of the workhouse had sought fresh air and recreation. There was a little gate office next to the mortuary, where a set of pigeon holes, constructed out of slate slabs, was designed to receive coffins, and where the gas meter took up most of the room . . . the cellars and basements of the building are of the most ancient and grimy description.

The building was not encouraging, nor was the RAMC colonel in charge of converting it: 'Good God, *women*!'

He was probably very much aware that these were a particular breed as well: suffragettes. As the workhouse was reconfigured and the equipment arrived, there was no doubting that the female staff were card-carrying members of the Votes for Women brigade. Louisa Garrett Anderson had served a month in prison for breaking a window. Flora Murray had joined demonstrations, treated those roughed up by the police and tended women who had been force-fed in prison. Members of the women's movement headed like moths to a flame to join the hospital: it was a wonderful opportunity. It had to be a success, and it was.

One of the orderlies summed up the core message of her training. 'We had this drilled into us: you not only have to do a good job but you have to do a superior job. What would be accepted from a man will not be accepted from a woman. You have got to do better.' A sentiment that is still recognized by many working women today. The army, wondering what it had started, had a strong feeling that the whole enterprise would soon collapse under a heap of bandages and petticoats. They decided that arm's-length association was the best approach and left its running entirely to the women, unwittingly cementing Endell Street's independent and individual character.

Coping with the stream of patients, flat out with work, the WHC started to deliver innovations and strategies of its own. War frequently accelerates improvements in medical techniques, and in 1916, having employed their own pathologist and begun clinical research in their laboratory, they were the first hospital to run clinical trials of BIPP. This antiseptic paste, first introduced by Dr James Rutherford Morison in one of the Northumberland VAD hospitals, is still around today. That women should be innovating and writing up their results in official reports again broke new ground: getting published in the *Lancet* meant a great deal in the profession.

All of this encouraged a warmer public view of the suffragette movement. Here were people who had formerly been objects of much public opprobrium and derision: not only were they proving to be capable professionals, equal to men in their skill, but they were behaving as respectable and responsible members of society. It's easy to forget how much the years just before the war had seen women vilified and despised when they undertook violent protest. In an atmosphere where violence and destruction on a huge scale now overshadowed everyone's lives, a few cases of arson and window-smashing seemed to fade. Endell Street also began to attract very favourable comment from those who had been treated there.

Twenty-six thousand men – and a few of the women in the service units formed in 1917 – were treated in the hospital. Dr Murray claimed that only one man had ever announced that he didn't wish to be admitted to a hospital run by women: the story goes that he changed his mind and 'sent his mother to ask that he might remain'. The press spent a good deal of time trotting round the wards, with the *Daily Sketch* breathlessly running a headline after the Somme offensive: 'Wounded men in hospital staffed by women more anxious to praise doctors than to talk of the big push.' The many visitors (it became very fashionable to see this curious institution) remarked on the flowers and other feminine touches in the wards, the cheerful and sympathetic atmosphere 'just like home'. Nor was this incidental: like many other intelligent women who were working with badly injured men, the staff at Endell Street were recognizing the need for something more than surgery and medicines.

Across the country, many of the VADs soon learned that talking and listening were not luxuries for their patients. There were countless cases of men whose bodily injuries didn't seem so serious, but who were clearly in a terrible state and not getting better. Severe attitudes to 'malingerers' and those considered to have 'lack of moral fibre' were still prevalent. 'Shell shock' wasn't recognized at the start of the war and was perplexing doctors with a range of disturbing symptoms. Mental health treatment was still in its infancy – the very building the WHC were inhabiting still contained the workhouse's fearsome 'lunacy block' when they first moved in. Treating the whole person was not an automatic concept. Providing 'comforts' and entertainment was understood as a charitable act; now there was a growing understanding that psychological problems were causing a great deal of concern alongside the physical wounds. Louisa wrote to her mother:

> I like still more the opportunity of being a little good to these bruised men. Their minds are full of horrors and it is a help to them to come into a soothing atmosphere with decent food and soft beds and our gentle merry young orderly girls who feed them with cigarettes and write to their mothers and read to them. . . . We are going to have Scotch songs tomorrow instead of hymns and I fear even a gramophone may appear for a short time. All the men are shocked by what they have been through – and normal comforts and little pleasures are a help to them and make them sleep and forget a little.

Endell Street was instrumental in introducing the idea of men being treated by women: it hardly seems revolutionary, but its rejection hitherto was probably the greatest barrier to women fulfilling their professional role and using their training to best advantage. Their ground-breaking work in surgery and interest in psychology would take years to be fully developed. Even today, there are divisions of labour within the medical world and battles within the hierarchies. In spite of their immense success, the women running the military hospital were still refused any kind of rank. Status means power.

Ability didn't equate with authority. The former suffragettes knew this, but had expected their efforts to generate a greater acceptance into the wider world of medicine. Their patients had no doubts: according to one young Australian soldier, who wrote to his father: 'The Women's Hospital Corps hospital is the best in London. The management is good, and the surgeons take great interest in and pains with their patients. . . . The whole hospital is a triumph for women, and incidentally it is a triumph for suffragettes.'

CHAPTER 10

TWELVE HOURS OF DANGER PER DAY

Did you sleep well? A polite and frequent enquiry, especially when you're away from home. In my case, the answer is nearly always, 'Very well, thank you.' Not because of comfy bed or quiet surroundings, but because I've always slept very deeply. Or, to frame it in the language of my childhood: 'That child doesn't sleep – she has a short course of death.' When very small, asked if I was frightened during the night's thunderstorm I always replied, 'What thunderstorm?' What may have added to this was my deafness, undiscovered until I was blown up by a grenade explosion three decades later in Beirut, and was informed by a specialist that the inflammation would soon disappear – but as I was obviously half deaf anyway, from birth, I shouldn't worry. So I wasn't surprised one morning in 1992 in Sarajevo, in a city which during the Bosnia conflict shuddered and jumped to the sounds of rockets, mortars and machine-gun fire day and night, that I'd again slept through a major event.

The Holiday Inn Hotel – an embarrassing name

to have in the centre of a battleground – was a part-ruined yellow edifice which already bore the scars of countless hits, being inconveniently located very near one of the city's front lines. The top five storeys were already burned out. The bedrooms facing the river were uninhabitable, being directly in line of fire from snipers in the high-rise flats a few hundred yards away. Window glass – well, who needs it . . . it just flies in and causes damage. Electricity made rare and brief appearances. Water was probably in greater supply in the Gobi Desert. On the other hand, the hotel carried on as if nothing untoward was occurring, the waiters serving 'siege soup' – soggy grey rice pilfered from the UNHCR supply convoys – and the barman ducking automatically below the counter when the incoming AK-47 bullets whizzed through reception. We sometimes stayed there, particularly when our office, a tiny garage workshop under a car-park ramp next to the PTT building, seemed to be attracting larger than usual shells.

In the early days of the war I'd been aware that I slept better than some of my colleagues – even though I'd spent some nights wrapped in a sleeping-bag in the bath, there being no chance of water and a big chance of incoming mortars. I crawled out of the bathroom one morning to hear a great deal of shouting in the next room. Peering into the corridor, I saw a bunch of young men hard at work with a bucket and a dustpan and brush. Inside the room – which no longer looked even partly trashed, but seemed to have experienced a kind of splintering transformation into a wood-chip store – was a shell that had part-exploded. The remaining explosive was being eagerly harvested by the lads. They were gone in a trice, leaving an empty shell and a lingering whiff of their cigarette smoke. . . .

Some weeks later, video footage arrived of the local makeshift munitions factory: rather scary pictures of lumpy explosive being thwacked enthusiastically with rolling pins and hammers and rammed into salvaged shell casings. It was no consolation to know that Bosnia had been home to many of Yugoslavia's ammunition factories before the war, so that at least a few people knew what they were doing . . . and, it being somewhat tense and hard work, that cigarette-smoking was deemed essential. Nor was it comforting to realize, after hard scrutiny of the shots of this 'factory', that it was the innocent-looking further education institution next door to us. When it exploded the following year, surprise was not one of our reactions. However, even I was surprised that I had slept through it.

The Bosnian Muslims defending their city in a siege could easily explain that you must take your opportunities where you can: the whole city was under bombardment, so locating an ammunition factory was merely a matter of finding a convenient building that was relatively well built and wouldn't attract attention. No one was safe, so no one thought twice about having a concentration of explosives in the middle of a city. Human beings have an ambivalent relationship with explosions. As a child, I was the pathetic little girl who didn't like her balloon to go 'pop'; I squealed at Bonfire Night bangers. However, I've come to appreciate fireworks, though I drew the line at one of Colonel Ghadaffy's eccentric celebrations when a dustbin full of waste paper was dragged into the press pen, had several seven-foot rockets stuck into it and the paper was then lit. We fled, and the ball of whooshing sparks hit the car park, and incinerated a truck. The Libyans gleefully announced: 'Just like your Gay Fox Night.'

The Chinese are the experts, having been busy with pyrotechnics for over a thousand years: fireworks have been one of their greatest exported inventions, and the rest of the world has happily copied them. Scaring away evil spirits may have been the primary use, but in the long term the battlefield has proved a much greater consumer of gunpowder. The Chinese 'fire arrows' morphed into rockets and mortars across Europe, and the medieval world of knights in armour and strong-walled castles literally gave way to cannon balls and bullets. The recipe of charcoal, saltpetre and sulphur spread rapidly.

Gunpowder was originally a very localized business: powderworks, as they were called, sat on riverbanks the length and breadth of Britain – small, often family ventures, supplying quarries, local militias, gun-owners – and firework displays. Rivers and streams delivered power for the mills and eased transportation, willow and alder produced good charcoal. They were a normal part of the working landscape, and in 1676 John Evelyn recorded in his diary that at Chilworth in Surrey 'I do not remember to have seen such a Variety of Mills and Works upon so narrow a Brook, and in so little Compass; there being Mills for Corn, Cloth, Brass, Iron, Powder etc.'.

Until the nineteenth century the powder mills had a family-centred workforce which automatically included women, usually stitching bags and filling them with explosives. Few precautions were taken and the massive grinding stones produced sparks. Explosions were common – and frequently huge. At a time when life was shorter and infinitely more perilous for the ordinary citizen, references to 'greate noyses' emanating from gunpowder mills rarely caused widespread alarm. Rural birdsong was punctuated frequently with appalling blasts, and as the towns grew the mills continued to grind in residential areas. Not a great deal of care went into transport or storage, either.

The residents of Regent's Park in central London have the pleasure of overlooking an elegant canal. At 5 a.m. on 2 October 1874 'a most terrible explosion occurred'. The report in *The Illustrated London News* gives a description worthy of live twenty-four-hour news:

> Such was the force of the blast that surrounding houses were severely damaged and their roofs and walls blown down, and some were near ruins. For a mile to east and west, windows and fragile articles were broken, and . . . sleepers were woken by the noise as their beds rocked, doors burst open, plaster fell from the ceilings, and everything shook and trembled.
>
> The noise and shock were perceived in every quarter of London, and in many instances ten or twelve miles away, both on the north and south side of the Thames. . . . Women and children rushed out of the houses, screaming for help, some in their night-dresses, others wrapped in blankets, and were not easily pacified by those of cooler mind whom they met. People from every quarter hastened towards the thick column of smoke which rose up from the great blaze . . . some began helping the Police and the Fire Brigade to save what remained and search for the lost. The confusion was so great that a detachment of Horse Guards was sent from Albany Barracks to keep order and it was feared that the wild animals might escape from the park.

A train of five 'light barges' – narrowboats – had been moving west from City Road Basin. As one of them, the *Tilbury*, passed under a bridge she exploded, killing three men and a boy. At the inquest her cargo was described as being 'chiefly of sugar and other miscellaneous articles, such as nuts, straw-board, coffee and some two or three barrels of petroleum, and about five barrels of gunpowder'. The exact cause of the explosion was thought to be an unexplained 'spark, coming from the Bridge', though it was also observed that 'there was no restriction on the lighting of fires on boats so laden'.

For over two hundred years, the eclectic *Gentleman's Magazine* frequently featured articles about gunpowder from the scientific, military and defence angle. Writing in 1748, one of its contributors colourfully described a huge bang in 1647, opposite Barking church in East London, where

> some people [were] barrelling up gunpowder, at a ship's chandlers . . . by some accident the powder took fire, and blew up the house, and demolished 50 or 60 others, among the rest the Rose Tavern, which, at the time, was very full of company, it being the parish feast . . . when they came to dig out the rubbish, they found heads, arms, legs, half bodies, and some whole bodies, not so much singed. . . . But the most remarkable thing of all was, a young child was found the next day, blown upon the uppermost leads of Barking church, in

a cradle, alive and well, and not the least damage done to it.

Making gunpowder was dangerous, the argument went, so what did anyone expect? At Chilworth mills in Surrey, established in 1626, accidents only got a mention when, for example, after a particularly loud bang a church on a hill half a mile away collapsed in 1760. It took nearly a century to rebuild, only to have a wheel and a large beam hurtle into it eighteen years later as Chilworth continued to experience accidents.

This was dangerous work, but vital to a country with an army frequently in action abroad and a navy intending to rule the waves. And the workforce had to be flexible, dependent upon a monarch or government's decision to wage war; small family concerns absorbed the fluctuating demands more easily. But as the Industrial Revolution changed working practices and employment systems throughout the country, the mills began to attract engineers and military commanders who wanted ever more efficient and powerful powders for demolition and ammunition. With larger numbers of workers involved, the hazards multiplied.

From the Kyle of Bute in Scotland to the mines of Cornwall, from the gentle chalk streams of Hampshire to the huge arsenal at Waltham Abbey in Essex, the munitions industry thrived – and suffered spectacular accidents. The Waltham Abbey site finally closed in 1991. A curate, Thomas

Fuller, once remarked that 'those mills in my parish have blown up five times in seven years'; he was writing in 1662.

And while the image (rightly) is one of dangerous work, the ubiquity of the mills and the frequency of accidents must always have been common knowledge across the country – and part of many families' memories. Women had always been involved in the work. Filling cartridges was fiddly, and nimble fingers were necessary. In days when both housework and farm work meant hard physical labour, everyone pulled their weight, and work in a gunpowder mill was just another local business. However, the only reliable statistics about the danger of the mills before the age of industrialization tend to come not from official reports but from the gravestones of women who died in explosions. There are fewer of them than for the men, but that's only because the women were often not counted as part of the workforce.

In World War I, the first indication to my family that the manufacture of ammunition might affect women was when one of James Adie's tweenies gave in her notice and disappeared to nearby Tyneside from his large Victorian house in Sunderland. One of two young women whose first task at half-past six in the morning was to lug buckets of coal up four flights of stairs, she regularly woke my adoptive father Wilfrid as she clanked up the last few steps to light a welcoming fire in his bedroom grate. Years later he recalled the consternation in the household as the second tweenie made off to a local war hospital kitchen. The housemaid and the cook stayed on, despite the extra work, and cannot have been unaware that domestic service was shifting from an inevitability for many working-class women to just one option in the employment market. The assumption often made today that the war *initiated* the decline in domestic service is gainsaid by the frequent moaning in the press in the Edwardian era that 'girls will not now contemplate the role that sets them on the road to competent housewifery'. James Adie's tweenies might well have picked up their own local paper in early 1914 to read that the local Labour Exchange was having a lot of trouble persuading young women that being a servant was what they could and should be.

The North-east didn't have the tradition of 'mill-girls' as in the Lancashire and Yorkshire textile factories, or of the Staffordshire potteries which employed tens of thousands. Away from these areas, working in a 'factory' was often a big decision which involved travel or staying away from home in a hostel or lodgings. However, the emotions that swept the country in 1914, coupled with the lure of better wages and the growing dislike of domestic service, made munitions work seem quite attractive. Quite, but not overwhelmingly. Everyone knew that explosives were dangerous. The work was dirty, and 'powder accidents' or 'blows' regarded as nearly inevitable, despite efforts at safety legislation in the late Victorian era.

It took a mammoth government effort to acquire the necessary workforce to supply the voracious demands of the front line, but it was an effort which eventually supplied just under a million workers. At the time women were, on average, so badly paid that the wages offered in the munitions plants seemed like a golden opportunity.

Munitions work was an absolute necessity, so official attitudes to those who went into the factories were underpinned by an acknowledgement that the war could not be won without them. There was little mention that such employment might be 'unsuitable', and that the very making of ammunition might conflict with the conventional view of women as live-givers, not life-takers. One might expect today that the danger would be cited as an obstacle – however, more than three centuries of recorded explosions were woven into the image of the industry. It was seen as a terrible, but seemingly unavoidable, inevitability – and women had not been excluded from that history. And the other traditional industries – iron and steel, shipyards, the textile mills, could be very daunting and risky too: open furnaces, no guards on machinery, constant fires, poor maintenance. 'Health and safety' was not a familiar concept then; indeed, most precautions were aimed at keeping the factory itself safe, rather than the employees, so that production was never halted. Caring for employees was a notion which insinuated itself only gradually, based on the desire to get the best out of workers who perhaps needed better food.

Patriotism gilded the wages' lily – this was a job which, for example, raised a domestic drudge to a valued national employee. And as the war progressed there was also a growing sense that this was, in some way, another trench in the 'Home Front Line'. Coming back from the trenches of France in particular was a picture of the most appalling sacrifice. Facing the risks involved with TNT seemed justifiable at the time.

Right at the war's start the Secretary of State for War, Lord Kitchener, had written to one of the old-established mills at Faversham in Kent about 'the importance of the government work upon which they [were] engaged. . . . I should like all engaged by your company to know that it is fully recognised that they, in carrying out the great work of supplying munitions in war, are doing their duty for King and Country, equally with those who have joined the Army for active service in the field.' Such stirring words must have been needed two years later when the worst-ever explosion in the history of Britain's industry tore apart the mill, killing 115 men and boys. The blast was heard as far away as Norwich; shop windows shattered in Southend-on-Sea. The only reason no women were casualties was that it was a Sunday, their day off. But then, no one had to be told that munitions work had its risks.

'Risk' was not a word that appeared on the posters encouraging women to head for the factories in 1915. The impression given was of a worthwhile and patriotic job, underpinning the efforts made by the men at the front and paying relatively decent, regular and regulated wages – because it was wartime. By tradition women already worked in munitions plants, but as low-paid unskilled labour. And as more men left to enlist and the new employees were signing on in their thousands, a perfect storm ensued. There was a full-blown national scandal in progress about the lack of shells at the front. The demand for them – specifically high-explosive and accurate enough to cope with trench warfare – was desperate. But employing women meant grappling with age-old prejudices, a cat's-cradle of interwoven habits, attitudes and fears in the workplace. All of which rested on the acceptance of women as second-class workers.

Skilled men feared that their prized status would be threatened by unskilled women working alongside them. If the women managed to do the same work – and were, as usual, paid less – then the men's hold on their own jobs might be threatened. On the other hand, giving equal wages to the women was unthinkable in a world where men were expected to support families. And if married women were to come into the factories, this again would break a social taboo: wives were not meant to work, they were meant to be dependent. (It was also thought that it might 'lower the moral tone' among single women. It's easily forgotten that sex was rarely mentioned, even intimately, and that ignorance of the 'facts of life' was widespread and considered wholly appropriate in young girls.)

Necessity drove the government, which embarked on some complicated manoeuvring with the trades unions, management and entrenched traditions. Its motivation was not the improvement of women's status or earning power, but the need to resolve the situation so that production increased and industrial relations were kept calm. The result was 'substitution' and 'dilution', two ways of introducing women into men's jobs. This entailed either training a woman and paying her less for the same work, usually supervised by a man, or splitting a man's work into smaller component jobs to be taken by two or three women or carried out on more efficient new machinery. Ironically, the most iconic job – filling shells with high-explosive – was not part of this argument. It had nearly always been done by women and was seen as unskilled work. And above all, the words 'for the duration' hung over everything. This was not to be permanent: conditions of employment for women had changed because there was a war on, not because of any national resolve to improve their employment prospects: war is a bubble in time – in which mysterious forces are at work: women can do this – now: what is unspoken, indeed ignored, is that, in the future, they should.

Across the whole of heavy industry some of the resentment emanated from the belief that women were a docile flock, more susceptible to arguments from a cunning management and without any idea of how to bargain. Women were suspected of demanding less and seeing assertiveness not as a quality but as a flaw, and for this alone they were not particularly welcomed by the trades unions. Those male officials who did argue for equal pay for women knew perfectly well that the employers would get rid of such 'expensive' labour immediately the war ended, for female labour had always been 'cheap'. At least this eventually led to larger numbers joining women's unions by the end of the war (an increase from around 350,000 to more than a million) and greater awareness of the concept of concerted action – due in part to women now being able to afford their union dues.

On the whole, those who initially headed for the munitions plants were unconcerned with the earnings shenanigans: all that mattered was that the wages were going to be better than those on offer elsewhere. And the bait of higher earnings was spiced with pride, often expressed as 'helping the boys' – it was a potent driver of the work ethic. Perhaps a stronger emotion was that of 'being part of the war effort'. A woman's individual labours could be seen as a necessary and purposeful contribution to the whole nation's future. This was new, and meant that even ramming powder into a shell with a mallet somehow connected with being a citizen. You were a vital cog in the war-wheel. And with the government taking control of production, you were paid – by the government.

It was the first time that women had come on to the government payroll in significant numbers.

Many of the images – photographs, paintings, cartoons – which were made of the vast munitions industry show breathtaking rows of shiny shell-casings in immense sheds, or serious-looking women pausing for a camera moment next to mounds of cartridges; or lines of workers intently manipulating hefty shells amid pulleys and chains and huge machinery; or cute girls clutching a shell. For the press, much of this substituted for direct coverage of life at the front in France: censorship, red tape and the monotonous mudscape of trench warfare made pictures of young women in novel surroundings irresistible.

And they were wearing trousers. If any single image caught the eye of the public, it was a pair of straight-legged, definitely untailored white trousers, modestly part-concealed beneath a tunic. 'Disgusting' was a much-used description. In some ways, women's legs were a measure of their emancipation – or lack of it. Those who might think it romantic to swish around in long skirts never had to brush the mud and street muck from the hem every day. Or play tennis with several petticoats slowing down the race for the drop-shot. Or navigate the London Tube at rush-hour – 'Mind the skirts' should have been substituted for 'Mind the doors.' Or tried to roll heavy shells around a munitions plant. The filthy, greasy-floored munitions factories weren't conducive to efficient work with clothes which tripped their wearers up and snagged on machinery. Even so, a great deal of the engineering work saw no switch to trousers. Only those in munitions, followed by coke-heavers and cleaners of railway engines and other gritty jobs, made the giant leap. It caused consternation in some quarters, but trousers were worn with pride – and relief – by the munitionettes. And because they weren't 'fashionable ladies' whose outrageous couture could be satirized in the upmarket magazines their change of garb was more serious and more influential. They were working-class girls, and they found the trousers rather smart, as well as comfortable. Their monarch might be horrified, their mothers might be upset, the maids' former mistresses might fear for their morals, but trousers had arrived.

However vital the work was, it wasn't glamorous – it was hard, undertaken in unpleasant conditions, boring and relentless. Heavy shells were predominantly produced from the many factories on Clydeside; sheer brawn was demanded of the workforce, many of whom were drawn from mining areas where there was a tradition of 'pit lasses' who sorted coal and shale. The shifts were often a merciless twelve hours, for less wear and tear was involved in running machines for two twelve-hour shifts than in three of eight hours. Sylvia Pankhurst noted that 'Family life is impossible. Mothers and grown children make munitions, younger ones suffer neglect at home. In the lodgings of munition workers beds are never empty, rooms are never aired, as day and night shifts prevent this.' Tales circulated of the eighty- and one hundred-hour week, and of workers almost dead on their feet at the end of the shift, as seen by one munitionette on Clydeside: 'I have seen her, hammer in hand and type in the other, fast asleep. Then all of a sudden she would realize herself and stamp a few more, then off again. . . . Another time I was looking at an Operator threading safety caps, believe me, she was threading as fast as she could, and yet fast asleep, until she had the whole squad of girls in an uproar, whose noise awoke her.'

The press was not inclined to print stories about the downside of this vast industry. Physical stress, unhealthy conditions and increasing arguments about wages from those who could see they were doing the same as men was not the image that was projected: these were fit, patriotic workers. The government held ammunition production as a precious process to be protected at all costs. Censorship blanketed rumblings of discontent, strike action and demonstrations; nothing was allowed to puncture the picture of pulsing, continuous production.

New factories sprang up across the country: some, such as the huge sprawling Gretna Green complex, had to import the workforce, causing another social taboo to be confronted. A young woman was not expected to leave home in those days until she married. There was neither the money nor the accommodation nor the social approval for her to strike out on her own and find a job further than a bus ride from her family. Grappling with thousands of new jobs in scattered locations, the Ministry of Munitions requisitioned and converted buildings, compiled lists of lodgings, built hostels and little townships, and mobilized welfare organizations such as the YWCA to provide facilities that allowed 'modern activities', such as smoking and dancing as opposed to Bible study and teetotalism.

Despite the long hours, the independence from home and opportunity to meet new colleagues from different backgrounds possibly had more impact on women than the actual job. This was a liberation which they had not had to fight for, and had not expected. To have money to spend, be able to go to a pub without the family or neighbours tattling, or choose to go dancing or to the cinema without asking anyone's permission, was freedom indeed. Unmarried women, even in their twenties, were meant to submit to their fathers' wishes – such as 'Be in by ten on Saturday – or else.' It was an era in which many young women were told that wearing make-up was 'fast' or 'common'; keeping your wages rather than handing them over to your parents was unheard of in some families. However, there was no domestic revolution in progress: patriarchal authority was being circumvented rather than challenged. It was the country that was making demands, not the women themselves. In many households it would be decades before these restrictive conventions would be modified, let alone completely removed.

The press was full of stories of giddy girls frittering money in public houses in the company of young men. Countless disapproving reports of ribbons and fripperies, cheap jewellery, saucy hats, showy gowns and drink – 'the thriftless manner in which some working-class women are squandering money' said the Sheffield Weekly Independent. The language says it all: out-of-control females busy blowing wages on luxuries. In one sense the country had got itself a new army, a vast cohort of women with a united purpose, wearing uniform and prepared to face danger – and if it got a bit unruly on Saturday night, what did you expect?

Most of the changes that were wrought in women's lives during the war were tinged by a public bout of moral panic. The munitionettes, more than most, excited the press and many commentators, who saw the emergence of working-class women into a more assertive role as highly undesirable: 'assertive' meaning being able to go into a pub and order a drink; to buy little luxuries in respectable shops; to smoke and to swear; to have fun in their time off rather than dutifully sit in church or chapel on their only free day. To the puritans, all this pointed to the road to immorality – without there being much evidence to support the fear. Statistics on drinking, illegitimate children and venereal disease did not bear out the notion of wholesale misbehaviour so fixed in the conventional respectable mind.

Showy clothes were a particular red rag to the puritan bull. Factory workers – like ladies' maids in the nineteenth century – were suspected of upsetting class divisions by dressing above their station. Added to this, any display of finery in the pea-hen was seen as a likely step on the road to being a tart. 'Dressed like a prostitute' is an age-old criticism, and the sight of munitionettes enjoying a new-found freedom to choose some pretty clothes raised the old cry in many quarters. 'Modest dress' – one of the weasel-word phrases which reappears today – tends to be used by a more conservative group to dictate the clothes of another; 'modesty' had a field-day during the war, pointing fingers, as the hard-working munitions women exercised their ability to buy bright and sparkly things. Time and again, the moral panic brigade were proved wrong: there was no mass flight down the road to perdition. On the other hand, there was a gentle drumbeat towards a greater confidence. Better wages meant choice, decision-making and more individuality – in themselves, quite disturbing for those who feared change. The *New Statesman* reported a factory supervisor saying that 'they appear more alert, more critical of the conditions under which they work, more ready to take a stand against injustice than their pre-war selves of the prototypes. They have a keener appetite for experience and pleasure and a tendency quite new to their class to protest against wrongs even before they become "intolerable."'

It was soon realized that the senior managers (all male) were neither keen on, nor particularly adept at, dealing with this new kind of workforce in the plants. Supervisors were imported, usually middle-class women who by their very bearing and tone – and proper modest dress – expected to be obeyed, possibly responding to this kind of advertisement: 'Lady Ammunition Work Supervisor, of high social status, required by engineering company on government contract, employing women; no technical knowledge necessary, chief qualification being tact, power of control, and ability to maintain a correct tone. Box.495, *The Times*.'

As with everything where such large numbers were involved, there were complex results. Some were of great benefit to the munitionettes, with intelligent concern focussed on their grievances, while others were not, such as irritation engendered by women who were seen as 'Lady Muck' ordering the lower classes about. Much has been made of the mixing of social strata during wartime, with aristocratic ladies on lathes next to scullery maids, and middle-class overseers dealing with unexpected pregnancies, fights and sorting out girls half-dead with inhaling acid and sulphur fumes, yellow with TNT poisoning. Again, no radical revolution took place, and when the workforce headed for the canteen social hierarchy dictated different buildings, a segregation of the sexes and sometimes different table settings – were you tablecloth or oilcloth?

What became clear was that for many there was a beneficial effect: canteens, rest rooms and first aid facilities. For women who were used to meagre food, with the best portion going to the man of the house, regular meals were a boon. It may not have been exciting fare but it kept them going on long shifts. Whether women's health overall benefited is difficult to gauge: those grappling with large shells and heavy machinery over long hours were unlikely to feel fit as fleas whatever they ate. Given the nature of the job there was a high turnover in the factories, notwithstanding the wages. Even so, one thing was abundantly clear: the women *could* do it. The never-ending palaver about skills, the threat to men's position and promotion, the undermining of traditional hierarchies, all continued, while numerous reports and analyses of the women's work showed they were doing what a man did. They were learning new skills, mastering new machinery, enduring long hours and hefting chunks of dangerous metal around cold and often risky places. And for less money. And only 'for the duration'.

We would now consider munitions establishments as 'high security', probably rather secretive for both military and commercial reasons. In 1916 distinguished writers, government propagandists, official photographers and ordinary hacks trotted regularly through the lines of cutters, grinders, fuse-assemblers, shell-forgers et al, grasping for adjectives to convey the mammoth production system. When stumped for a word to describe the workers, they usually fell back on 'splendid', hinting at a flash-in-the-pan kind of admiration; a wonderment that the war-machine relied on ex-tweenies who had popped up from below-stairs to manhandle monstrous ammunition and who apparently had taken to it like proverbial ducks to water; or on married women who were also keeping a family going while their husbands were at war.

One such onlooker was L.K. Yates, who in 1918 published his impressions of the industry under the imprint of the Ministry of Propaganda. Even so, his description is one of the most detailed and he was full of genuine pride in what he had seen (narrated in the kind of trumpeting tone familiar to anyone who ever sat through Pathé or Gaumont British newsreels many years ago). But behind the 'highly chuffed with our women' approach is the authentic view of munitionettes which probably prevailed with much of the population after several years of war. The initial surprise has faded, the admiration for what they could do is genuine, and his is a quaintly chivalrous voice which still hints at reservations as to whether this is what women should be doing, always emphasizing that the way women approach work cannot be anything other than 'womanly'.

> the average woman has, at the initial stage in the munitions shops, to overcome an instinctive fear of the machine. Occasionally, the fear is intensified into an unreasoning phase of terror. 'One has to coax the women to stay with such as these,' said one understanding foreman, pointing to a monster machine with huge-toothed wheels. 'We don't ask a woman to sit alone with these at first, for she wouldn't do it, so we put a man with her, and let her sit and watch a bit, and after a while she loses her fear and won't work with anything else, if she can help it.

He wouldn't get away with it in a government pamphlet these days. But this was 1917, and it was axiomatic that there should be a softening glow which would evince approval in those still disturbed by the influx of women into the engineering world:

> Sometimes, they have volunteered to work throughout the night when air-raids are in progress, at other times, women-workers have returned to the danger zone immediately after some bad experience there; and in every case, the woman worker in the filling factory cheerfully sacrifices much which she holds dear in life. It may signify but little to a man to give up his small personal possessions whilst at work in the

> danger areas, but to many a woman worker it means much, that she may not wear a brooch, or a flower, while on duty, and that her wedding-ring, the only allowable trinket, must be bound with thread while she works. Her tresses, which she normally loves to braid, or twist into varying fashions, must also be left hairpinless beneath her cap. She must relinquish her personal belongings before going to her allotted task; no crochet hook or knitting-pin may accompany her into the zone where friction of steel, or hard metal, might spell death to a multitude of employees. Yet this sacrifice of individuality is given freely by the woman in the filling shop, and she is still merry-hearted and blithe as she fills the small bags with deadly power, or binds the charge which shall fire the shell.

You can't fault him on the detailed picture; it's the frame which doesn't stand the test of time.

What would we think today if we had toured the same factories? We would be struck by the dirt which those who worked in heavy industry took for granted. Even in a munitions plant where precautions were taken against explosions, there would be rubbish and accumulated grime, and very few safety precautions with dangerous machinery. Few industrial premises would be heated in the winter or cooled in the summer.

Protective clothing was unknown, and pictures show long skirts flapping next to lathes, ordinary shoes among the heavy shells being moved, fingers gripping unshielded machinery, and overalls filthy with daily work. Where there are hundreds of women assembling fuses, making cartridges, ramming explosive into shells, the work is clearly mind-numbingly repetitive, with no thought given to varying tasks or spreading skills. The noise in some of the plants was taken for granted, preventing ordinary conversation and adding to the pressure of the job.

When just days before it was finally decommissioned, I walked through the huge building in Birtley in County Durham, built in 1915, I realized it was a rare reminder of what 'heavy' industry really meant a hundred years ago: daunting, clanging, sooty-smelling and austere. We have few of these buildings left, and it is hard now to convey the idea that people once accepted these demanding conditions as normal. The 'facilities' were very basic: prior to the war it was rare for employers to provide more than a simple lavatory; washrooms were rare. And as the factories were often far from residential areas, an hour or so's travel could be added on to the twelve-hour shifts. Discipline on a factory floor was sharply enforced: there were no tea mugs to be seen in the work areas, no places for 'sitting out'. Indeed, not until the final months of the war did anyone seem to think that twelve hours on your feet shoving shells about might be a tad wearying for even the healthiest worker: the Minister of Munitions had given it some thought and 'made an order requiring the provision of sitting facilities for all female workers employed in any process in turning or machining shells or shell bodies, so as to enable them to take advantage of any opportunities for resting that may occur in the course of their employment'. The announcement was careful not to be too indulgent of those with tired limbs – the Minister didn't stipulate whether it should be one chair, bench or stool each, or one chair, bench or stool shared by everyone. Depends on local conditions, was the guidance and no seating whatsoever need be provided 'if the proximity to the machines is impracticable or undesirable'. Consideration for workers' comforts only went so far. . . .

The army of munitionettes naturally attracted the attention of the enemy: despite black-out precautions or remote locations, the Zeppelins, and later the bombers, came hunting for them. This was the kind of activity which the press was not invited to witness – the ignition of Faversham's 200 tons of TNT and ammonium nitrate only reached the local *East Kent Gazette* on 29 April 1916 – twenty-seven days after the event. Elsewhere, it was probably more luck than defence that spared the sprawling sheds, though the Armstrong factory on the banks of the River Tyne boasted a new-fangled anti-aircraft emplacement – two guns out of retirement from the Boer War. If a raid began, the lights were turned off and the workers crept out, sometimes to the canteen, sometimes outside. Several accounts by the lady superintendents charged with evacuating the buildings acknowledge that there wasn't really any place of safety. Mrs G.M. West was at Waltham Abbey and was constantly herding her charges out:

> The hooters sounded about 6.30 before the girls' supper hour – there are no real shelters for the girls who have to leave the danger sheds & crouch under the clean-ways. There are raised gangways which lead from one shed to another. The ground underneath is often very wet, & covered with nettles, also there are some rats, & always plenty of slugs. These small matters make it extremely difficult to get the girls to go under cover, & still more difficult to keep them there.

The four hundred women under the care of Mrs Geraldine Kaye at Woolwich Arsenal impressed her during raids as they waited in the dark in the sheds: 'wonderful pluck'. However, when she moved to another Vickers factory she initially found that everyone had to huddle indoors with the lights off – and with all the windows and doors locked from the outside. At least when they could head to the canteen for a meal, rather than endure a twitchy wait for engines overhead, the munitionettes would happily order a plate of two sausages and mashed potato as 'two Zepps and a cloud'.

The traditional problems with explosives were

ever-present, but it is hard to gauge how much they were in the thoughts of the workers. We look back on it as a risky business, with few of the precautions expected nowadays. Coming from a shipbuilding town, I was aware at an early age that heavy industry produced men with fingers missing, nasty cuts which putrefied, slices off shins which were ignored by men 'not wanting to make a fuss', and women who suffered from numerous chronic conditions which they seriously believed were inevitable and had to be 'put up with'. The world of manual labour and dangerous machinery exacted a heavy toll, and the level of tolerance was far greater than today. You expected to feel 'poorly': 'our skin was perfectly yellow, right down through the body, legs and toenails even, perfectly yellow . . .'. These are the words of a 'canary girl', Mrs M. Hall, describing the result of ten hours making munitions in Perivale in London – ten hours during which she had been absorbing TNT, which could be fatal.

The authorities were somewhat coy about illness and deaths: censorship extended to the munitions industry, and not all accidents were reported. Some, however, could not be ignored: in July 1918 Chilwell Filling Factory in Nottingham produced a massive blast which sent a cloud of smoke and debris high in the sky. Local residents ran to help: 'What a scene of horror met us. Every available vehicle had been commandeered to take the casualties to the hospitals. Men, women and young people burnt, practically all their clothing burnt, torn and dishevelled, their faces black and charred, some bleeding with limbs torn off, eyes and hair literally gone.' When the Brunner Mond factory at Silvertown in East London exploded in January 1917, there were plenty of eyewitness reports: 'There were shouts of "fire", well, you could not miss it, the whole place was lit up. We were all outside looking. I went upstairs to get a shawl. Suddenly I was downstairs and the house was on top of me. It's funny, but I can't really remember hearing the explosion . . . our house was blown down right enough.' Sixty-nine workers were killed and four hundred were injured, though there were suspicions that the casualties were considerably higher. Most of the East End of London was roused from bed, and Woolwich Arsenal across the river looked likely at one point to join in the disaster.

Usually incidents were confined to a description such as 'a factory in the north', but time and again the flames in the sky and the shudder of the explosions defeated the censors. Ardeer in Scotland was home to one of the older plants, Nobel's Explosives Works – the largest in the world before the war and with an experienced workforce, many of them women. They had had their accidents in the previous century, but in July 1915 the TNT building detonated repeatedly, turning night into day. A mile away 'the glare cast over Irvine is so bright that it is possible to read the newspapers'. Kilmarnock, seven miles away, shook violently. The local press knew that there were numerous casualties, but could not get past the official censor for accurate numbers.

Every so often, individual acts of bravery were given some prominence. Mabel Lethbridge was one of the first women awarded the CBE: one of five munitionettes operating a shell-filler at Hayes in Middlesex, she lost a leg and suffered multiple other injuries when the machine malfunctioned and the other women were instantly burned alive. She had started work a mere week before and was only seventeen, having lied about her age to escape from a cloistered upbringing and join the thousands streaming towards their new jobs. Other women did not get recognition: a letter to the Imperial War Museum after the war reveals another casualty at Port Glasgow:

'Dear Sir or Madam this is the Photo of my Dear daughter this is the only sort of Photo that I have to send the loss of her has been very great to us and for ever will I never will get over her Death she was so Good and never was abstant [sic] from her work and was at her work when she was killed my Dear Girl it is with deep regret I write this. Yours with kind regards Isabella Crouthers Sen. Mother of the girl.'

CHAPTER 11

HA'WAY THE LASSES

I went to my first football match when I was twelve. I remember the extraordinary sound of fifty-odd thousand voices bellowing and echoing round Roker Park, filling every particle of air with the famous Roker Roar. I thought it thrilling. I don't remember a single thing about the game.

Rather strange to take a twelve-year-old girl to a Saturday football match? Not in Sunderland, where football has always been an alternative religion. The question 'Are you a fan?' is a redundant remark to a Wearsider. As with most religions, you are born into it – there's no choice. And we have little red and white stripes on our eyeballs as well.

In the second half of the twentieth century, there was a continuation of the industrial decline from the heyday of shipbuilding and coal pits and glass-making. As the totems of work diminished, passion and a sense of place became ever more focussed on the football team, reaching the point now where it is the one reliable point of contact with the wider, richer world. Being part of the internationally famous Premier League (well, most of the time, teeth gritted, fingers crossed) enables us to put down a marker and start a conversation almost anywhere in the world. As a journalist, and a woman, I find it a passport into the strange land of male conversation; men immediately feel confident and I desperately try to remember how the ref refused an obvious penalty last Saturday. I may watch football, but I have no talent for the minutiae.

At school in Sunderland, we played a lot of sport – the legacy of that late Victorian enthusiasm which built on the idea that a healthy body would lead to a healthy mind, i.e. one that didn't spend every waking moment dreaming about boys. We played netball, tennis and rounders, attempted lacrosse but found no one else in the North-east to play against, and were encouraged on to the hockey field to undertake what was seen as armed rugby (but still healthy). Cricket was occasionally suggested, probably because all good wives were supposed to understand the meaning of silly mid on and why Test matches are a sacred ritual. Football was never mentioned. Like all religions, it was seen as the Province of Men, run by them, featuring them and with women as followers. I cannot remember a single instance of anyone ever discussing whether girls should put on football boots. Clearly, even in this football-mad town no one remembered the Sunderland Daisies and the Southwick Lilies.

In the school reception area there were faded

sepia photographs of hearty Edwardian girls in long skirts brandishing lacrosse sticks and posing snootily in high-collared shirts with tennis rackets, and we possessed a large assortment of battered silver trophies and sports shields. Even if the clothes were unsuitable by modern standards, there was a strong sense that the Victorian crinoline had been dumped and the odd ankle was going to be on show. At the turn of the century, sport for ladies was becoming respectable. Tennis, rowing, fencing, archery, golf, swimming and many more pursuits were gaining ground, and girls' schools were organizing leagues and competitions. Some sports, however, were deemed out of bounds, and on 23 March 1895 the very sight of ladies kicking a football in North London prompted a great deal of harrumphing and trumpeting in the press:

> There was an astonishing sight in the neighbourhood of Nightingale Land Ground, Crouch End, on Saturday afternoon. Crouch End itself rubbed its eyes and pinched its arms. . . . All through the afternoon trainloads of excited people journeyed over from all parts, and the respectable array of carriages, cabs, and other vehicles marked a record in the history of Football. Yet all that this huge throng of ten thousand had gathered to see was the opening match of the British Ladies' Football Club.

The *Daily Sketch* might be excited, but two days later the *Jarrow Express* delivered the north-east view: 'The members of the British Ladies' Football Club have played their first match in public. We hope it will be their last.'

The *Manchester Guardian* took a more liberal line, noting that

> their costumes, of course, came in for a good deal of attention, but, thanks to the illustrated papers and the recent developments of gymnastics and cycling, the general public has become so familiar with 'Rational Dress' that it no longer creates anything like a sensation. The ladies team of the North wore red blouses with white yokes, and full black knickerbockers fastened below the knee, black stockings, red beretta caps, brown leather boots and leg-pads . . . one or two added a short skirt above the knickerbockers, but this rather distracted from the good appearance of the dress, as the skirts flapped about in the wind and rendered movement less graceful.

The *Sketch* got down to the actual game – and took aim:

> It would be idle to attempt any description of the play. The first few minutes were sufficient to show that football by women,

> if the British Ladies' be taken as a criterion, is totally out of the question. A footballer requires speed, judgement, skill, and pluck. Not one of these four qualities was apparent on Saturday. For the most part, the ladies wandered aimlessly over the field at an ungraceful jog-trot. A smaller ball than usual was utilised, but the strongest among them could propel it no further than a few yards. The most elementary rules of the game were unknown, and the referee, Mr C. Squires, spent a most agonising time.

Newspapers up and down the land carried letters and articles about 'this astonishing sight', fuelled by more matches in Brighton, Bury, Reading and Bristol. The driving force in the team was Nettie Honeyball, who played as a defender and was quoted as saying: 'If men can play football, why can't we?' A swift answer was published in the pages of the *British Medical Journal*: 'We can in no way sanction reckless exposure to violence, of organs which the common experience of women had led them in every way to protect.' Undeterred, the club advertised in the *Daily Graphic* for members to play 'a manly game and show that it could be womanly as well'. The club's president was Lady Dixie, the Marquess of Queensberry's daughter, well known for her progressive views on women's rights; she had already made her mark as the 'field correspondent' for the *London Morning*

Post during the First Boer War fifteen years earlier. Florence Dixie lent the club respectability and publicity. Florence had well-known views on women's rights and took equality seriously, stating that 'the girls should enter into the spirit of the game with heart and soul'. She set the pattern which was to emerge later, charging an entrance fee which was donated to charity. The club went on tour – Brighton, Bristol, Bury and Newcastle, where a crowd of eight thousand turned up at St James's Park, and played several games in Scotland. Whether the crowds came to see a game or, as suggested in numerous reports, to ogle the legs on show, is difficult to judge. It needs to be stressed that women's legs were in the same category then, as breasts are on American family television today.

On the whole the footballers were regarded with the attitude that was automatically taken to women who did not toe the conventional line: a mixture of patronizing amusement and disapproval, and definitely a one-off with no future. However, there were indications that the turn of the century would see a change, as the *Sportsman* reported a week later: 'I don't think the lady footballer is to be snuffed out by a number of leading articles written by old men out of sympathy both with football as a game and the aspirations of the new women. If the lady footballer dies, she will die hard.'

After that first season and the deluge of comment there were only a few sparks still alight, one of which – inevitably – turned up in Sunderland. In

1889, the *Sunderland Daily Echo* carried an item about the Sunderland Daisies and the Southwick Lilies who were looking for games with other female teams, all correspondence to be addressed to the Secretary, the Dog and Pheasant Hotel, Coronation Street. The Craven Angels responded. It's not clear what happened match-wise, but the *Echo* published a letter from 'A Father': 'Sir . . . I think if the Southwick Lilies, likewise the Craven Angels and the Dog Daisies were to go home and attend to house duties, and kept the old man's boots clean, it would look much better than learning the art of football.' The game was getting a toe-hold among young women, but with no public encouragement. It was in a different world from the tennis- and golf-playing middle classes, and it lacked organization: the Football League ran the national men's game, and many clubs had decreed initially that women's part in it was to accompany men to watch the matches in order to prevent unruly behaviour. Locally, most men's teams were connected either to church or pub – neither of which were wont to regard women as equal. And so things remained, right through the Edwardian age. It was the war which provided a new springboard for a short-lived flowering of female football.

Crowded together in their thousands in huge factories, women found a new sense of cooperation. Admittedly they had little spare time, with those ten- or twelve-hour shifts and almost no time off. Lateness and missed days could result in hefty fines, backed by law. A good proportion of the workforce was seriously undernourished. In households where money was tight, women always came a poor third after the husband and children. If there was occasionally some meat on the table, the lion's share went to the Head of the Household. Few would have questioned the arrangement, especially where men were in labouring jobs. Even in the 1960s, I remember my elderly landlady in Newcastle producing fatty mince every night for us students. Our timid enquiry as to whether there might be a change of menu provoked outrage: 'Lasses get mince and should think themselves lucky! Only men need real meat.'

When the munitions industry powered up in 1915, the government eventually had to take an interest in what women ate so that they could be kept fit to work under intense pressure. The concern was entirely centred around production figures: few of the men in authority felt responsible for the health of their workforce – and all classes of men took no interest whatsoever in what went on in kitchens. That was woman's work. Canteens appeared, providing plain but nourishing food. The lady supervisors in some factories noticed that many of the women were completely unused to being served food: they carried their meal from the counter and initially stared at their well-filled plates with some incomprehension. Then they began to realize that, sitting down together, this could be a pleasurable time – if quite brief. Those who had been in service in a grand house might have dined in a servants' hall, but there would have been a hierarchy among the staff as stiff as at any aristocratic table. Most of those who came from domestic work in an ordinary home had often worked on their own. The canteen was a revelation. Being together. Food and gossip. New friends and fun. All reinforced by a shared sense of doing a job that was valued, however dirty or tedious it might be.

Unsurprisingly, the munitions works found themselves the cradle of women's football. Many of the workers wore trousers, so there was less of a leap into 'unfeminine' kit. Fresh air appealed – the working conditions were frequently ghastly, with no thought given to ventilation, dust, dirt and noise. And compared to what had been experienced in their parents' generation, the publicity for their pioneering sport was much better.

It has been called something of a hidden story. However, one glance at local newspapers shows that reports of games figured regularly – and on the sports page rather than in the oddity section. In the North-east papers it was headed 'Association Football', classifying the matches as properly run, and was sandwiched between the regular reports on boxing, cricket, racing and the popular but quaintly named pedestrianism (an early form of race walking, with a great deal of betting attached). As teams sprouted from munitions firms, heavy engineering, rope-making and shipyards, the women's game gained acceptance because of its charitable aims: a large crowd meant more funds for the myriad war chests needed for soldiers' welfare.

The reports are a little snapshot of the war's reach into everyday lives. Most of the snide comments have disappeared – the women may be playing football, but it's acceptable because there's a war on. They play for their employers – the heavy industry which needs them – but thankfully without having to have it emblazoned across their shirts: having Armstrong-Whitworth's No. 43 Shop (Elswick) on your back would have been a bit of a squeeze. They are part of the immense charitable effort to alleviate the effects of the fighting: Wallsend Slipway Munition Girls play the Blyth Spartans Munition Girls in Northumberland and the proceeds are 'devoted to the widow and family of the late Peter Mackin, the popular local footballer who was killed in action last Easter Monday'.

Indeed, the tolerance of the women's teams was perhaps increased by the lack of professional men's football, which was suspended at the end of the 1914–15 season. Apart from the distaste which was felt at men being paid to play a game while other able-bodied men were losing their lives in France, the sheer numbers who joined up made it nigh-impossible to carry on normally. In County Durham alone in 1915, over three and a half thousand local footballers were already in the forces, along with a thousand officials.

Nor did the crowd just consist of friends and family. Thousands thought it worthwhile to turn up: it's not every day that you go to the University Ground at Durham to see that 'Mrs Shafto, attended by the Mayor, kicked off.' Fifty pounds was raised for the Durham Light Infantry's Prisoners of War Fund. In Lancashire, a POW's wife was persuaded that her colleagues who enjoyed kicking a ball around in their lunch-break should raise money for soldiers' charities. Grace Sibbert became part of the most famous women's team to emerge from the war.

The Dick, Kerr factory in Preston made shells, engineered bridges and produced pontoons. It also produced the outstanding Dick, Kerr's Ladies, who fulfilled the Prime Minister's wish that life in the munitions factory could be made attractive to those yet to join the female workforce and replace the men needed for the ever-hungry army. They hit the headlines with their first major outing: in a slight moment of madness their office manager, Alfred Frankland, had hired Deepdale, Preston North End's stadium. On Christmas Day 1917, the Ladies trounced Arundel Coulthard Foundry 4–0, in front of a crowd of ten thousand. The sports reporters smiled upon them: 'they suffered less than their opponents from stage fright, and they had a better all round understanding of the game. Their forward work, indeed was often surprisingly good, one or two of the ladies showing quite admirable ball control.' Lots of publicity, steady contributions to charity and all on a professional club's hallowed turf.

Over the length and breadth of the country teams turned out, from Scotland to Swansea to Sunderland's Ropery Works to Hackney Marshes National Projectile Factory. They sported a variety of strips: trousers at Elswick, long jerseys at Haslemere, striped shirts for Dick, Kerr's Ladies. And in many cases they wore shorts: the novelty, the shock, even, of a row of ladies' knees must have been considerable to traditionalists still fussing about slowly rising skirt hemlines. Many of the munitionettes proudly appeared with their work caps – some quite frilly – perched on their heads. In Blyth, the Spartans' appearance was defended in the local *News* by a fellow (male) munitions worker:

> I have heard more than once, some very uncharitable and uncalled-for criticism of the respectability of the young women playing these matches, certain of the 'unco guid' ['the rigidly righteous'] asserting that it is not decent for them to appear in public in 'knickers' – pardon my mentioning the article of clothing that has raised their ire. . . . May I say these girls are doing an excellent work of charity in playing. I am working with these girls and I am proud of it. Some of them are a bit boisterous, but they all have hearts as big as a lion. If some of the weak-minded

> and weak-kneed could only have seen them stick in manfully during the recent inclement weather they would feel reassured that there is no possible doubt of our winning the war while we have such women (heroines I call them) as mothers of the race.

Most of the matches were 'friendlies', though the North-east ambitiously planned a Challenge Cup. It was sponsored by a glassworks in Sunderland and eventually known as the Munitionettes' Cup, though the title did not prevent teams competing who represented the whole range of jobs from transport to mills and shipyards. At Newcastle's St James's Park Blyth Spartans had a goal-less draw with the steelworks team from Teesside of Bolckow, Vaughan's. The replay saw the striped shirts of Blyth win 5–0. The team photograph shows a determined cross-legged front row (knees showing) with the rest of the team behind, all arms folded. Just like any other football team (male), and so very different from the image of women just a few years earlier.

CHAPTER 12

LADY POLICE AND LOOSE WOMEN

In 1922 the Home Secretary, Sir Edward Shortt, summed up the job of women police as 'welfare work . . . not proper'. Their task was in fact seen by both its opponents and its supporters as almost exclusively confined to women and children, and had begun in response to wartime conditions. Sir Edward was trying to abolish the women's patrol section of the Metropolitan Police, part of a raft of post-war government cuts in public expenditure. But after he was roundly attacked by Viscountess Astor, the first woman MP to take her seat in the House of Commons, his proposal was effectively watered down.

The debate in the Commons has a contemporary ring, with cocaine, child abuse, sex-trafficking and prostitution all figuring in the detailed exchanges – though using slightly different language, such as the 'white slave trade'. A view unlikely to be heard today would be the one expressed by Ronald McNeill MP, that 'members feel that so far as possible we should keep women uncontaminated from contact with the under-world of crime or with that part of society which is always on the brink of crime, and especially a very unpleasant class of crime'.

In the late nineteenth century, the police had employed 'matrons' to supervise or escort female prisoners, but the practice was not widespread and the wives of policemen or prison warders usually undertook the task. Mr McNeill's worries about 'criminal contamination' were commonly held, especially by the middle classes, and no respectable woman would have been induced to associate with the 'under-world of crime'. The militant suffragettes who found themselves under arrest in the first decade of the twentieth century were dealt with exclusively by men – and often very harshly. Theirs was 'ordinary' crime – public disorder and attacks on property – and their treatment, by and large, was regarded as appropriate, especially by the authorities and the press.

Dreadful though their treatment was in prison when on hunger strike, many of those in the suffrage movement were fiercely engaged in wider questions about women's encounters with the law. They discussed and debated how the all-male aspects of the justice system impinged on their lives and controlled them, and how poorer women were especially vulnerable where sex crimes and prostitution were concerned. They had to take into account the fact that women were thought responsible for the nation behaving 'decently': they were its moral guardians. Many of them based their own demand for the vote on a progressive 'moral' drive to improve society, believing that women with the vote would usher in a fairer and more civilized world.

In the first few weeks of the war, the sheer scale of disruption which resulted from thousands of men applying to enlist in the forces caused alarm. Large camps were being set up, railway stations swarmed with recruits, barracks overflowed with men, and even policemen were heading for the recruitment depots. 'Everywhere problems of order and decency in public places cried out for an urgent solution,' remembered Dorothy Peto – later to become the first woman Superintendent in the Metropolitan Police – who, appalled that the forces of law and order were being thinned out, promptly set about joining one of the newly set up 'women's patrol units'.

The perceived problem involving troops and women is age-old, and for centuries garrison towns and naval ports had always been seen as dens of vice. Moreover, in 1914 the new recruits were actually seen as vulnerable to 'not very clean' women. A strand of popular thinking at the turn of the century had planted the idea that the British Empire's 'racial stock' was being weakened: the impoverished or criminal classes, abetted by loose women, would not produce fit, strong young men for imperial service – critical now there was a war to fight. As ever, the answer was sought in controlling the women, rather than the men. Working-class women were specifically targeted because they were assumed to have a poorer sense of moral behaviour and would therefore be likely to cause trouble in the streets. One of the difficulties with the suffragettes in the previous decade had been astonishment that well-educated, supposedly 'gentlewomen' had had to be arrested for stone-throwing and arson. There was surprise that they *could* do it, never mind that they thought they should, confusing both the police and the courts. In 1914 the initial enormous enthusiasm, dubbed 'khaki fever' by the newspapers, exacerbated the fear that things might get out of hand. Young women were described as excited and uninhibited in their appreciation of men about to serve their country; and though the first burst of fervour ebbed away, the fear that women's behaviour could and would change never went away.

Those in both the suffrage and the women's trade union movement, alongside social and charitable workers, had an attitude to women's safety and prostitution rooted in the circumstances of the age. The law did not side with women, who were seen as temptresses and harlots, and those campaigning for women's rights felt that young girls and poor women should be offered protection. It may seem patronizing from today's point of view, but was thought necessary back then when they were considered responsible for prostitution: they were Eve, tempting Adam. So the first responses to the 'khaki fever' were aimed at preventing women being victimized by it.

Within days, the arrival of Belgian refugees in

Britain prompted a prominent campaigner against trafficking, Margaret Damer Dawson, to suspect that men were coercing displaced women into prostitution. Alarmed, and determined to intervene, she headed for Sir Edward Henry, the Chief Commissioner of Police. However, another women's organization, the National Union of Women Workers, was already on the case. They had written to *The Times* proposing 'voluntary women's patrols' which should be 'neither police nor rescue workers, but true friends of the girls, in the deepest and holiest sense of the word'. Using their extensive network of union members they were swiftly engaged in forming several hundred patrols nationwide, beginning in London. In order that the right sort of candidate should apply, they contacted the Headmistresses' Association and the University Women's Federation. They had the blessing of the War Office, in particular, for emphasizing their desire to clean up the goings-on which attached to military camps.

To begin with, the members of the voluntary patrols just wore a badge and carried an officially issued card; but soon, like other emerging wartime groups, they acquired a uniform. This was partly out of the widespread desire to show that they were as patriotic as the troops they were unable to join, though with heavy skirts just above the ankle they were unlikely to be involved in the hectic pursuit of miscreants. Interestingly, they appeared – at least in reports – to be able to impose their authority without resorting to imitating the military. Society was not used to women raising their voices in public – reaction to suffragettes addressing public meetings had often been hostile purely on the grounds that it was 'unwomanly', regardless of what they said. The women patrols relied heavily on using their class and their confidence, benefitting from the public's approval that they were 'doing good' and the fact that they were unpaid.

Their task was ambivalent: reassuring women, and at the same time endeavouring to 'prevent immorality' – not that it hindered them in any way. They patrolled streets, parks and train stations, and headed for the music halls and cinemas to check for impropriety. Pouncing on couples whose only chance of privacy was in the dark in the park was a particular feature of the job:

> A military policeman came up, evidently very perturbed, and said he had been watching a couple (man a civilian) for some time, and would the lady patrols try and get the girl away? They found the couple indicated partly screened by bushes, but with other couples all around and in disgraceful position. . . . Yet later, when the patrols passed the same spot, they noticed that all the couples, though lying on the damp grass, were in decorous attitudes. . . .

It is difficult to assess the way 'respect' operated in these situations. Middle-class women expected, and got, politeness and a certain deference in many situations, though should they break the rules of their class and their gender, like the suffragettes, the general public of all classes was likely to be hostile. Clearly a quasi-military uniform and a firm delivery in educated tones seemed to work in most cases. And at times, nothing needed to be said: 'A special duty from the very first was to turn girls and lads out of the deep doorways and shop entrances. This is a job the police constable did not care to do, owing to the amount of abuse he got. But we never have any difficulty. Indeed, the rule now is that as soon as we appear, out they all come of their own accord, some sheepishly touching their caps with the remark: "All right, Miss." And yet we have not said a word.'

Their attitudes today might seem disapproving and narrow, but considering what few legal rights women could rely on, how rape, single motherhood and illegitimate children were all regarded as the woman's fault, as well as the immense pressure on women to be 'moral guardians' and not behave like men, their efforts can be seen as springing mainly from genuine concern for women's safety rather than prurient interference. The latter was evident in many letters to the press about 'khaki fever', but it was a useful umbrella under which to help young girls avoid grim consequences. The contraceptive pill was far in the future, other methods were folksy and unreliable, abortion was often murderous; girls with an unwanted pregnancy were traditionally 'turned out of doors' – and poverty thwarted any chance of a decent life.

Wearing large round-brimmed hats, shirts and ties, the voluntary patrols toured the flesh-pots, though still had no authority other than their own confidence. Their presence was a complete novelty: never mind public speaking, women did not 'keep order' in public places. Many welcomed their presence, as the National Union of Women Workers, though in favour of getting the vote, was a pressure group rather than a campaigning society, and had many working-class members who understood the vulnerability of young girls whose poverty gave them few choices.

Margaret Damer Dawson was also busy organizing a uniformed unit: briefly called the Women's Police Volunteers, then the Women's Police Service (WPS), they too were in dark blue uniforms – long skirts and military-style jackets – and a large felt hat, described by their wearers as 'inverted soup-plates'. Dawson came from a different tradition – she was a seasoned campaigner against sex trafficking – and teamed up with two suffragettes, Nina Boyle and Mary Allen, both with militant histories. Allen had broken windows and been to prison three times, having been force-fed twice. Boyle too had served three prison sentences, and both had direct experience of abusive behaviour from the police and male prisoners. All three women were well educated, from comfortable backgrounds, and unlike most of their peer group wanted to put into practice the suffrage campaigners' demand that in a police force women should deal with women.

While Dawson had been worrying about Belgian refugees, Nina Boyle had been advertising in a suffragette paper for 'Specials', having heard Sir Edward Henry at the War Office calling for volunteers for the police force. Sir Edward got wind of her efforts and said that only men would be suitable. Undeterred, she continued to recruit and joined forces with Dawson, who had already put together her own committee. She had secured the blessing of the Commissioner of Police that women might be trained and deployed, as long as they remained resolutely unofficial.

The speed and efficiency with which the myriad voluntary organizations delivered their services was extraordinary: official discouragement was ignored, money was raised, and committees utilized to ease paths to the doors of influential officials. Having argued and demonstrated for women's rights for years, none of them missed the opportunity to show that they were capable of equalling men in their rush to the colours.

The WPS formed a tiny group initially, but on film and in photographs its members look formidably serious. Their training had included first aid and signalling, and some form of self-defence; the uniform suggests the latter might be rather limited, but Dawson herself was an experienced Alpine mountaineer who clearly believed in fitness. Starting in London, they took their moral responsibility to considerable lengths, tending to follow Dawson's view that new jobs, working away from home and more money might easily result in the young women of Britain joining the drunken criminal classes. The patrolling uniformed 'gentlewomen' – the WPS was decidedly educated and well connected – became known for their insistent presence, or more likely prowling, and tendency to lecture on behaviour. They gave prostitutes a hard time, though never thought to remonstrate with their clients. They were also busy separating people who had had the temerity to use a public park for a private act, one of the few duties which the Commissioner of Police thought worthwhile at the end of the war: 'I don't think it is quite the thing for a full-blown constable to go and stir up ladies and gentlemen lying about in parks. It had far better be done by women police.'

All through the war, sexual behaviour, prostitution and the law were seen as a matter to be dealt with urgently because of what it might do to affect fighting men. The problems were recognized as linked to women's status and rights, but no satisfactory conclusions were drawn and all the arguments about the laws on prostitution have continued to this day. Discussion of the consequences for women who fell foul of the law in these respects was also hampered by the regular habit of 'clearing the court', leaving only male officials and legal personnel: women police were not welcome to stay in court rooms, and not until the war was over were women permitted to serve as magistrates, barristers or solicitors. Juries were all-male as well. So the justice system was entirely operated by men.

The courts might not have been friendly, but the WPS was exploring new avenues: petty crime committed by women, drunken brawls, women flat out in the gutter as a result of drink, fights in brothels and trouble in pubs. Policemen very gradually and very grudgingly acknowledged – or at least noticed – that the WPS had quite a lot of success without resorting to fists and truncheons in a mêlée. The idea of patrolling spread, but that was as far as official thinking was prepared to go. According to the *Daily Express*, reporting that lady typists had been engaged for the first time at New Scotland Yard, lady police constables were not envisaged by the senior ranks: 'No, not even if the war lasts fifty years,' insisted an official.

The people of Grantham in Lincolnshire were wondering how to cope with the growing army camp on its outskirts – nearly twenty thousand men descended on this modest market town. Margaret Damer Dawson persuaded them that women police would be of great benefit and two of her colleagues arrived to march in uniform through the town from the station, having been 'requested to keep an eye on alleys, courts, yards and passages'. The locals were nonplussed at the sight, falling about with laughter and hooting loudly at their appearance. By day the two women reverted to plain clothes and set about the thankless task of dissuading country girls from seizing an opportunity to earn a little money. It cannot be said that they reformed the place, but they did have some impact, for the local bishop was moved to propose that their role should be extended nationally. The two women headed for the city of Hull, which was trying to introduce volunteers into the lively port area, while in Folkestone the local watch committee was debating what to do about those attracted to the thousands of troops waiting to cross to France. Not just prostitutes, complained the committee in exasperation, but 'enthusiastic amateurs'.

Sheer force of character must have been their greatest strength, for they had no powers of arrest and were hardly acknowledged by many chief constables, who were loath to pay them adequately. And class difference was an element of control: working-class girls were familiar enough with middle-class bossy-boots types who spoke differently and expected obedience. Even so, the WPS drew many of its members from the suffrage movement, and that alienated many of the respectable-minded rate-paying business community: these 'police ladies' had not long ago been out-of-control women themselves who had shown no respect for order and property. The *Sussex Times* timidly voiced some of the fears about women in police uniform on London streets:

> If the women police act with tact and discretion, there is useful work for them to do in the West end of London, but the average Cockney seems at present to resent their presence in the streets. The suffragettes are to blame for this in large measure, for in the public mind the 'Copperettes', as the girls are called, have come to be associated with, quite erroneously no doubt, the women who used to break windows, and shout, 'Votes for Women' in Parliament Square.

However, the Ministry of Munitions was at a loss to know how to keep order: the migration of thousands of workers into the immense new munitions factories was fuelling worries about 'trouble with women'. The factory supervisors reported that fights and insolence were not uncommon, and the WPS was asked by the Ministry to second members to keep order. Miss G.M. West volunteered in 1916, remarking that most of her fellow recruits were 'ladies or middle class women, all are in a better class than the average policeman'. She was stationed first at a Welsh munitions plant, where nearly four thousand women produced explosives:

> The girls here are very rough, so are the conditions. Their language is sometimes too terrible. But they are also very impressionable,

> shrieking with rage one minute, & on quite friendly terms the next. The previous Sub Insp had only one sergeant and three constables under her, & they managed to get themselves heartily detested by the workers, with the result that for a policewoman to so much as show herself was a signal for all the girls to shriek & boo. They several times threatened to duck the Sub Insp, & did once throw a basin of dirty water over her.

Miss West, paid by the Ministry of Munitions but having had to buy her own uniform, exercised what authority she could over the women: 'Some of them come down from the sheep farms in the mountains, & speak only Welsh, or a very little broken English. Then there are the relatives of miners from the Rhondda & other coal pits near. They are full of socialistic theories & very great on getting up strikes. But they are easily influenced by a little oratory, & go back to work like lambs if you shout at them long enough.'

Outside the factories, there was widespread public grumbling that young women were out and about spending money on fripperies and drink. They were in high spirits, according to some newspaper reports; they were rowdy hoydens, according to others. The sight of hundreds of very young women heading out on the town was enough to cause apoplexy in some people. That working-class girls spent money on ribbons and hats and brooches and drink suggested to the strait-laced that they were completely without a moral compass, former maids imitating the mistress and clearly on the road to ruin. Despite the long shifts they had occasional time off and were determined to enjoy themselves. This was a different kind of work pattern from that of the small world of domestic employment, with a mistress who was nosey about how you conducted yourself. There was the novelty of being in a crowd of fellow workers, the sense also that you were on 'official' work that you could take pride in. And nearly all were earning more than they had ever dreamed of before the war – even though it was nowhere near the wages of the men next to them. No wonder they wanted some fun.

There was grumbling in the countryside as well, as the girls in the Land Army kicked over the traces. Shocked squires and vicars complained to the newspapers that girls were out and about at late hours, and going into pubs. Even when they were at work, passers-by muttered that they had divested themselves of overalls and their breeches were for all to see. The Land 'Army' was unable to deliver military discipline, and charged its welfare officers – older, middle-class ladies – with delivering stern tickings-off to those who misbehaved. Away from home, like many of the munitionettes, free for the first time from family disapproval, they found wartime life – though full of hard slog – unimaginably liberating.

Patronizing attitudes still abounded – in Hartlepool,

the chief constable had taken it upon himself to ban women from buying drink in the local pubs 'in the interests of public morality'. The very sight of women 'congregating' and 'pubs becoming meeting places for women and men at a time of national crisis when so many temptations abound' had been enough to prompt his action. It was implied that wives of soldiers and sailors serving abroad, and girls working away from home, were not to be trusted and had to be supervised.

The voices which lamented the arrival of rowdy behaviour in groups of young wage-earners bent on enjoying themselves tended to be louder than those which sympathised with victimized women; however, the moralizing attitude which had underpinned the police work initially had begun to decline as women claimed the right to enter into public space as citizens. Towards the end of the war, Victorian concepts of female behaviour had been modified and in some cases abolished altogether – respectable young women went out in public on their own, and there was greater acceptance of the idea that girls who enjoyed themselves in pubs and cafés were not all 'loose women'.

The women police had been given the chance for 'women to police women', but in a very limited way. The numbers in both the WPS and the voluntary patrols were never very great, though again the publicity given them spread nationwide. Being prepared to go out on the streets, into pubs, brothels and factories, and represent law and order – even without the policeman's warrant and authority or power of arrest – was a statement that women could do it. The idea that women should deal with women took hold – a victory at the time, but one which later came to be seen as a restriction in the job.

However, even if the public was impressed by their stern and serious demeanour, one group was not wholly enthusiastic: policemen. After women were partially granted the vote in 1918, the voluntary patrols, rather than the WPS, were chosen by the Home Secretary to train to work under the Metropolitan Police; but still without the powers of an ordinary constable. The experienced members of the WPS were rejected as being too closely connected to militant feminism. The Commissioner of Police was quoted as saying that its members were too well educated and his men would be both irritated and intimidated by them. A flavour of his reluctant attitude crept out a year later when he declared that his new force of women police should not be 'vinegary spinsters' or 'blighted middle-aged fanatics'.

The *Daily Mail* was mildly welcoming at the prospect of women police in peacetime, but had reservations: 'Women are likely to be firm and efficient constables – Our urban life will be cleaner by the presence of the woman constable. . . .' However, 'Man is apt to be merciful with man – and woman. Woman is not to be cajoled. When a woman has a sense of duty, she is inflexible. There is some amusement in the prospect that those who hear the chimes o' midnight will have to be wary of women police. These would be ill days for Sir John Falstaff.'

Two weeks later, Margaret Damer Dawson expressed her thoughts by turning to the heart of the matter: the women that women police would have to deal with.

> It's all so one-sided, so unjust to women. They talk as if men were innocent angels, helpless in the hands of wicked women – many of them [prostitutes] have worked for the starvation wages women used to get, and they have found a way of earning as many pounds in a night as they used to earn shillings in a week. . . . It is strange that all those [who have discussed this] are agreed as to the general responsibility of women for all wrong doings. That equality of men and women which has made so much headway in the world of labour is unknown here. In the realm of morals we have not advanced beyond Adam and Eve.

CHAPTER 13

PRECIOUS LETTERS

There was one word missing from the appeals and advertisements for women to help the war effort, and 'career' rarely makes an appearance in any of the contemporary comments on the new occupations on offer. Women did not then have careers in the modern sense, and the few distinguished practitioners of medicine or headmistresses were seen as successful individuals who had made their own way through many obstacles. It was a given that they would be single, and the term 'blue-stocking' was often used. When the men left for the forces, a vacancy was created, not a path to advancement. Just before the war, a Parliamentary Select Committee had enquired into wages and employment at the Post Office and took evidence from a founder member of the Women Clerks' Association:

Committee Chairman: '. . . in other words, so far as the clerical staff of the Post Office is concerned, there should be no distinction of sex at all?'

Miss Cale: 'Exactly.'

Chairman: 'You contemplate a Lady Secretary to the Post Office?'

Miss Cale: 'Yes, certainly, and a Lady Postmaster General eventually.' (Laughter)

Chairman: 'That really is your claim?'

Miss Cale: 'Yes, that is our ambition.'

There was much laughter, amused rather than cynical, about much of the war work. The 'natural order of things' was something established and, for many, unquestioned, and the war was an emergency which would have a certain duration, after which life would return to its traditional pattern, wouldn't it? This had been enshrined in much of the employment legislation and also underlined attitudes to women in unfamiliar uniform undertaking unfamiliar activity. The world was not about to be turned on its head, but was just a little topsy-turvy for the moment, and inevitably, large numbers of girls and women took up work with no great expectations. But when the Post Office started hiring, they at least knew they were joining one of the great institutions of the land.

The Post Office was huge: to join it was prestigious, even in a humble capacity. Women had worked for it in the previous century, though most were classed as 'non-established', which meant the lower ranks of the institution. It also meant that married women could be employed, as there was an official bar on wives in 'established' positions. The marriage bar was one of the pieces of legislation which confirmed the 'natural order of things', initially intended – and endorsed by women – to ensure that single females had a better chance of supporting themselves at a time when married women were expected to be provided for by their husbands. School boards, the civil service, many professional organizations and commercial firms automatically operated it: it merely reinforced that 'natural order'. It was determinedly operated within the Post Office, whose view of the 'natural order' extended to segregating women from men as much as possible when at work. Photographs of row and rows of telegraph operators tend to show no male, other than a supervisor; the male operators were in another room. Across the world of work, this helped shore up the idea of difference – different place, different gender, different pay. Historically, clerical duties occupied both single and married women: Flora Thompson's semi-autobiographical novel, *Lark Rise to Candleford*, attests to 'sub-postmistresses' in late Victorian times, and here and there, where distance or isolation intervened, they were actually allowed to carry the post-bag and deliver (but as 'letter-carriers', never 'postwomen').

If anyone in 1914 doubted female ability to cope with delivering post they could have consulted a book by Bristol's postmaster, written in 1899. Mr R.C. Tombs proudly recalled postal progress from the 'dropping of letters' in the mid-eighteenth century (while avoiding prowling highwaymen) to the introduction of the telegraph and telephone by the end of the nineteenth, and he had a list of formidable – and vintage – 'postal dames'.

> Martha Pike, now in her 93rd year, represented the Department until quite recently in the charming village of Wraxall. When nearly 90 years old she had a three hour letter round every morning up hill and down dale. . . . Hannah Vowles, the sub-postmistress of Frenchay, who, after performing the active duties of that position for forty-seven years, resigned when within five years of 100 years old. . . . Hannah Brewer commenced to deliver letters near Bitton when a mere child; recently, though, she had to give up the work, as having attained the advanced age of 72 years and walked her quarter of a million miles, she felt that she ought to take life more easily than hitherto. In distance, her round was eleven miles daily, and the route was a very trying one on account of the steep hills she had to traverse, and of great exposure to the sun in summer, and to the wind, frost, and snow in winter. It may be interesting to record that Hannah Brewer, although she had to serve a district sparsely populated, was never robbed, stopped, nor molested in any way.

Mr Tombs took immense pride in his job and in his employees, and had many observations that would resonate today. Bristol was full of 'ferocious bulldogs and snappish terriers' who went for his posties, and he thought the handwriting of fifty years earlier was 'much superior to that of the present day'.

The service was seen as a major pillar of civilized life and its public face was the postman. Delivery was a man's job, seen by the PO mandarins as the reliable face of the organization, sturdy and dedicated – on your doorstep, if you lived in the large towns in 1914, up to twelve times a day, a statistic that takes some swallowing a hundred years later. A quarter of a million people were employed to keep the vast network whizzing; it was considered to be the biggest single employer in the world, and handled nearly 6 billion postal items a year. The British wrote letters: some wrote every day, some wrote several times a day. Telephones were rare in all but the richest households and the telegram was for emergencies. No radio, no TV – the letter *was* communication. By no means did it have to be a lengthy literary epistle; society ladies thought nothing of putting literally a few words on the page in the morning and expecting a few words back that afternoon. In many ways, it was very like texting today, obviously not so quick but brief and to the point. Today's mobile phones, Skype and emails are eroding letter writing, which has thus come to be seen as something longer and more composed than other communications. In 1914, just a few lines from across the Channel were seen as marvellous and precious – and meant the world to those separated by war.

The men at the front saw writing home very much as part of daily routine, and the Post Office was also on a war footing in every way. Thousands of its employees had enlisted early, many of them serving in the three battalions of the Post Office Rifles. To replace them, over thirty-five thousand women were engaged in just the first two years – temporarily, it was emphasised – and even married women could apply.

A huge operation to service the needs of the forces swung into action: Regent's Park in London housed an enormous wooden structure covering five acres which became the chief sorting office. Mail was a priority alongside ammunition crossing the Channel, and special sorting offices were set up in France. Meticulously sorted to regiments, camps, hospitals, canteens and the trenches, the letters and parcels were carried through mayhem and mud; the system took the post by train and lorry and horse as far as possible into the battle zone. There were 'field post offices' flying a little red and white flag in barns, cellars and tents, where more sorting took place for the units in the front line. Writing as an accredited war correspondent, Basil Clarke described such a post office operating by candlelight in 1917:

> I spent half an hour in a dug-out post-office in the valley of the Somme. You climb down it by twenty muddy steps made of planks . . . in feeling your way down in the dark you invariably touch the stove pipe and burn your fingers. At the bottom the place looked more like some pirates' or smugglers' den than a post-office. A sergeant postmaster was in charge and along with him were two corporals as assistant postmasters. They were opening the mail bags, newly arrived and sorting the letters into companies and platoons. The sound of the guns and dropping shells not far away lent a curious unreality to it all. To see a soldier in shirt-sleeves, struggling patiently to read a badly-written name and address while guns were booming not many yards away, was unlike any preconceived notion of a post-office.

Each unit came and collected their bundle and headed back to their trench. The Post Office reckoned it took, on average, less than two days for a letter from London to reach that trench. Men could expect every morning a delivery of letters that were part of sixteen thousand mailbags crossing the Channel each day – some 12½ million letters a week. And the network stretched to all the theatres of war – Egypt, Mesopotamia and beyond: the War Office saw post as morale-building.

At home, the Post Office had decided that women could be allowed to deliver. Smart uniforms and navy blue panama straw hats were supplied, along with the all-important large bag. Again, this was one of the jobs which brought home to the general public that the old order seemed to be changing. The post went all over the country, to every kind of household. Having a woman perform a vital and highly recognizable task carried the message of capability further. In many remote places, she would also be expected to bring news and keep country people informed; and on top of that she would be delivering leaflets and paperwork about allowances. The postman was a very public official; and so was the (now official, but only temporary, remember) postwoman.

Women helped sort, helped deliver, and of course wrote. Over the years, keeping in touch by post became a necessary part of surviving separation. Perhaps in many instances the very touch of the paper which had come from another hand was the most important element, for in many of the letters there was little more than gentle longing or chirpy chat. Censorship – which relied heavily on 'honour' – denied any details of military action or location and restricted description of living conditions. However, the kind of details which obsessed the censors were unlikely to intrude on the emotions of the recipients. Military historians feel the lack of description of battles and precise locations: to most of those at home, 'France' was a distant unknown place, the war a complicated situation. Only the wealthy travelled for pleasure; that a soldier was 'abroad' was an acceptable description.

What the families wanted from the letters was reassurance and the human touch, and in the early months of fighting local newspapers published these letters: mothers and wives read them and almost immediately went to the papers' offices to ask for them to be printed and read by the whole town. They were not circumspect in their tone: Mrs Tinkler of Sorley Street in Sunderland heard from her son on 9 October 1914. He was in hospital in Manchester, having been shot in the mouth in the battle of the Aisne: 'I crawled away to a cave four miles away and lay there for a week. Two of my chums fell in the same battle – never to rise again. There were only two of us out of twenty-eight who got out of my trench.' The following week Mrs Allan of Durham Street brought a letter from her son William: 'Dear Mother, it would make all England weep to see the sight of our wounded. I am in the pink at the present but don't know what might happen. I was driven out of one place by the Germans and we were a bit lucky to escape. . . .' Percy Snaith of the Royal Engineers was trying to reassure his mother in Sea Lane: 'We are having hot times here, but up to the present I have managed to escape being hit. I will be very careful for your sake.' Private Green's mother in Deptford Terrace was probably less than reassured, with her son writing to say that he had three wounds in the head and two in the arm:

> The Germans charged our trenches and eleven of us never received the order to retire, so we had a hand-to-hand fight, bayonet for bayonet. About fifty Germans to eleven of us. We fought on till we all fell. The Germans thought they had killed all of us so they started to bury us. The Inniskilling Fusiliers just then opened fire on them from 300 yards and cut them down like grass. I and another were found to be alive, so I am one of the luckiest chaps alive.

These letters, all published within ten days of each other in the *Sunderland Daily Echo*, cannot have left people in much doubt as to the nature of the fighting. Private Green even went on to list his narrow escapes before he was wounded, ending with 'Three men I was standing talking to had their heads blown off. I have been in the thick of the fighting for two months. I was in the battle of the Marne, lasting 22 days.'

Sometimes there was little to glean from the thin bits of paper and postcards which arrived. Upbeat, soldierly phrases abounded: 'We smashed up the Germans a bit and we drove them back a long way with heavy losses on their side, and we are still gaining ground. Don't bother about sending any Christmas puddings out here, as I might be home.' Driver Frank Davison of Monkwearmouth filled his letter with his main preoccupation: 'I got a beautiful ball from the Sunderland Football Club, and it put joy in the hearts of all the boys. We have not had a chance to have a game with it yet, but, when we do, won't we enjoy a game with it!' Just a few streets away, Private Wood's wife got more home-town longing: 'I call my dug-out "The Daisy Inn" and the Sunderland chaps who pass it say "I wish it was, mate." Then we have a chat about Sunderland. Some fellows I talked to I found were schoolmates of mine. The war makes a fellow think of home. I have had "narrow squeaks" but I'm still all right.'

The letters to wives and mothers formed a picture of the complexities of the front line, but the idea which is commonly expressed that the women on the Home Front lived in total ignorance of the hard reality is scarcely borne out by the stream of information which got past the censor's pencil. Many ordinary soldiers didn't spare their mothers descriptions of corpses floating in their trench or men drowned in lakes of mud. As the months went on, such conditions became a commonplace and even these were laced with the optimistic and patriotic sentiments that came naturally at the time. They would be home by Christmas, they would keep their spirits up, they were proud to be defending their country. Please send more socks and fags.

The early stages of the war seem to have produced some of the liveliest correspondence, naturally upbeat but also starkly realistic. As trench warfare took hold, many began to take the grim conditions for granted – and the newspapers were no different from today in tiring of the same old story, however vital to the individuals involved. At home one only had to glance at the horrifyingly long and never-ending daily columns of casualties to know that the scale of the slaughter was terrifying.

Alongside the blunt descriptions of boredom, death and misery there are also thousands of bland or brisk communications: it's hard to know how many men wished to conceal from those at home what it was really like. A well-known consequence of their experiences was the extraordinary number of men who never mentioned World War I for much of the rest of their lives. They didn't talk about it freely when they came home, and only in their seventies did some of them begin to describe what they went through, in detail and with much emotion. So it isn't surprising that it's missing from their correspondence. However, it's also the case that men returning from the war wouldn't automatically think to tell their nearest and dearest their innermost thoughts. Reticence, especially about emotional issues, was considered the norm. What is now taken for granted, indeed encouraged – the expression of the deepest feelings and anxieties – would have been regarded as absurd or self-indulgent, even weak. Men in particular weren't expected to show a great deal of emotion. It wasn't manly – that was women's territory. Marriage involved sharing, but only up to a point. Having a 'heart-to heart' conversation sometimes meant stilted exchanges by today's standards. Pouring out everything would have been met with embarrassment and not a little disgust. There has been such a sea-change in how we display our emotions and share them that it's very hard to understand what was acceptable in 1918. A whole generation buttoned up its memories – silence on the subject wasn't questioned until decades later.

Even so, the letters going to and from front line and Home Front are not without feeling and warmth: food figures in great detail – monotony and fear concentrate the mind tremendously on the amount of meat in the mess tin, and there are yearnings for home cooking. Squashed cakes, favourite biscuits and tasty pie turned parcels from home into manna from heaven. Being in a foreign land, where the odd glimpse of the locals hinted of an alien culture, never mind the 'funny food' in nearby villages – this was something to tell the missus at home. In a world of no radio and TV, it was an introduction to exciting differences: a glass of *vin ordinaire* was an exotic experience. The post kept spirits up. It was the lifeline to normality and the lifeline to all that was longed for. The enormous effort made to keep the postal service functioning in the midst of chaos was no sentimental 'comfort' for the troops, but a major factor in sustaining fighting spirit.

But just being in touch, expressing love, saying how much you missed someone meant a huge amount to men who had never left their home village before enlisting; men who had large families – 'five brothers, three sisters, twenty-two cousins, and not one of them written', as Basil Clarke quoted one unhappy soldier – and who missed female company in a foreign land. Above all, the Post Office delivered a letter which *should* mean that someone was still alive; but even with the swift postal service, it was often being read when the writer was not.

On 2 October 1916 Nellie Nye wrote:

> My dear husband, just a few lines hoping to find you in the best of health as I am please [sic] to say, I am well as can be expected at these times, you may have two to see instead of one this time. Well dear we have been to Hernebay today to see Jack and really we did not know him he is just so thin and when he came home from Hospital he was so fat his legs have been trouble to him he as [sic] a job to walk. My Dear many thanks for the PC now I think I will conclude as things are about the same here. I remain your loving wife Nellie.

Her letter from Whitstable in Kent to her husband Sergeant George Nye in the Queen's Royal West Surrey Regiment chatted companionably about relatives, illnesses and the weather. Buried in it was a shy hint at her condition, showing the delicate circumspection that existed between even husband and wife on such matters.

I wondered if I was reading too much into it, so followed up Nellie's details – twenty years old and just married. This must have been her first letter to her husband and she was three months pregnant. She sent him a second letter on 4 November which was mostly about the weather and Jack, with her mother's worries about him. There was no mention of her pregnancy, except that she ended by saying, 'Well dear excuse this short letter as I do not feel like writing, so will conclude with love from your loving Wife Nellie.'

Her son was born in March 1917. Not surprisingly, she called him George, for exactly a week after she wrote her second letter her husband was dead. The letters, along with his cap badge, ID disc, a charm, his Bible and a lock of hair, were returned to her in May. The postal service recorded life and death in a way that officialdom could not.

It also showed the compassion which men had for those other than their own families. For every death or injury, there were expressions of sympathy or concern – the battlefield was not an impersonal place where only numbers counted. A single casualty meant someone's friend, or a link in the chain of command, or a man who had talked of his family. The postal service bulged with notes and telegrams and letters keeping people in touch, gossipy stuff about having met someone in a hospital, being asked to pass on information, making contact with old friends. There was no phone to pick up, so you wrote.

On 2 June 1917 an officer in the Royal Field Artillery had his horse blown from under him and suffered severe injuries. Several dozen telegrams and letters criss-crossed the Channel as he lay in hospital. His wife, his family, his brother officers, their wives, staff officers and officials at the War Office sustained a network of information, made arrangements, gave support. The fate of people he knew were part of the swirl of news which wound through his regiment by post. The initial telegram about Bernard Massey to his wife Irena in Leicester was terse: 'Regret to inform you 2nd Canadian Casualty Clearing Station reports June 3rd 2nd Lieut B.W.A. Massey R.F.A. D/180 Bde dangerously ill gunshot wounds face Left arm Right // foot right Leg penetrating abdomen regret permission to visit Cannot be granted further report sent when received.' Mrs Massey was already writing to obtain permission to head for France, and her husband's senior officer, Major Harry Cheyne, had already sent his own letter to her:

> Dear Mrs Massey
> You will be surprised to hear from me but I am writing for your husband as he

unfortunately cannot do so himself tonight. I am very sorry to say he was wounded this evening when bringing up ammunition. He tells me the first shell got him in the left arm and knocked him off his horse and a second shell got him on the right knee & foot. These are bad wounds and I am afraid you must be prepared for your husband being laid up for a long time. Your husband probably will not be able to write to you for a few days but I told him I would write you tonight and tell you not to expect to hear from him.

He is just going off to hospital and I fear we will not hear from or of him as he will be moved down to the Base as soon as possible.

If I hear any further particulars I will let you know and I will be very glad if you will let me know when you hear anything.

We are all very sorry to lose your husband – I think I can say we all got on excellently together. He was developing quite a keenness for straffing the Huns and was proving most useful in many ways.

On 4 June Mrs Massey was busy contacting the rest of the family, who replied the same day, as a second letter arrived from Major Cheyne. On 5 June Lieutenant Charlwood was on the case:

Dear Mrs Massey
I am writing this at your husband's bedside. I am pleased to tell you that so far he is making good progress, he maintains a wonderful brightness considering. His left arm and right leg have been rather *badly* injured & he may have to suffer the loss of a limb but you must not worry. Just thank God he is alive & that you will have him back soon. I expect he will be in England in a week or ten days.

He was ever so brave, & the officers of the battery are all very proud of him his Major particularly.

Cheer up.
Yours faithfully
Ed Charlwood, 2Lt RFA

On 6 June, despite his injuries, Major Massey was describing everything to his wife (who was still busy sending letters trying to get to France):

Well I will tell you all about it! On Saturday I again went up with ammunition as on Friday, and I had a glorious ride without a check, so that I hoped all was going smoothly to the end. However at 9.15 or so, as I was about 500 yards from the battery position some seven or eight shells began to come over. The second smashed my forearm, hit my right knee, broke Poppy's forelegs and brought me to the ground. I was wondering how I could manage to shoot Poppy with my revolver, which I carried loaded for some such purpose, when a fourth shell killed her and smashed my right ankle. The men with the leading wagons behind me 'cleared out' and I lay in the road with a Royal Engineer man, and called for help for a quarter of an hour or so, till at last a Colonel came along and went for help. The R.E.'s brought a stretcher and carried me into a dug-out. Then the doctor from our Brigade came and bandaged me up. Major Cheyne came and promised to write to you; and our other officers were there. There I had to lie till midnight before a motor ambulance came, – suffering pain, pain; but even so I knew how lucky I was. My wounds might so easily have been much more *dangerous*; and moreover I knew that my part in this bloody war was over, and that before very many weeks were past I should see my Ilka and Halszka again! The ambulance brought me to a dressing station in that little town to which the wagons had returned without me the evening before. Here my wounds were dressed again, and then I came on in an ambulance to where I am now, namely '2nd Canadian C.C.S., B.E.F.' [British Expeditionary Force] three miles behind our Wagon Line (C.C.S. meaning Casualty

Clearing Station). *Everybody* is so good and gentle here,– the surgeons, the sisters, and the orderlies. I am very fortunate in finding here an excellent surgeon, Major Gase, who has just come in view of operations which are expected, and another good Major as well.

As I had lost a large quantity of blood the sisters worked a quantity of 'saline solution' in through the nipples of my breasts. This supplied *bulk* but not the necessary cells; and as I was looking very very weak and ill they had recourse to 'transfusion' – that is they took a quantity of blood from a healthy man who volunteered to give it to me, and injected it into my right arm. They now say I have proved a '*wonderful case*'. My temperature and pulse have *improved every day*, until to-day they were actually normal. On Sunday morning they cut off my left arm above the elbow, and I have had no pain in it since. My right leg was still painful, so on Monday morning they took that off above the knee,- since when I am free from all pain. I am *very happy*, and *you* are to be too, for they will give me very excellent artificial limbs; I shall be able to ride a bicycle, and pick up pins. And I have my right hand and can write as you see. Also my left leg. And as I say my part in this bloody war is over. To-day I move on to the Base, on the coast near here. Soon I hope to be in England, and as soon as I am cured and fitted out I shall quit the Army and come HOME! I hope the Govt will give me a pension. Anyway I can take up my work again – and shall have *no suffering*. So you are to be *happy*. Good bye from Boy

Berny

There were then several telegrams from the War Office, another letter from Major Cheyne, the family at home writing to each other, and finally a second letter from Lieutenant Charlwood which showed the desperate need to keep in touch in desperate circumstances:

Dear Mrs Massey
A few very Sad lines to tell you that poor Major Cheyne was killed two days ago. He & another new officer a Lt Robinson were killed a few yards from our mess by a stray shell. It is a terrible loss to me & I can hardly realise it. I find myself the last officer in the battery that formed in last July 1916 – and this is the third Major we have lost. Your husband, Hart, Blythe, the Major & Lt Robinson, it is a sad record. If your husband is well enough tell him that I had the Major buried in the same place as Major Hart & with full military honours. 70 odd

men from the Battery attended also Staff Captains and Brigade Officers. I should so like to hear how your husband is progressing please ask him to write *me* a line if he can & tell him I am still Carrying on but a *very* miserable person, also that by *chance* I discovered I was a Lieut since Feb last. I find myself now second in command, but it is all So different!! All my friends have gone. Lieut Spriggs went on leave & is now in Military Hospital Eastbourne. I don't expect him back to the battery. We have had a hard time lately & all pray for the End soon, but the latest news seems to put it a long way off. I must conclude & write a few lines to my wife.
Sincere regards to your husband
Yours very sincerely
Ed. Charlwood
Lieut RFA

There were hundreds of thousands of women who read and reread every precious word from the front line. The news of the war was contained in every envelope, often as vivid and direct as anything we see on screens today. The post came several times a day. Families didn't live in ignorance of the fighting or its consequences. The postwomen who were the bearers of this news must have had dedication and courage to continue delivering it. Throughout the war, carrying a mailbag, running the local post office counter, sending parcels of goodies from home and receiving packages that were all too obviously the personal possessions of yet another casualty were more than just a job: they constituted yet another major contribution to the war effort because they delivered the most personal news.

CHAPTER 14

FLYING COLUMN

In the years before 1914, foreign travel was the preserve of the wealthy and privileged. For the majority, travel for pleasure was on home ground, if at all: a visit to relatives a few miles away, who could put you up; or a few days at the seaside, where you removed none of your clothes to sit in sunshine on the sand. Beaches were crowded with women in corsets, long skirts and large straw hats, accompanied by men in dark suits, ties, and hats or caps. The cheap foreign holiday was more than half a century away. The very idea of going somewhere foreign was followed with the question 'Why?' In rural communities it was common for many people never to leave their village, except perhaps for an occasional visit to the nearby market town.

There was, of course, work to be done in the far-flung Empire, and you could expect travel if you joined the army or Royal Navy. Thousands, mainly young single men, headed for Africa and India, and sometimes their families joined them. But holidays to such places would have seemed odd. A handful of doughty and determined

Victorian females blazed individual trails to distant lands, but most ordinary women were never likely to set foot on foreign soil unless they emigrated, a journey often of regret or desperation.

It must have been an extraordinary adventure for those who found themselves heading across the Channel in the war years, not only to France and Belgium but to Serbia, Egypt and Mesopotamia. Any form of travel, unless you were rich and took your servants, was a challenge, and with the exception of the odd mosquito net or stout boots few concessions were made to local climate, customs or conditions. Women still packed their stays, wore a hat in public and usually insisted on riding side-saddle. Moreover, the war offered a different form of travel: the purposeful adventure in the service of others. And the army of women on the Home Front provided the flying columns to faraway lands, for specific jobs in the face of danger and hardship.

Not that anyone asked them to. A good number of the successful ventures in the war were achieved *despite* official opposition or apathy, particularly those which appeared to be unorthodox or merely not expected of females. The First Aid Nursing Yeomanry (FANY), the Women's Convoy Corps and the Scottish Women's Hospitals all experienced a cold hard stare of indifference, sometimes accompanied by a small official smirk or a blank look of incomprehension. It was famously summed up in the reply to Dr Elsie Inglis: when she offered to organize a thousand trained women doctors and nurses to serve in any war zone, a senior War Office bureaucrat told her, 'My dear lady, go home and sit still.' However, many women hadn't been sitting still for some years, having anticipated that there could be a role for women who were ready and able should the rumblings of conflict become a reality.

The FANY had been in existence since 1909, dreamed up by Sergeant-Major Edward Baker. He had been wounded in the Sudan and reflected afterwards that battlefield medicine lacked a vital element: a troupe of ladies on horseback who would gallop to the rescue and scoop up wounded men. How they might actually heave an inert man in full army kit onto the horse wasn't entirely clear, but the idea took off. He advertised in the press, stating: 'Our mission is to tend Britain's soldiers on the field and prove ourselves worthy country-women of the first and greatest of Britain's army nurses.' The reference to Florence Nightingale and his own military background somehow persuaded the Royal Army Medical Corps (RAMC) that he might at least be allowed to try it, perhaps with horse-drawn ambulances as well.

His initial call for volunteers had strings attached: must have own horse – therefore severely limiting the class of people able to join. On 24 February the *Daily Graphic* sent a reporter ('a mere male') to the London headquarters, where he was clearly bedazzled at the scene he encountered:

> On giving the password to the pretty sentinel at the door, he found himself in the presence of a busy band of aristocratic amazons in arms. Their purpose was peaceful. In their picturesque uniforms, they were engaged in recruiting work. There was a constant stream of lady callers, most of them Society folk, whose patriotism had impelled them to enrol in the Corps which is being formed to enable women to help their country in wartime. Surrounded by gaily garbed sergeants and corporals, Lady Ernestine Hunt, the eldest daughter of the Marquis of Aylesbury, who looked dashing in her uniform of scarlet tunic and dark skirt relieved with white braid, was hard at work.

Those 'without horse' got lessons in riding side-saddle. With over one hundred members they attracted coverage whenever they made an appearance, principally when exercising in places such as Hyde Park, where they organized 'Hunting for Casualties' and 'Wounded Rescue Races'. But it quickly dawned on them that they should pursue less fashion and more field-work. The RAMC offered serious training, and soon the members were skilled in preparing tents and buildings as temporary hospitals, along with first aid and stretcher drill. The latter was carefully analysed, to avoid any embarrassing public accidents: 'No more than ten minutes' carrying work for the first few drills; and a good squad could then 'carry a heavy man for two hundred yards over rough ground without difficulty' ('stalwart guardsmen' did duty as patients). They had also ditched the scarlet and blue for khaki and risked scandal by riding astride, before taking driving lessons and switching to cumbrous mechanical steeds.

This kind of detail had become essential. They wanted to be taken seriously, while the general public wanted to laugh and reject their efforts, for it seemed inconceivable that any of this would ever be of real use. Battlefields were reserved for men. When war did break out, the services of the FANY were offered at once to the government. It responded by saying it couldn't think how to utilize them in any way. Undeterred, they offered themselves to the Belgian army and Red Cross who snaffled them up immediately, whereupon they headed across the Channel.

In December 1915, being by now well blooded in coping with hazardous conditions, the FANY once again went to the War Office to suggest they employ women drivers for ambulances on any British bases. No, came the reply: 'It was not considered practical to employ women to drive for the British wounded in France.' This time the British Red Cross Society proved more amenable, and on 1 January 1916 the first British FANY convoy started work. In that first year alone, it carried eighty thousand wounded. In October they were asked to do the 'Service of Bombardment', which meant having to be ready to work during air raids or naval attacks. By then they were also running canteens and a mobile bath unit, and organizing troop entertainments.

All the time, their efforts rested on the fund-raising machine on the Home Front. The FANY members themselves were all unpaid volunteers, except for a few trained nurses, and they bought their own uniforms – which may account for the fur coats which transformed them in winter into a Mammoth Hamster Unit. Every month, a new camp or hospital or service was deemed necessary and continuous donations were needed. Experienced drivers, able to deliver vivid accounts of their exploits, returned home to give talks and lectures to audiences up and down the country. Individual appeals were sponsored by local charities, wealthy individuals and contributions from ordinary workers. The Workmen's Relief Committee at the massive munitions plant on Tyneside, Armstrong-Whitworth, 'gave largely', following a personal appeal from the FANY Commandant, Mrs Grace McDougall: it bought hospital supplies, surgical instruments and mattresses, as well as a large supply of soap and bandages.

This somewhat piecemeal system was typical. The various Red Cross societies made large contributions, but the endless round of supplication formed the core of the work at home: from five guineas sent by Her Royal Highness Princess Louise, to pillowcases and towels from Broughty Ferry, and £600 from Aberdeen for a motor ambulance. Appeals for supplies, appearing regularly in the official *FANY Gazette*, were precise and detailed:

> For Camp de Ruchard: Readers, please note – We want hair brushes, combs, toothpaste, soap, razors, pipes as luxuries – (think of it, and look at the four or five brushes on your dressing-tables!) and we want *at once* – Cigarettes, tobacco, cocoa, chocolate, biscuits as necessities. There are none so blind as those who will not see – so please read the above over again three times, and then *act*, don't think about it!

The time and energy expended in travelling, acquiring supplies, sorting, packing and transporting them abroad are hardly recorded. It represents the most enormous amount of daily effort by an unsung and huge number of women. Volunteers gathered in church halls, drill halls, town halls and front rooms. Any local newspaper of the time contained scores of small paragraphs and personal column notices about this work: low-key, humdrum and relentless. Garnering no medals and mostly ignored by the official historians, it was small beer compared to the horrifying statistics of the military campaign; but every last little bandage and bar of soap kept the wheels of the war machine turning.

The contrast between organized fund-raising at home and work in the mud of Flanders couldn't have been greater. The FANY diligently chronicled their work, and it was regularly published in magazines and picked up by the press. No one can have been in much doubt as to what life was like for them, as Mary Tombour described on 22 February 1915: 'Thompson, Waite and I set off for the Front in order to take £10 worth of woollies and shirts and 200 tins of cigarettes and tobacco . . . and we had a splendid run to Oostkerke. A lieutenant and three soldiers accompanied us and helped to carry our gifts and on arriving at the first line of the trenches we, three girls, distributed our things to the soldiers whose eyes filled with tears of gratitude.' Heading up to the main trenches, wearing 'rubber Wellingtons reaching to our thighs', they had

> advanced at 100 metres, crossing the wire entanglements, when the Lieutenant came running back and said I must return as the Huns were sending death in Tabloid form [i.e. from aircraft] all round the Poste and that there were also several blesses [wounded]; on hearing this, I absolutely refused to go back but insisted on accompanying him to render First Aid to the wounded, the object for which the FANY came to Belgium. Seeing it was

> useless to protest further, he warned me to double up and run to the Poste Avance. On arriving there was a terrific explosion from a bursting shell, which for a moment almost stunned me; then pulling myself together I crawled to the nearest Blesse but alas on examination I found he was beyond human aid; then having rendered First Aid to the Blesses, the Lieutenant and I returned with the most severely wounded, when the Huns, who are no respecters of the Red Cross, started shelling us and as the three of us made an excellent target for the enemy, the Lieutenant urged me to run back to the Blockhouse.

The essence of FANY character comes over in their despatches to various magazines and papers. One of the very first drivers at the wheel of her 'plucky little Ford' described a typical run to the front line, to deliver medical supplies:

> on and on, under the bridge which marks the frontier between France and Belgium, until we saw the town of Furnes looming ahead – Furnes, once such a gay and beautiful little city, now looking like a fairy town of ruined houses and battered walls. Poor 'Flossie' had become rather overheated in the slow procession from Dunkirk, necessitated by the awful state of the road,

and we decided to stop to refill her radiator, whilst in the midst of this operation, we were suddenly surprised by a big Rolls Royce ambulance. A man looked out from the front of the car and shouted 'Clear out of here just as fast as you can! They've been shelling this place hard every half hour or so, and the next lot is about due.'

We didn't argue! We just put back that radiator cap in a flash, started up the engine (which, happily, responded to the first pull), and were out of that market square before anybody could say 'Knife'.

As we crossed the railway we heard the singing of a large shell tearing its way overhead, followed by a sickly thud in the town. We drove on for about three miles, then, as it was lunchtime, we decided that it would be wise to encamp ourselves in the nearest dry ditch to regale ourselves on bully beef. We found a spot where 'Flossie' could be halted, well out of the way, unpacked our rations and attacked the little meal while we watched distant shelling. Just as we were about to start again, we were nearly shot out of our ditch by a most violent explosion, which apparently proceeded from some innocent-looking seedy bushes not far behind us. We saw a big flash, followed by a loud report. We had been quietly lunching within a few yards of a camouflaged Belgian battery.

It's a serious but jolly-hockey-sticks approach, which gives not an inkling of the phenomenal courage shown by these women. Perhaps they had the advantage that no one expected them to be doing this work, and there were no expectations that they should be heroic. They had none of the pressures which are always felt by male soldiers to be brave and not to show great fear. The army of volunteers could set its own standards and wasn't bound by the rigid conventions which have always been demanded by men and of men on the battlefield. They didn't have to acquire or be trained in the often alien imperative to kill or maim the enemy; they only had to follow an instinctive impulse to help and to rescue in order to fulfil their task. They could sensibly scuttle into a ditch or run for their lives, propelled by common sense and the need to survive; they didn't have to conform to those disciplines which keep armies moving forward, unquestioningly, to an unknown destiny.

The FANY all write candidly and vividly about their experiences, not restrained by any need to avoid describing the appallingly destructive side of war. They didn't have to conceal, as often happens among soldiers, the fact they weren't prepared for what they saw. Of course they weren't – and they felt no difficulty in saying so. It gave them immense strength to cope with month after month of ghastly scenes. So this is war? It's dreadful; we are frequently frightened; but as long as we can help we will do our best. This was the kind of fulfilment that supplied the strength to carry on, and combated the wave of emotions that fighting and destruction brought. The one note of despair always seemed to come from the sheer numbers involved:

> we have carried 3,646 sitting cases and 283 stretcher cases through the month of February . . . yesterday a large [mine] sweeper blew up near the coast, men were drowned and a few rescued: two of our cars were sent for; it was a ghastly sight to see the crowd waiting to see who was saved. . . . In October, the numbers carried are 5,323 cases, 864 stretcher cases and 13 dead. Three of our cars were specially chartered to assist in a big military funeral, as there were not enough hearses in Calais. This is probably the first time that women have had to drive in a funeral. . . .'

Some of the reports and letters deplored the wastage of human life – but it didn't lead them to question their own role: they had men to care for and to help. If there were doubts about the war – and many wondered about the purpose of the carnage – it didn't undermine their commitment. Unlike some soldiers, they felt utterly justified in what they were doing.

In between the casualty statistics were descriptions

of trying to keep life normal: picnics, impromptu concerts and singsongs, letters from home, how to conjure soup from a tin of bully beef, going down with the measles, delight in an unspoilt area of countryside, and hearty instructions on how to heave a large car out of an immense shell-hole. Most of the FANY drivers were from confident middle-or upper-class backgrounds, but this kind of attitude was found among other volunteers too: the same straightforward can-do approach which was free from any need to pretend to be brave. That so many were exceptionally courageous was not a product of public expectations: they were merely proving what they could do – and thought that they should do.

The FANY received countless citations for bravery from the French, Belgians and many of the other Allies. Individual acts of bravery included those of women who entered areas that had just been gassed, drivers who went through shell-fire without stopping, and women who evacuated the wounded with cool disregard for their own safety. A modest letter of 1919 in the Imperial War Museum collection gives a list of decorations awarded to the FANY: twenty-five women had been decorated by the Belgians and the French, including the award of the Légion d'Honneur and the Croix de Guerre, and there were five British Military Medals. This was just part of the FANY's total of ninety-five decorations and fifteen Mentions in Despatches. The postscript reads: 'A good record, isn't it?' They would probably have replied larkily:

> Three little Fanys went to see the
> Trenches
> They journeyed on a Camion, being saucy
> wenches.
> One little Fany, going back to Blighty
> Stopped in Paris on the way, to buy a
> naughty nightie.

'The only way of showing that women are capable of taking a real share in National Defence is to *prove* it – by *practical demonstration.*' Seven years before the war began, Mabel St Clair Stobart hit the nail on the head. No one took any notice. A woman completely convinced that action, not words, was the key to progress, she found herself among the early suffrage campaigners who, she sighed, were 'very busy writing, very busy talking . . .'. She had already demonstrated a taste for action, having lived on a farm in South Africa just after the Boer War, combating locusts and bush fires and every so often leaving her first husband at home while she trekked through the remoter parts of the Transvaal. Back in Britain, her children grown up and she herself now a widow, she remarried, embarked on a career in journalism and observed that the prevailing preoccupation with a possible war in the near future completely ignored any role for women. She didn't contemplate the idea that women should fight – but instead, with every suitable male in the front line, she believed women should be trained to undertake all the supporting roles: drivers, orderlies, stretcher-bearers. She had found a cause and set about pursuing it.

Her first efforts met with indifference and mild amusement, but also a clutch of volunteers for her Women's Sick and Wounded Convoy Corps. As with the FANY, there was emphasis on a uniform (divided skirt and Norfolk golf jacket) and practical first aid, with an annual camp, the first of which was held at Studland in Dorset, where bemused locals watched fifty women marching past in blue-grey uniforms, carrying haversacks. (Women were not expected to march: it was 'unwomanly' and even the early suffragettes tended to walk briskly on demonstrations rather than fall into step.)

Recruits were trained in signalling, wagon drill and 'Improvization work in field and hospitals'. The latter was at the heart of Mabel Stobart's efforts. Like Sergeant-Major Baker, she believed that nursing should be left to the professionals but was concerned that the entire army system ignored the importance of getting the wounded to hospital as quickly as possible: 'Precisely during the precious first hours, or it may be days, when most care is needed, least is procurable.' (This was something that has had to be relearned time and again in subsequent wars.) Unlike the FANY, the Convoy members didn't swoop up the wounded into the saddle; instead, wagon-driving skills were prioritized.

With a small band of enthusiastic women, the Convoy scented its first challenge in 1912 when war broke out in the Balkans, where the Serbs, Bulgarians, Greeks and Montenegrins were fighting the Turks. Mabel went to see the chairman of the British Red Cross, Sir Frederick Treves, offering to go to Bulgaria. Sir Frederick rejected her idea. She then saw Viscount Esher, who was president of the London Territorial Association. He objected on the grounds that help should not be sent to warring foreign armies, even when it was in the form of 'well-meaning, philanthropic and earnest folk patching up wounded'.

Mabel Stobart wasn't to be thwarted, feeling that the Red Cross would send men who 'knew more about the rules of football than hospital work'. Frustrated, and furious because she kept being told that there was 'no work fitted for women in the Balkans', she countered that these people only *imagined* such a thing. 'I knew better,' was her reply. Her mind-set didn't improve when she opened her newspaper and saw advertisements placed by the Red Cross advising women *not* to enrol in the Convoy for Bulgaria.

However, in possession of a steam-rollering ability when confronted with conventional prejudice, she decided that British big-wigs should be bypassed and direct action employed. Having selected sixteen members for her Convoy, she herself made the two-day railway journey by Orient Express to Belgrade in Serbia, immediately touring a huge military hospital containing six hundred wounded soldiers. She was unimpressed by the smell and the overcrowding, and the fact that the non-medical staff were hopeless: 'local ladies of society and peasant women, utterly untrained for their grim, gigantic task'. However, she felt that the hospital wasn't near enough to the action for her Convoy to operate and so headed for Sofia, the capital of Bulgaria, where she saw Queen Eleonora, herself a trained nurse.

In the next few days of travel around Bulgaria Mabel experienced a microcosm of early twentieth-century warfare: civilian chaos and railway trucks full of eager young men going south to the front line – 'sturdy sunburnt peasants', passed by trains going north 'full of human wreckage returning from the front – white-faced, mutilated – with bloodstained, tattered garments'. The hospitals were inadequate: an improvised one in a boys' school contained '200 beds which were occupied by 250 patients – lying three in two beds close together – and staffed by one surgeon and five nurses'. It took five days for the wounded to be brought there by jolting ox-wagon.

She acquired hospital equipment, hired interpreters, got blankets and cooking pots from the Red Cross, cabled friends in London for large sums of money to buy more supplies in London, and obtained permission to work behind the front line. The kind of organization that was going to be needed in just over a year's time, but on an unimaginably greater scale, was being put into practice. Mabel Stobart had never doubted that it could be done, and when her sixteen-strong all-women team arrived she piled everyone into ox-drawn carts for a seven-day trek to the front. Once at Adrianople she learned in a trice how to requisition a house for hospital use, and then everyone got down on their knees and scrubbed for hours. A line of wagons disgorged the first fifty patients and the work started. The next few weeks saw the kind of problems which reappeared time and again in the following war: mud and poor accommodation – though plenty of rats – language difficulties, post interfered with by censors, illness among the Convoy members, continual military and official visitors, the sound of gunfire and a stream of wounded men.

Mission accomplished in this short campaign, Mabel Stobart reflected in 1913 that 'The purblind policy of shielding women against their will from a knowledge of truths, however unpleasant these may be, is disastrous not only for women, but for the community at large.' The 'men only' policy of the Red Cross struck her as signifying that 'a prominent organisation in Great Britain is still breathing the atmosphere of the times of our grandmothers, and fails to realise that women can no longer be content to float idly upon the surface, but feel it is their duty, at whatever cost to themselves, to plumb the depths of life.' She cannot have realized how prescient she was.

A year later, she was speaking at a peace rally in London alongside many senior members of the suffrage movement when they heard that war had been declared. Before leaving Kingsway Hall, she had already begun setting out her ideas and collaring her colleagues; the next morning saw a headquarters set up and the Women's National Service League sprang almost fully formed into life. Recruiting, fund-raising and equipment-ordering started immediately and, unsurprisingly, a path was beaten to the door of the Red Cross again. And once again Sir Frederick Treves dusted off his argument and trotted it out . . . there is no work fitted for women in the sphere of war. This time the Belgian Red Cross snapped up her offer and she went to Brussels to set up a hospital for French and Belgian soldiers. But the fast-moving first few weeks of the war sabotaged her plans: before the unit waiting in England had time to leave she and her husband had to retreat from Brussels, only to be arrested and tried as spies by the Germans. The tale goes that she only escaped because she lived in Hampstead Garden Suburb, which the German judge had taken a shine to on a visit just before the war.

After returning to London she took a League unit to Antwerp, which operated for only ten days before the Germans were on the doorstep again.

By now, she was making headlines. Stories about women found ready publishers – they had pages of military manoeuvres, maps and official despatches, but here was something different, unusual. Local newspapers being the main source of information for most people, the syndicated snippets got a wide audience: the very fact that an all-women unit was somewhere in the war zone was an extraordinary novelty to readers in 1914: The *Sunderland Daily Echo* followed her progress with fascination, possibly boggling at the news that the team of British women had been under bombardment in their hospital and led or carried their patients into a cellar: 'During the hell which followed, Mrs Stobart and the doctors and nurses of her staff walked unconcernedly through a rain of projectiles to and from the convent across the way to obtain supplies and food for their patients.' Having found a lorry to take the patients to the Dutch border, Mabel Stobart commandeered three motor buses loaded with ammunition and they made their escape.

Few of the newspaper articles carry the name of a reporter or agency and it is quite clear that the numerous first-hand descriptions of women's organizations during the war came from the members themselves, or from the many supporters who travelled abroad to see their work. Those who had been in the suffrage societies were keenly aware of the value of publicity and the possibility of hostile coverage from traditionalist male editors, so suffrage branches around the country were assiduous in delivering any reports they received to their local journalists. They knew that war was always covered from the male standpoint – strategy and interesting weaponry. One of the major special publications was the *Illustrated War News*, which appeared throughout the war and was hugely popular: its forty-plus pages chronicled the minutiae of the fighting in pictures. Tucked among the official images of troops and detailed illustrations of guns, tanks and ships were the occasional photographs of women serving both at home and abroad. It usually managed one page of print on 'Women and War', adopting a tone of cautious enthusiasm for their new-found occupations (change was coming – but let's be careful about it). And when lost for a word to describe what women were doing, they always used 'splendid'. The old hands from the suffrage campaign knew that more was needed, and the doings of people like Mabel Stobart were seized on. She didn't let them down, for she was establishing another hospital near Cherbourg in France.

Up and running smoothly, after several months it wasn't enough of a challenge. It was too comfortable, she said to herself, and seized upon news of a widespread typhus epidemic in Serbia – and a shortage of medical staff. She was a graceful and commanding figure, someone who negotiated well with her peers and picked up languages easily. In the Balkans, after several months running dispensaries for civilians she was put in charge of the First Serbian-English Field Hospital, giving her the opportunity to get as near the front-line fighting as possible. However, she and her two dozen-strong team almost straightaway found themselves in a desperate military retreat, tending the wounded while on the move. With winter approaching, a gargantuan column of troops and fearful civilians – possibly several hundred thousand – headed for Albania through the mountains of Serbia and Montenegro.

It was an epic trek in horrendous conditions, with 'The Lady on the Black Horse', as she was known, leading her staff in cars and lumbering ox-wagons and having to cope with non-stop cases of wounds, disease, accidents and total exhaustion – often the result of the earlier terrible epidemic which had killed thousands. Twelve weeks and eight hundred miles, at a snail's pace, at the mercy of blizzards and bandits. At the age of fifty-three she spent eighteen hours a day on horseback, plodding up the treacherous narrow passes, and recalled, 'Whichever way you looked, oxen, horses, and human beings were struggling and rolling and stumbling all day long in the ice and snow.' Tens of thousands died – the Serb estimate is well over a hundred thousand, many of them young boys, and mainly of exposure and starvation. Mabel Stobart's unit was one of the few which survived the ordeal.

Several of her nurses kept diaries and detailed records of the event, and published them immediately they returned home. The Balkans were an exotic location, full of minarets and mosques, gypsies and peasants in traditional costume. This was war in a far-off land where the battles were between a bewildering array of armies across borders which were loosely defined. However, Serbia had assumed a special place in the war narrative, with much popular support in Britain for its people – and there was an array of British and Allied units operating in the country: the Red Cross, the Association of Wounded Allies, the Young Farmers' Ambulance and Lady Paget's Hospital in Skopje among many others.

Once home, the Convoy veterans spread the word about the dreadful state of the country and Mabel Stobart herself embarked on a series of talks and lectures. Pictures of the retreat, with black scarecrow-like figures trudging through the snowdrifts and slush, appeared in all the press, and the figure of a woman in long divided skirt and a large floppy hat leading a horse spread Mrs Stobart's reputation. She never omitted to press her ideas along with her account of the amazing journey, and thousands must have heard her saying that not only *could* women be part of a country's defence – but *right now*, they *were*.

Was everyone impressed? Not the chairman of the Serbian Relief Fund in London, who reprimanded her for 'having exceeded her instructions, and having led her Unit into unnecessary risks in accompanying the Army to the Front'. To which one can only imagine she replied 'Hah!'

While serving in Serbia, the Stobart Convoy found itself alongside units of one of the largest volunteer medical groups in the war, the Scottish Women's Hospitals (SWH). They were ahead of the field in many ways, and got publicity not only in the press but in the cinema. The Scottish Screen Archive has footage of an operation, probably in a hospital in Romania in 1917, with an all-women team round a patient who is having shrapnel extracted from his leg. Wielding the forceps is Dr Elsie Inglis, fulfilling a dream she had had for many years.

If you desired to be a doctor in 1914, and were a woman, you had to have a tenacious spirit as well as the requisite abilities. Medical schools didn't welcome you – some still refused places to female students. Your skills were limited to general practice work or traditional specializations: children and birth. Many hospital boards were wary of recruiting women, and the army flatly refused to have them in its Medical Corps. All this in a society in which it was almost impossible for some women to contemplate a male physician examining them, such were the pruderies and pressures of the time.

Just over five hundred women were registered as qualified in 1914, and Elsie Inglis already had a reputation in Edinburgh as an outstanding doctor. She had pursued her medical goals with her father's encouragement (a rarity in the 1880s), studying in Edinburgh and Glasgow. Most of the medical schools still practised segregation, especially when anatomy was taught. One Glaswegian professor confronted Elsie outside the lecture room with a downright refusal to let in a female while 'certain parts of men's bodies' were being discussed and possibly displayed in pictures.

Despite this, Elsie, determined and diligent, passed her finals with flying colours and found herself inevitably drawn to the cause of suffrage, partly because of the way in which women were at the mercy of the law when ill. On one occasion, having just left a patient who needed an operation, she went straight to a suffrage meeting to tell them that 'the woman was to be left to lingering suffering from which only death could release her'. The woman's husband had refused consent – a necessity if a married woman needed an operation.

The moment war was declared, she headed for Edinburgh Castle and the War Office. Pointing out that the male doctors would be taken on by the military, she offered to supply qualified women doctors and nurses for whatever foreign theatre of war needed them. To this offer had come the famous reply that she should go home and sit still. This response encapsulates much of the dismissive and patronizing view which many encountered – and in some cases expected – from the men who were running the war. It says a great deal for the suffrage movement and the practical attitude of those who knew that they could and should be of use that they took no notice of such remarks.

Within days, the National Union of Women's Suffrage Societies (NUWSS) in Scotland was organizing at full throttle, raising money and approaching the Red Cross with the offer of a fully staffed hospital unit. However, as the War Office had the final decision, it refused. At least the government was consistent in its approach to women volunteers. Two hospitals were planned and, while the NUWSS appealed in print, Elsie headed for London and a big meeting at Kingsway Hall called 'What Women Can Do to Help the War'. She declared that 'the need is there, and too terrible to allow any haggling about who does the work'.

The need was coming from the governments of Belgium, France and Serbia, and initially a dozen women hurried to Calais to combat typhus among refugees. The Oxford Women's Suffrage Society spotted an opportunity to swat the Red Cross fly in the ointment and wrote to the *Oxford Chronicle* that

> it is not generally known that the British Red Cross Society will not make use of the suffrage hospitals, because they are staffed by women doctors. All they have allowed us to do yet is to send two women doctors to Calais to take charge of enteric [typhus] cases under the supervision of a man doctor. At present their small hospital has the lowest death-rate in France, and it is

> gratifying to learn that it is entirely staffed by British nurses, which is perhaps the reason for the low death-rate.

The suffragettes were not letting up in their campaign.

Meanwhile, a much larger permanent hospital was set up near Paris. The draughty, gloomy abbey at Royaumont was a splendid relic of medieval times, but not obviously suited to up-to-date medical work; to begin with it had no water supply, so water came in by the bucket – for all the floors had to be scrubbed – and mattresses were stuffed with straw. Typically, it was seen by the volunteers as a challenge. As money poured in the wards were quickly furnished, with many of the beds individually sponsored – a fund-raising wheeze that was immensely successful and established links with schools, societies and individuals the length of Britain, generating both publicity and sustained donations.

Royaumont garnered great attention: the well-known actress Cicely Hamilton had volunteered and was keeping up a stream of articles for the suffrage magazines and the rest of the press. The *Nursing Times* delightedly picked up articles from around the British Empire and republished them at home, with one from the *Daily News* particularly enthusiastic about

> an army of British women uniformed in workmanlike greys and blues with a gay

> touch of tartan on collar and hat-band. The combination of a half-ruined monastery with this energetic army of women in charge is not more strange than the contrasts in the hospital itself. Everywhere there is electricity, supplying to the finest x-ray apparatus in the whole district, so that military and civil doctors bring cases from all over the country round to be dealt with by the little lady expert from Scotland and her electrician-orderly – a girl barely 20.

Surely the novelty of having women proving to be professional and efficient would wear off quickly? It seems not. So entrenched were views of what women ought to do and what they should not that articles and letters and discussions swirled in the public forum throughout the war. There is no doubt that proving they could face up to the rigours of service in a foreign land, sometimes in danger, coupled with their evident ability to do a job competently, not only drew admiration, but also disturbed and frightened: if these women could do this in the worst conditions, what was to stop them coming home and taking over the jobs normally filled by men? Few voiced these feelings in public, for it would sound unpatriotic. However, the constant reminder that it was war that produced this excellent display from the ladies accompanied a lot of the praise, underlining the 'temporary' nature of their efforts. And search as one might, there are no public statements from government or hospital boards to the effect that the rules and regulations restricting women's training and employment would be swept away. Nor even *should* be swept away. Sometimes press comment on the hospitals in France harked back, rather than looked forward:

> British nurses are very businesslike in their methods, and their bedside manner has no excess of sentiment. So that when Sister Ben Nevis caught Dumanet at the wrong end of the ward and ordered him back to bed he knew better than to argue about it. He might understand the 'good angels' better if he knew that in the days before the war many of them were militant suffragettes and walked about London with wicked little hammers up their sleeves, itching to break shop windows.

Visitors from many countries were intrigued by the scale of the undertaking and the fact that women ran it, carried corpses to the chapel and performed surgical operations. Eventually the unit treated over ten thousand servicemen.

Elsie Inglis was meanwhile getting the Serbian unit under way, and touring Britain giving talks and gingering up local suffrage groups. Everything was financed by donations: every bed, every knife and fork, every bandage had to be acquired either by gift or by public funding. The Serbian hospital was to have 250 beds, and the *Evening Standard* carried the call for 'robust young women who are prepared to start for Salonika right away'.

When the first unit arrived in the country there was news of casualties – nurses died of typhus, and later from enemy action. But no brake was put on any of the activities and there was no suggestion from their supporters at home that they should withdraw further from the action, nor was there any reduction in the number of volunteers. Elsie was able to draw on the considerable experience of women working in the medical service in Edinburgh, for the city had established itself as a place where women could study, train and practise. But look a little closer, perhaps at just one girls' school, and there emerges an extraordinary list of pupils and old girls who were part of the war effort. It gives an idea of the immense involvement of ordinary women. Two of Elsie's nieces had been educated at St George's, and she had known the school's founder. Like so many other schools, they produced an inordinate amount of knitting ('woollen, men's size, No.8 Mittens should have ½ finger if possible') and raised money for hospital beds in France. They set up and funded their own VAD detachment for convalescent soldiers ('the girls personally digging and arranging the garden'). Two former pupils, Florence McLeod and Lucy Smith, went to Serbia as orderlies with the SWH and sent letters back to the school:

Kraguievatz, January 1915

We have actually started our hospital. We are relieving a Serbian doctor who ran this building single-handed, and is now absolutely exhausted. The wounded were lying on sacks of straw on the floor, and everything was horribly dirty. We have had the wards whitewashed and got our beds put up, and things are looking very nice. The men are charming and tremendously brave. One man in my ward had most of one heel blown off and two wounds in the leg: he suffers horribly, but he smiles and says 'Dobro!' (right, good). Another, who talks French fairly, said he was so glad he had English sisters, as he would soon be back to fight the Austrians again. We have lots of Serbian orderlies, mostly prisoners of war, Slavs, Croats, etc., who surrendered to the Serbian army with the greatest joy. I have three orderlies under me. One is a Russian, a student from Lemberg, who was sent to fight against his will. Another is a poor Hungarian, who can get no news of his wife and children. It was hard for the Magyars, living on the plain, to go up into the mountains to fight the Serbs. One poor man died the other day. The other patients asked leave to sing their National Anthem while he had his last cup of coffee. I am awfully happy working out here.

You get a sense of another world into which young Edinburgh women had been tipped: a mass of foreigners, grim medical cases. However, their interest in the individuals, their can-do attitude and their humanity shine through.

Having arrived in April 1915 to take charge of the unit which had been dealing with the outbreak of typhus on top of everything else, Elsie Inglis spent much of her time trying to combat the filthy conditions and the general lack of trained medical staff in Serbia. However, with more units now established in the country she was able to turn to her great passion: surgery. There had been little opportunity for that back in Britain, and in any case it had been mainly connected with women and childbirth. In Serbia there was ample opportunity to operate on grown men, and she relished being able to use her skills.

However, autumn brought the enemy to Kragujevac and she and her staff elected to stay at the hospital where they were swamped with Serbians – now prisoners like themselves. They coped with hundreds of wounded men and stood up to the enemy, she herself refusing to sign a document crediting them with 'good behaviour'. This was a tough but wise decision, for the Germans in particular were desperate to gain propaganda credit following their execution of Nurse Edith Cavell for alleged espionage – about which Elsie knew nothing. By the end of the year the small group had been repatriated, and finally arrived home in February.

Dr Gertrude MacLaren was another St George's old girl who had been at Kragujevac before retreating with her patients in the face of the Bulgarian army's advance:

> The roads were crowded, horse carts and bullock wagons blocking the middle, while soldiers and refugees jostled each other at the sides. The first day we walked about twenty miles, and slept in a stubble field. . . . A quarrel arose amongst some Serbs, and one of them fired his rifle at random, wounding one of our sisters in the chest. Three of us remained behind with her, spending the night at a Serbian Field Hospital, and next day she was carried into Rashka on a stretcher by some Serbian orderlies. One other sister and I stayed with her there for a day or two, and then brought her on by automobile to another Serbian Field Hospital, stationed between Rashka and Mitrovitza. While we were at Rashka an Austrian aeroplane paid us a visit and dropped a few bombs, one falling in the courtyard of the hospital and wounding a patient. And always the endless procession of bullock wagons, soldiers, and refugees was passing. . . .

What is often omitted from these reports is the harshness of the conditions. In the Balkans a century ago most of the villages and their inhabitants would have lacked basic sanitation, electricity and education. The mountain areas were isolated, the way of life tough, sometimes brutal. Many of the women who came to nurse the wounded were equally shocked by the state of the civilians, and tried to help where they could. It was commonplace to have fleas and lice, a monotonous, unhealthy diet and to die of easily curable ailments. Superstition was rife and the obsession with the 'evil eye' as the source of disease or the 'devil's mark' as the cause of mental illness interfered with attempts to treat patients, especially children. The houses looked quaint, especially in the areas of Turkish influence, but were damp and dark. Nor was there much possibility of change: it would be at least half a century before the central Balkans began to acquire some of the comforts of modern life. Even so, rarely is a patronizing tone heard from the volunteers, who emphasize welcome and friendship, helpfulness and gratitude. Taking everything in her stride, Dr MacLaren recounts acquiring accommodation in a monastery. The monks were kind but somewhat surprised by the arrival of thirty British women, who went on to spend two nights in Pristina, sleeping in 'a Turkish harem'.

Back home, the current and former pupils of St George's followed the exploits of the SWH in letters and in the press and may have been inspired – or just as likely were patriotically inclined – to add their own efforts. A hundred and seventy-five (by no means all, apparently) are listed by the Old Girls' Association, and this is a selection of their roles: nurse, VAD, in the YMCA in France, in the Red Cross Room at Waverley Station, munitions worker, cook, with Scottish Churches' Huts in France, with the Forestry Branch of the Scottish Women's Land Army, member of the Almeric Paget Military Massage Corps, in the Soldiers' Washing and Mending Clothes Bureau, Chairman of the Biggar and District War Gardens Cooperative Society, in the Wicklow and Avoca harvesting and land work depot, Inspector of Factories, in the YMCA flax camp, in the Eastern Mediterranean Secret Intelligence Bureau, nursing Russians in Kazan, worker in the Kensington Splint Department, collecting and sending one hundred pairs of socks a month to the Royal Scots, sphagnum moss picking, teaching French to the 16th Battalion Royal Scots, and violinist in one of Miss Lena Ashwell's concert parties in France for three years. Just one school's part in the war.

And in Serbia, the SWH was just one of many medical missions: other British women were serving with the Red Cross, the Association of Wounded Allies, The Young Farmers' Ambulance and Lady Paget's Hospital in Skopje. One of the features of the St George's girls' exploits is the large number of young women who, having served with a unit and returned home, immediately set out for another front. The lead came from women like Elsie Inglis who, back from Serbia, found herself feted by press and public but was still determined to return to the front. Funds were flowing in to the SWH and in August she was off again, to help the Serbian army fighting Bulgarians and Austrians in Romania.

The press were hooked by now, and gave prominence to those setting off from Liverpool with the headline: 'British Women's Heroic Sacrifice' – they had had their hair 'cropped boyishly short'. Columns of newsprint followed their seaborne progress to Archangel in northern Russia, then by train to Odessa in the south, from where they headed to the chaos of the Russian front and the huge military camps in the area. Moving to Romania, they found conditions no better, with retreating forces, aerial bombing and little organization on the ground. Elsie eventually established her unit in the town of Braila, setting up an operating theatre and treating mainly Russians, but then had to retreat to nearby Galati. The pressure was immense, a thousand wounded arriving every day. 'The night we opened, we got 109 cases. We began operating the next afternoon at 2 o'clock and went on until 5 o'clock the next morning.' They were moved to yet another town, Reni, still with a never-ending number of wounded men to treat. A freezing winter, followed by the Russian Revolution in the spring, complicated everyone's lives.

It was probably here that she was filmed in her surgical whites, operating amid her all-women team. This would have been not only fascinating to the audiences at home, but astounding; in general, there was complete approval for women to be nurses in the war zones, but that they should be elevated to doctors – and then to surgeons – was a huge step. The public might have read about women surgeons at the Endell Street Hospital in London, but this was proof that women really did perform battlefield surgery. The film clip itself raises questions – was this a real operation or only for the camera? In 1917 there were few accepted rules about this relatively new-fangled medium; what we would call staged or fake footage was clearly judged acceptable at the time, as long as it showed what *had* happened. The War Office had happily done so during the Boer War, finding Hampstead Heath a good substitute for the South African veldt, and had no qualms either in Flanders when staging scenes of men going 'over the top' from the trenches. However, considering the medical workload of the Balkan campaigns and others it is unlikely that fake needed to be substituted for real: Elsie and her staff worked non-stop. And it is not to be overlooked that film – by now the most popular way of reaching large audiences – was a marvellous vehicle for the women's cause, showing what they could do and indeed were doing.

However, at this point Elsie herself was diagnosed with inoperable cancer, having known for a year that she might have it. She eventually headed home from her last hospital camp in Bessarabia via a tortuous fifteen-day trip across Russia to the port of Archangel, and thence by ship to Newcastle. She died in the Station Hotel there on 26 November 1917, her two sisters and niece witnessing a peaceful passing.

To the end she had put her duty first, as the press reported her having 'brought her unit safely back from Odessa, succeeding also in the brilliant feat of bringing her forty tons of hospital equipment home almost intact, and while dying she had superintended the landing in England'. That phrase was a mere footnote to the tributes: she was mourned by the nation, and by her friends in the Balkans. Her determination and kindness were mentioned by all. One Serbian message read: 'In Scotland they made her a doctor, in Serbia we would have made her a saint.' Queen Mary wrote personal letters of condolence and the people of Edinburgh stood to watch her coffin taken to St Giles' Cathedral, where she was buried with full military honours. The *Daily Sketch* asked: 'Inglis had received the highest Serbian decoration, the Order of the White Eagle. Why no VCs for women?'

The hospital supplies whose safe landing in Newcastle she had supervised soon headed back to Serbia with the newly formed Elsie Inglis Unit, and by the end of the war there were fourteen SWHs in France, Serbia, Macedonia, Russia and Salonika. When in Romania, she had heard that the House of Commons had begun to discuss a

Bill granting the vote to women over thirty. That it was women's work in the war that had supposedly won the day caused her to comment: 'Where do they think the world would have been without women's work all these ages?'

Those who had the social position and money that engendered confidence and clout often pursued an individual project in a Boadicea-like style. The largest voluntary hospital in France – which bore her name – was one of many ventures in the colourful life of the Duchess of Sutherland. Millicent was beautiful, rich, energetic, a fabulous hostess of glittering soirées, and an unstoppable force when intent upon philanthropy. Already known as 'Meddlesome Millie', and calling herself 'a liberal at heart – a little bit of a socialist', she had supported spinners and weavers via the Sutherland Industrial Society, set up a technical school in the Highlands, and persuaded her husband to build a gasworks and install gas lighting in his tenants' cottages. She was muttered about in high society as the 'Red Duchess' and satirized by the novelist Arnold Bennett as 'Interfering Iris, watching over the mental and immortal welfare of everyone in the village'.

For her, the declaration of war was like a trumpet call to action. Leading her own unit of eight nurses and a surgeon she ploughed into the confusion of the first few weeks of fluid front lines, treating Belgian and French soldiers in a convent at Namur. As the Germans approached, she sensibly buried her revolver under an apple tree in the garden and eventually intimidated enough junior officers to gain access to their general. Social clout and charm in fluent German were now applied, involving Millicent's personal acquaintance with the Kaiser; she and her colleagues were soon safely back in England. With an eye on returning to France with another ambulance unit, Millicent instantly produced what must have been one of the first books about the conflict, *Six Weeks at the War*.

She set a pattern for many others – publicity, fund-raising, substantial social backing (the millionaire Andrew Carnegie among them) and endless determination. When she met with the same official indifference as everyone else, and the Royal Army Medical Corps ignored her, she cajoled the First Lord of the Admiralty, Winston Churchill, to enable her to respond to an invitation from the French Red Cross. The very efficient hospital she set up near Calais eventually worked with the British army for the duration of the war.

Millicent was an example of an Edwardian woman who used all the advantages of her class to achieve her aims. The upper-class leisured way of life also insinuated itself into the running of the hospital – she and her nurses sat and talked to patients, listened to their stories, tried to entertain and amuse them as they had been taught by their governesses and mamas. In the hellish aftermath of battles Millicent would spend as much time as possible on the wards, dressed elegantly all in white with a small row of pearls: 'She used to look like an angel', wrote Hugh McCorquodale, novelist Barbara Cartland's husband, who had been wounded at Passchendaele. 'She came round, looking so beautiful, that men who were actually dying revived because she gave them hope, gave them something they longed for. She was like a dream to those men.' The staff, too, were not exempt from the country house experience, for Millicent insisted that 'play should alternate with work, to ease the strain. We would come from the wards and find the guests she had sent in, spread about the Mess, waiting for us to join them, and we would dance to the gramophone till twelve o'clock.'

There was more society elegance at the Duchess of Westminster's hospital along the coast at Le Touquet. Young and pretty, the duchess not only ran the hospital but, sparkling with diamonds and accompanied by her large wolfhound, would tour the wards every evening, believing implicitly in morale-building, and saying 'It's the least we can do to cheer up the men.'

The public learned a great deal about their ventures: the titled belles of society had appeared regularly in the social columns of the papers before the war. Indeed, royalty, aristocrats and 'respectable' actresses were the staple diet of most of the magazines of the age. The press took little notice of ordinary folk, especially women, and the 'human interest' story was almost unknown. The lives of working-class or poor women were not chronicled, except in statistics or in generalized fashion, or glimpsed through the reporting of court cases. Therefore these privileged individuals' forays into war work had more impact than might be assumed. If a duchess could roll up her sleeves and clean a wound, why shouldn't others do it? Nor were their efforts a decorative diversion on the fringe of grim action. The army needed the voluntary medical units, their standards were high and they were keen to innovate, often leading the way with new methods of treatment. Inevitably there were times when chaotic conditions, inexperienced helpers and busybody do-gooders managed to ambush the best of intentions, but above all their desire to care shone through.

Nursing won general approval. Being astride a motorbike – when ladies were hesitant about abandoning side-saddle on horseback – was pushing things a bit in 1914. Even though the Post Office delivered several times a day, notes and letters and parcels went by hand. Banks and businesses employed a small army of messengers, and only a few had risked frightening pedestrians and horses by acquiring motorcycle couriers – not the most obvious mode of transport for women, one might think.

In Edwardian times opinion hadn't quite decided if this was a 'proper' activity for women. The motorcycle was still seen by many as a bicycle with a motor attached, and cycling was considered healthy and liberating for women (without in these early days, any hint of 100mph bikers and roaring Hell's

Angels). On the other hand, the machines weren't yet very reliable and riding one had to be accompanied by the ability to repair one – grease, oil and dirt obligatory. Nor was there consensus about the correct attire for lady enthusiasts: advertisements suggested long leather skirts under a 'motoring coat'; some riders experimented with leather breeches, jackets and caps – dashing but rather daring. To be candid, these matters interested only the tiniest handful of people – there were perhaps only a few dozen lady riders before the war. However, after it began the army ordered a large number of machines for messengers, and the motorcycle began to gain in popularity.

Couriers were eagerly embraced by the voluntary organizations (lady administrators and committee members wrote dozens of letters a day, since the telephone was still considered by many to be somewhat exotic) and the Women's Emergency Corps found itself with two couriers who were to become nationally celebrated as the 'Women of Pervyse'. Elsie Knocker and Mairi Chisholm had met through their mutual enthusiasm for motorcycles; they had applied to the Corps immediately and been employed riding round London's decidedly non-bike-minded streets, among large unwieldy motor cars, horse-drawn buses, taxis and tramlines. After a month, Mairi's drop-handlebar racing bike weaving speedily through the traffic caught the eye of Dr Hector Munro, busy recruiting a small team to go to

France as an ambulance unit. So began an exceptional tale of bravery and hard work, where two women defied all the conventions and spent nearly four years only yards from the front line in Belgium, running a first-aid post. They did exactly what women were not supposed to do – position themselves intentionally and permanently in an active war zone.

Hector Munro was an unusual man for his time, recruiting women for his unit in a crusading belief that they should be allowed to show they could cope. Elsie Knocker was a thirty-year-old trained nurse and midwife, who had the rare distinction of being a middle-class woman with a young son who had determinedly divorced her violent husband. Few women had either the money or the courage to initiate divorce proceedings – courts were not sympathetic to them, and the loss of social standing and respect which almost invariably followed was not for the faint-hearted. Mairi Chisholm, of impeccable Highland stock – her grandfather being the chief of Clan Chisholm – was an eighteen-year-old who fitted Munro's ideal of a spirited volunteer, keen and adaptable. Twenty-five-year-old Lady Dorothy Feilding joined them; daughter of the Earl of Denbigh, she had trained in first aid and would go on to be the first woman awarded the Military Medal for bravery in the field.

Along with doctors, orderlies and drivers, the unit crossed the Channel on 24 September 1914 and within a month had seen sights which encapsulated all the horror of war and were to be a permanent feature of their work: mutilated soldiers, ruined landscapes, desperate refugees, stinking corpses. In the confusion and danger, their unit was already of interest to the press at home – Dot Feilding's name ensured coverage – and they were in the thick of it from the start, collecting wounded troops and negotiating shrapnel and shell-holes to get them to hospital.

After several months they established themselves in the cellar of a ruined house close to the front line in the Belgian town of Pervyse – Dot Feilding having opted to drive ambulances for the Munro Unit – and ran their own show, having to cope with an almost never-ending flow of injured men. Elsie wrote: 'Our house . . . was a woeful sight. There was not a pane of glass left whole, the roof had fallen in, the walls were ominously cracked, and everything that was any good had been taken or looted. It was right on the edge of the village, nearest the tottering church and the trenches, and the stream of shells which the Germans lobbed across the water meant that we should have to sleep, cook, and nurse in the cellar. I could not wait to move in!' They served soup and hot chocolate, gave first aid, bandaged wounds, ferried injured soldiers, picked up corpses and took them for identification.

The women were convinced that being at the centre of the action enabled them to save more lives: too often, men had died on the way to hospitals way behind the lines. They resisted all attempts to move them from the town and when shelled-out relocated to other rickety buildings. Regularly risking their lives and always enduring tough conditions they could claim to be the only women working in a zone which had been forbidden to their sex, the Belgian army authorities having set a three-mile men-only exclusion zone behind the front line. They gained both respect and affection, and not only for their battlefield work.

Troops in the area knew that they would receive a hot drink or have their minor ailments dealt with by these brisk but sympathetic women. Military medical aid concentrated on war wounds and, as Florence Nightingale had realized sixty years earlier in the Crimea, the ordinary soldier's health was never a major consideration for the top brass. The Belgian army was typical: full of men with swollen feet, cuts turned septic, boils and a fair amount of VD – Mairi remembered that she 'wore long rubber gloves and used a lot of mercury'. The average soldier in any army fighting this war would have been used to indifference to his health, for working men in civilian life were used to enduring what would now be considered treatable conditions. Chronic chest complaints, unpleasant skin infections, rotten teeth, feet that sometimes went to bed in their boots . . . all the difficulties brought about by dirt, deprivation and poverty. Working-class women at home spent much of their lives swilling, scouring, scrubbing, trying to keep some of the disease and infection at bay. Life in the trenches was indescribably dirty, squelchy and full of furry vermin, fleas and lice. A little hot soup or chocolate, a cut cleaned up or a dose of patent medicine from the women's supplies meant a great deal.

Elsie and Mairi's lives, though, were not lived unnoticed; they were chronicled with regularity and saw a stream of visitors. One of the notable features of the war was a kind of unorganized battlefield tourism, with journalists, military officials, representatives of Allied armies, photographers, friends, family and royalty turning up frequently, often regardless of surrounding action. And Elsie and Mairi, like other volunteer workers, were very conscious of the need for funds: they relied entirely on donations for everything they had and were constantly in need of more supplies. Every few months they headed back home, not just to see relatives and have a short respite but to publicize and fund-raise. As they travelled the country, usually by motorcycle and sidecar, they attracted headlines and news stories.

They were perhaps the most photographed women of the war and the newspapers delighted in their image; the press had already dubbed Dorothy Feilding 'Our Joan of Arc in Khaki', and now they had the 'Heroines of Pervyse'. Added to this were 'Heroic Scottish Ladies', 'The Two', 'Angels of Pervyse', 'Women who work in the Danger Zone' and, especially for Mairi, who had spent much of her childhood in local Ferndown, the *Bournemouth Echo* delighted in 'Dorset Lady at the Front'. After three years the official 'kinematographers' arrived and filmed Mairi among the debris and ruined houses, wheeling out the machine with Elsie in the sidecar and heading off through the smashed and blackened landscape. Cinema had become one of the most potent means of reaching large audiences, and the scenes in Pervyse became part of a film on women's war work shown nationally.

Elsie and Mairi exploited their links with the bike-riding world, posing for the *Motor Cycle* magazine in boots and breeches and jokingly captioning themselves as being in 'Skirtless Dress in the Belgian Army'. Their simple, not to say gritty, domestic routine in Belgium was reported in detail in all its privations, though they were assiduous in ensuring they always looked 'nice and feminine'. A gushing *Tatler* article entitled 'Sandbags instead of Handbags' decided they were 'Ministering Angels' and 'The New Ladies of the Lamp'.

None of this sprang from a desire to be famous: it was all seen as a necessary accompaniment to keeping their first-aid post in existence. No one paid them, no army or government gave material support, so they had to campaign on the Home Front. The public had to be alerted, persuaded, asked for donations. In a pamphlet to spread the word for funds in 1917 they emphasized their continuing commitment:

> We wonder how many realise what it means to be going through a fourth winter in Flanders? Our work is endless, day and night; the sick and wounded in the front line cannot choose the time of their arrival. They come at any time and our door must be open. It is almost impossible for those at home to realise what the work is, or the tremendous area it covers. They do not know that *never* can we honestly say 'Now we are off duty.' They do not realise that even if we are sick and ill, we *must* exert ourselves almost to breaking point, in order to see the work carried through.

Photographed, lionized, interviewed, featured regularly in press reports, Elsie and Mairi were celebrated – though I wouldn't call them celebrities, with all the baggage that term conveys today. Nor were they 'role models'. They were seen as shining examples of courageous, individual dedication. It wasn't suggested that other women should emulate them: there was no appeal for other spirited, resourceful women to strike out on their own, away from the voluntary organized units already operating in tough circumstances. And thus they presented no threat to the general conception of men alone fighting on the front line, well away from women's sphere of activity. They had met and worked with many former suffragettes when couriers for the Women's Emergency Corps in London, but politics was not their motivation. They relished adventure and a challenge, and knew they could make their own contribution to the war effort.

Like many other inspirational figures, such as Elsie Inglis, their contribution to fund-raising on the Home Front, publicizing the needs of the soldiers, encouraging a war-weary public to redouble its efforts and keep up morale, was equal to their efforts in Pervyse. Having two women give talks in which they described the details of life under fire, the precise way that funds were spent on supplies and medical needs, the need to save lives wherever possible, brought the front line thrillingly into their listeners' lives, with the added piquancy of imagining how hard it must be for women to cope with lice, rats, mud and shelling.

They were each awarded the Military Medal – and fifteen other decorations.

CHAPTER 15

SHAKESPEARE AND SONGS IN THE MUD

When hundreds of thousands of men found themselves overseas, they were desperate for a taste of home. They could sing, perhaps, make their own music with a mouth organ – but there was no radio yet, and gramophones were precious and only turned up occasionally in the YMCA huts. Among the thousands in France, some would recall being recruited personally at a concert by Vesta Tilley, yet for all her patriotism she never appeared among the many visitors behind the lines to sing for them, and later wrote: 'I tried not to lose touch with the boys who had joined up on my appeal. . . . They used to write and ask why I did not go over to France and sing to them when they went behind the lines to rest, but I said I could not possibly do this. I should not be able to take over with me all my stage suits and props, and it would not have been "me" if I had sung to them in petticoats.' And in any case the songs which were popular in France differed from the rousing recruitment songs and sentimental ballads so popular on the Home Front.

The excitement of the recruiting refrains had led to a grim life in the mud of Flanders. The sentiment of 'Keep the Home Fires Burning' and 'Roses are Blooming in Picardy' did not apply to them. As the war dragged on, a mocking reality entered their own songs:

When old Jerry shells your trench,
  never mind
And your face may lose its smile,
  never mind,
Though the sandbags bust and fly
You have only once to die
When old Jerry shells your trench,
  never mind.

If you get stuck on the wire, never mind
And you face may lose its smile,
  never mind
Though you're stuck there all day,
They count you dead and stop your pay
If you get stuck on the wire, never mind.

All sung to the tune of 'If you're happy and you know it, clap your hands . . .'.

This was a war that gave you time to reflect – if you survived long enough. The previous century had seen campaigns waged across the British Empire, but nothing which resembled the huge concentration of men abroad for months, eventually years, on end waiting their turn for action. Never before had there been such a necessity to keep up morale. How to do it?

Away from the front line trenches in France – and the majority of time was spent in the rear, usually thirty out of every forty days – the main idea was to fill the soldiers' waking time: lots of drill, training and inspections; repairs to vehicles, movement of stores, occasional manoeuvres. Sport was smiled on, and football and cricket easily arranged. This promoted 'team spirit' – the army thought very much in public school terms. When there was some free time, cards and dominoes were popular among the men, as they smoked, gossiped and listened to music on someone's mouth organ.

Writing letters home was common to a vast majority, who were not only literate but had imbibed, willingly or not, a fair amount of Sunday school education. Newspapers and magazines were popular – and available behind the lines. 'Trench journals', edited and printed in makeshift offices in rest areas by soldiers, were also passed from hand to hand among all ranks. The *Whizz-Bang*, the *Wipers Times*, the *Minden Magazine*, the *Outpost* and many more mainly satirized life through the prism of soldiers' humour: the mundanity of daily chores, attitudes to the enemy and the proximity to death, nearly always described through jokes and lampoons, gallows humour and spoof poetry. In some there was sports news and articles about the stars and the fun of the music hall, reminders of what was being defended. Much of this was interspersed with a great deal of grousing – a way to let off steam. Thoughts about women lurked between the lines. And overtly. This was a single-minded preoccupation which couldn't quite be expressed in letters home. In the *Outpost* a drawing with the caption 'A General Offensive' showed an older officer eyeing up a very young Frenchwoman. It made the point that women were only totally absent from the front line of fighting; further back, the villages and small towns weren't short of French women and British medical and welfare volunteers. The *Wipers Times* openly advertised the Fancies and Plug Street – local brothels.

Many newsletters were written in pencil and reproduced using sheets of carbon paper. 'Have you ever sat in a trench in the middle of a battle and corrected proofs? Try it,' wrote the *Wipers Times* editor, Captain Roberts of the Sherwood Foresters, later adding that the magazine was 'produced when the air was generally full of shells . . .'. Those with printing presses in makeshift buildings away from the front found the eagle eye of the army censors on them. According to the editor of the *Minden Magazine*: 'We are not allowed to insert the names of the various places we go to; neither are we allowed to discuss too minutely the ins and outs of our prolonged misunderstanding and unpleasantness with the Germans.'

Every so often the army gave permission for visits to nearby estaminets, bars and, turning a blind eye, brothels, though most private soldiers had little money to flash around and were unable to emulate the officer class who could afford some of the wine and lifestyle on offer even in wartime France. But overall, the official mind was not initially receptive to the idea that a soldier should be entertained, especially at a cost to the War Office.

As the months stretched into years for men under arms, individual military units began to organize their own amusement, initially frowned on by the top brass but soon tolerated. After all, in an era before radio and television 'making your own entertainment' was the conventional answer to any boredom at home and there had been a tradition of rough-and-ready skit-and-song routines in the Empire's army in Victorian times, often involving soldiers in drag. In 1914 the vehicle for amusement was the concert party – which covered every sort of act.

The Optimists, the Bluebirds, the Duds, the Verey Lights – every unit began to produce men who could inject a little gaiety and humour into the scary routine of army life. Subversiveness abounded, words of popular songs got changed, and female impersonation flourished. A picture of the Dumbells' Divisional Concert Party shows Private Allan Murray as Marie and Private Ross Hamilton as Marjorie in splendid hats and high heels and with some impressive cleavage. One of Vera Brittain's friends, serving with the Sherwood Foresters, wrote to her that 'After tea we went to the Verey Lights, a concert party of—Div which was excellent. . . . The dancing and everything else was topping but perhaps this was due to the fact that there was a stringband as opposed to the ordinary blare without violins etc. The man who was Columbine danced perfectly and was a jolly good impersonator. Our div lady is hopeless; always mincing about and very gawky, grinning inanely the while!' And the poet Siegfried Sassoon described a show: 'It wasn't much; a canvas awning; a few footlights . . . [the performers] were unconscious, it seemed to me, of the intense impact on their audience – that dim brown mass of men. Row beyond row, I watched those soldiers, listening so quietly, chins propped on hands, to the songs which epitomized their . . . longing for the gaiety and sentiment of life.'

It slowly – very slowly – dawned on the War Office that entertainment might be a necessity rather than an obstacle in a theatre of war. They had been prodded by a very determined woman. Daughter of a sea captain, and born on a ship on the Tyne in Newcastle in 1872, Lena Ashwell embarked on a career in the theatre when the acting profession still trod a precarious path between fame and 'a not at all respectable way of conducting yourself'. By the turn of the century she was getting major roles on the London stage, and gradually became very conscious that the successful parts were either submissive females or sinful witches. She had been drawn to the suffrage movement and campaigned in the Actresses'

Franchise League, making her own mark by branching out into theatre management; her first production was in 1906 in my home town of Sunderland. After working under a succession of Victorian actor-managers she thought there might be a distinct advantage in taking the reins herself and getting the chance to stage dramas that promoted suffrage. A passionate believer in the value of the arts, she thought the whole community should benefit, not only those who could afford an expensive seat in the plush circle. She saw culture as essential to wellbeing, and the war presented her with the opportunity to spread this idea to the thousands of men enduring the fighting. But the War Office, she found, was not even lukewarm about the prospect when she first contacted them: 'in October 1914 I tried very hard to get the entertainment of troops put on national lines, and was interviewed several times on the scheme of "every camp and its own theatre," and the organising of the work by professional actors, but there was little interest shown'.

Part of the problem appeared to be that the army was not a little suspicious of actors, though various prominent members of the profession, backed by a few generals and bishops, were drafted in to vouch for the idea of recreation for the troops. Having been rejected, Lena headed for the Women's Emergency Corps, one of the many thriving volunteer organizations channelling the efforts of well-connected women determined to contribute to the war efforts.

A few months later, hope appeared in royal form. Princess Helena Victoria, granddaughter of Queen Victoria and busy as president of the Women's Auxiliary Committee of the YMCA, wondered if a concert party could be got up to go to France. Lena pounced on the chance, obtained a cheque for expenses from a wealthy friend and sent out the first group in January 1915. She herself longed to go but had other theatre commitments, though she found herself dealing with a wealth of detail which again hinted at the army's worries about the reliability of the acting profession. There was to be 'no advertisement, no making use of the war to aggrandise one's own personal popularity . . . every artist should be personally known to me, and . . . I should be able to guarantee their suitability to Her Highness and the Committee, and . . . every artist should become known to Her Highness, who became personally responsible for them and their conduct'. The YMCA was to organize the expedition and it too was nervous about the project. Lena wryly recalled the attitude:

> there is a great prejudice amongst a section of the nation against artists, especially actors. To them we are a class of terribly wicked people who drink champagne all day long, and lie on sofas, receiving bouquets from rows of admirers who patiently wait in queues to present these tokens of rather unsavoury regard. I think some expected us to land in France in tights, with peroxided

hair, and altogether to be a difficult thing for a religious organisation to camouflage.

There were thirty-nine concerts in that first fortnight's tour. They went well and in March Lena herself crossed to Le Havre and in the Harfleur valley had her first taste of life behind the front line:

> The valley was a sea of mud, with tents and a few huts, and as a pathway through this sea of stickiness there were duckboards to walk on. If you fell over, you were done in, for the mud was ankle-deep, and very often knee-deep. We wore top-boots. The winter had been very cold and abnormally damp, and the cold and rain and mud without made a great contrast to the fog of smoke and the heat within the huts and tents. There was a great concert in the new Cinema Hut, which we, the Concert Party, opened in great style. The Base Commandant and the officer of the Base were all present. The wooden hut was packed to suffocation. No one would ever believe now that human beings could take up so little room. The men had been waiting for hours and smoking incessantly. The acetylene lights were very new and very glaring, and quite suddenly they all went out. We were all sitting on the platform, as

> we always did, partly because there was nowhere else to go, and partly to save time. The concerts had to be fairly short – two hours at the most – and there was no time to spare for the entrances and exits. When the lights went out there was a rush for candles, and a row of candles was lit in front of us and along the side of the hut. No one can imagine how hot rows of candles can be. The heat of the candles, the smoke, the enthusiasm, the terrific roar of response to our small efforts were quite incredible. Ivor Novello, who was one of the party, had just written 'Keep the Home Fires burning,' and when he sang it, the men seemed to drink it in at once and instantly sang the chorus, and as we drove away at the end of the concert, in the dark and rain and mud, from all parts of the camp one could hear the refrain of the chorus.

In her account of her 'Modern Troubadours' Lena Ashwell never attempted to describe the scale and horrors of the military operations through which she led her concert parties. Instead, she conveyed an often intimate picture of men in impossible conditions who responded like a flame in dry tinder to the songs which connected them to their homes. She had absolute faith in the power of music, describing hospital wards full of those who had been wounded, blinded or gassed, and trying to bring solace or encouragement to individuals. All her players spent time with patients after the hospital concerts, some singing quietly to just one man. She describes an open-air drama production with all the audience in beds watching the actors as the heavens opened – and the show went on.

There were Shakespeare and Sheridan, popular comedy and poetry, string quartets and violin solos. The hours were exhausting and the conditions often primitive – and the professional performers were all volunteers, paid only expenses. In between tours, there was indefatigable money-raising on the Home Front. Ashwell produced plays for the London theatre, toured provincial cities relentlessly, spoke at public meetings, organized bazaars and wrote newspaper articles to stir up support. Mindful of the complex operation in France, she targeted the Prime Minister, Lloyd George, wanting to press the YMCA case that lecturers should be included in the recreation programme to give the men 'food for thought, having been informed in France that "military training to become an efficient fighting unit made little or no appeal to the brain . . ."'.

Theatre was to Ashwell just as important as music, and the actress Cicely Hamilton, having been at Royaumont Abbey with the Scottish Women's Hospitals for over two years, sleeping in monks' cells with bats flitting about them, wrote home as she was preparing to undertake a new venture:

> At present I am struggling to establish a small repertory company theatre for the troops in one of the army areas; the difficulties are enormous of course as one's arrangements are liable to be upset at any moment – one of the best actors has just been snatched away as a minor consequence of the German advance into Italy. All the same we get along somehow and Miss Ashwell (under whom I am working) is increasing my company as far as women are concerned.

There was a shortage of male artistes. By now the war was eroding the 'reserved occupations' at home and taking every able-bodied man to be found. The Prime Minister was cornered about this too. In particular, there was the need to provide what were called 'firing-line parties' – artistes who were prepared to go much further towards the front line rather than stay near the base camps. Lena proposed mixed parties, men and women, who would 'be grateful of the opportunity of more service to the Army'. The Prime Minister appeared to agree with her, but it took a full year for the war machine to grind into action on the matter.

Firing-line work was not for the faint-hearted: 'The concerts were often given in the open, punctuated by 9.2 guns, with one or two aeroplanes coming over the platform, which was two packing-cases of unequal height. Whilst the aeroplanes were being happily shelled, the party carried on. The big guns were firing directly over the concert, so the party was literally performing under fire.' On another occasion, during four hours of bombing and firing a young singer who had taken refuge with an officer in a ditch tried to distract the young man with light conversation until he pointed out to her that they were in the middle of an ammunition dump.

The lack of men led in 1917 to all-women concert parties, considered by many in authority to be a 'grave innovation'. Lena Ashwell declared them to be a 'tremendous success', adding the rather quaint observation that the soldiers were overjoyed 'to see a pair of slippers'. And there must have been a certain amount of pressure on the women, though Ashwell trips through a social occasion at a convalescent depot with a certain blithe insouciance. Three of her ladies had been asked to a dance – with a thousand men: 'the dance resolved itself into three congested groups of hopeful humanity, and in the centre of each group there danced a very hot, a somewhat breathless, and yet wholly happy girl. Thus do we help always in that one great task of bringing Blighty to the boys, pending that great day when they themselves can return to it.'

With several thousand concert parties under their belt, the Ashwell organization spread its wings and sent parties to other theatres of war in September 1916. They went to Malta, Italy and Egypt, travelling by ship, train and on camel; the reward was huge audiences at performances on the desert sand, in the Cairo Opera House and along the whole length of the Suez Canal. Letters went back to England, overflowing with gratitude: 'The camp and all the patients in our 800-bed hospital, and all the patients that could go were sent in field ambulances and the consequences risked, for it would be a very long time before we got a treat like this again'; and 'We are one and all sorry that the Lena Ashwell Party are leaving us. They have given us a glimpse of home out here on the desert. Singing their choruses has moved the sand from our throats and given us new life. We feel we are not forgotten.' In Ismailia they were almost overwhelmed: 'Thursday, there were 3,800 men, the next concert there were 4,000 men, and on Saturday, 6,000.' It had been the intention for the Egypt party to be away a few months; instead, it was two years before they returned to Britain. In the summer of 1917 the Egyptian heat prevented concert work, so the party ran a YMCA hut before getting permission to travel on to Palestine. There were open-air performances in Gaza and Jaffa, then Jerusalem, where they gave concerts on the Mount of Olives.

Lena Ashwell only lost two of her performers, the singers Emily Pickford and Frederick Taylor, when their car slid into the River Somme in icy weather at night after a concert – and this was two months after the Armistice was signed. Emily was buried in the war cemetery at Abbeville and her name is inscribed on the war memorial in her home town, Penarth. Later, writing about the work of over six hundred entertainers, including herself, Lena describes the risks in a businesslike way; she was not gung-ho, but determined to carry out what she believed to be a vital contribution to life behind the lines. Her conclusion was that it was impossible to describe adequately what they had seen and felt: 'the whole experience was so overwhelming, so moving, so terrible that one's littleness was stunned and could not find expression. It is easier to describe a little tennis-party at a country vicarage than seeing a world in arms – suffering, wounded, muddy, smiling, and tortured – try to express, try to give even a small impression – that is beyond description.' The worst moments, she felt, were when they watched one regiment after another heading for the front line 'going forward with a smile to death, sacrificing self for an ideal, for freedom of small peoples, for an empire in danger of destruction, for Country, for Home, for wife and child, that women might not be ashamed of them, that God might know that they could play the game, who can describe this. . . . The tears might blind one's eyes and mark one's face, but these signs of sorrow must not be seen, for we were there to help.'

CHAPTER 16

WE PRAY WE MIGHT BE HEARD . . .

'The churches emptied – people left in droves . . . it was the war that did it. . . .' I heard the phrase frequently as a child and, on asking why people 'left in droves', was always told that the very idea of two Christian nations fighting each other posed questions which went unanswered on Sundays. It resonated as a family historical judgement on the war, but there's no hard-and-fast evidence that such was the case nationwide. Church attendance had been gradually declining from High Victorian times, and anyway Sunderland was a well-known Babel of competing denominations, groups and sects. A prosperous Victorian town which had begun to decline at the end of the first decade of the twentieth century, it boasted multifarious chapels, churches, missions and tabernacles which aimed to divert the ungodly from the equally numerous pubs. There are no reliable statistics to confirm that the war tipped the balance dramatically, but on the brink of World War I the town mirrored much of the legacy of rapid industrialization and the energetic activities of reforming Nonconformists among the damp slums of the shipyard workers and the pitmen.

The Adies in Sunderland were staunch Nonconformists, to the point where James Adie, a prosperous, stiff Victorian to his fingertips, popped up in the pulpit of his local Baptist church and preached – lengthily, it was remembered – on various hellfire and brimstone subjects. The Adie family view, very privately, was that he personally might have been responsible for shifting a large number of people out of the pews towards the pub. But it seems his congregation of shipyard workers apparently appreciated a bit of threat and torment: rather like medicine, it only did you good if it tasted horrible.

James Adie knew his flock, because he was the superintendent engineer at the yards. He would peer down at the management in the ground-floor pews, then upwards to direct his major firepower at the workers in the gallery: religious observance did not alter the class divide. At least he could talk man-to-man, for the Baptists had yet to consider women in the pulpit. And working-class women only appeared at the Sunday evening service, as servants only got Sunday afternoons off.

Going to church was still a sign of respectability among large swathes of the population, although belief might not have been as fervent as attendance. Sunday school was immensely popular – a genuine element of education, aside from the spiritual teaching. Biblical language peppered the speech of those whose access to books was limited, and getting rid of the children from overcrowded houses for a few hours gave the parents a bed to themselves for an hour or so. . . .

Even if the concept of Hell and the Last Judgement occupied James Adie's puritanical mind, for his congregation it was receding in favour of Heaven. Sunday school hymns emphasized the crowns and harps and angels that would await a good child. Generally, English religious observance was more about a shared set of values which defined 'good' behaviour than fear of an eternity of damnation. Theological dispute was not a major issue for the everyday worshipper, and Sunderland merely noted differences in rituals. Anglicans knelt in prayer, Methodists crouched; Anglicans had one cup for all at Communion, Methodists each had their own little glass. What preoccupied senior clerics nationally hardly touched their lives – though mutterings were beginning to filter through to a broader audience from across the Atlantic.

In America, there had been a formidable pantheon of itinerant women preachers in the early nineteenth century; later, the demand for the vote and a greater say in society, coupled with the lack of male preachers brought about by the devastation of the male population during the Civil War, pushed the question of women in the Church to the fore again. The notion of the 'feminization of American religion' was met with stout resistance from the pulpit. 'This common movement for "women's rights", and women's preaching, must be regarded . . . as simply infidel': in 1879 Robert Lewis Dabney, a professor of theology in Virginia, had delivered a sermon in response to the frightening prospect for him of 'female preachers knocking at our doors'. He was astonished at the idea, and summoned up the Bible, history and the 'guilt of a woman six thousand years ago' to denounce their 'unnatural pretentions'. His sermons are still around today, helpfully recorded on CD and published on line, to bolster like-minded clergy in their modern battle against 'disastrous' progress. For the record, Dabney also defended slavery, abhorred mixed marriages – the 'feebleness of the hybrid' – argued against universal suffrage and expressed that all of this might lead to 'accepting negro presbyters to rule white churches and judge white ladies'.

Despite this, a number of American Nonconformists were already ordaining women. The Quakers and the Salvation Army were also ahead of the game and, with the suffrage movement in Britain very much to the fore in the decade before the war, trouble was brewing for the traditionalists in Britain. What James Adie would not have expected was the feminization of his flock.

A town like Sunderland would give a classic picture in 1914 of the effects of poverty. It had been fertile ground for several investigations into the urban poor in Victoria's day, especially since it had the dubious claim to being the English cradle of cholera: the epidemic which arrived in

1831, probably from the Baltic ports where Sunderland shipping trade was well established. Slums huddled round the riverbanks, rubbish and sewage piled up everywhere, and water was drawn from communal pumps and the industrially grubby river. The outbreak was handled badly: the government imposed quarantine, enforced by the military and a warship in the river mouth, with the colliers trapped in the harbour. The result was a furious campaign by local businessmen, who said it was a 'most wicked and malicious falsehood' to claim that the epidemic was actually cholera.

Unfortunately for them, the second man to die was Sunderland's only war hero, Jack Crawford, a young sailor who had nailed Admiral Duncan's colours to the mast after part of HMS *Venerable*'s mast had been shot away at the battle of Camperdown in 1797. He had been awarded a pension and a silver medal, but like many of his impoverished neighbours in the East End riverside he was a near-permanent drunk who had had to pawn his medal and about whom tales abounded – one involved riding a pig down the town's High Street. He died a pauper, his blackened body lying unburied for three days.

While the epidemic raged the row continued at full volume, not helped by many people dying at home among their families because they dreaded going to the Infirmary. In those days it was a place where many of the poor believed that 'body-snatchers' operated, making off with corpses to sell for medical dissection. The only good to come out of the town's misery was the work of Dr John Snow, who like many of the medical profession had headed for the North-east to witness this new and frightening disease. Years later he was to prove his idea that contaminated water supplies spread the contagion – usually at the public pump. Sunderland came out rather badly, according to the *London Medical Gazette*: 'The good people of Sunderland appear in no very favourable light, it seems very clear that the public safety is in their estimation a very secondary object when brought into competition with the sale of coals.'

But this is a snapshot of a northern town expanding rapidly as the demand for its merchant ships grows in the nineteenth century. Ignorance and dirt, rat-infested housing and open ditches for sewers, and above all the grinding poverty of the working class resulted in a fondness for religion or drink. Sometimes both. It was not all grime and grimness: the shipyards, pits and glassworks all thrived, and in the latter half of the nineteenth century there was affluence for the middle classes, able to afford substantial houses and fine civic buildings. And grand Gothic churches were built in leafy suburbs, mainly Methodist, for the shipyard owners were Wesleyans.

By the turn of the century the 'Sunderland Cottage' – a single-storey terrace house – served as a symbol of the earning power of the skilled workers, many of whom bought rather than rented their homes, which was unusual for Edwardian times. The riverside area was all noise and dirt as the claim to be the 'biggest shipbuilding town in the world' grew. Shipbuilding was fitful employment – each ship that went down the slipways left a hole in the order-book – and often meant a period of unemployment. But there were music halls and theatres and uncountable pubs, from huge brightly lit taverns to tiny stalls dispensing beer into bring-your-own jugs.

James Adie didn't drink, and his fellow middle-class Nonconformists in the town were only too keen to lecture others on the devil's potions. There was solid support for the Temperance Society – founded in 1832, just a year after the cholera epidemic – with many Nonconfomist churches getting people to 'sign the pledge' and renounce the consumption of alcohol: 'We agree to abstain from all liquors of an intoxication quality whether ale, porter, wine or ardent spirits, except as medicine.' This last was useful to many, as the two aged spinster aunts who inhabited James Adie's upper storeys were remembered as retiring to their rooms with 'a headache' every Sunday afternoon, clutching the medicinal brandy bottle.

Wilfrid, my adoptive father and James's son, recalled childhood just before World War I as a time dominated by strict religious observance, with church three times on Sunday at Bethesda Baptist and the shunning of any kind of entertainment where drink might be present. This was reinforced by the efforts of the Baptists, along with the Methodists, Congregationalists et al, to 'go a-missioning'. This involved descending from the leafy suburbs into the slum areas of the East End and holding hearty hymn-singing sessions in the tiny 'missions' – often no more than a room or a tin-built hut cheek-by-jowl with the raucous pubs. In the years before the war drinking began early, and Wilfrid, a timid small boy who rarely ventured to the East End, remembered seeing numerous men lying dead drunk in the lanes by midday.

As the war began, the yards got new orders. Restrictions on pub opening hours were introduced and the drumbeat of war was faced by all the Churches with mixed and complex reactions. And one interesting change occurred. As James Adie continued to preach he didn't see his flock diminish 'in droves'. Instead, he saw it alter: the pews were now filled with women. The clerks and foremen, along with the platers and riveters – the lower middle and skilled working-class backbone of the Nonconformist flock – had gone off to war in huge numbers. It was a change which has not been reversed in a century since.

Very quickly, the impact of the war on women left at home added to those who sought comfort in church. Bereavement, anxiety about men far away and fighting, changes in employment, Zeppelins overhead – all brought the women together for shared support. As has often been the case in other contexts, my family's carefully preserved memory of decline in the size of congregations was inaccurate. In reality it was a decline in the numbers of men; women – as in so many surveys of the population – didn't count as much.

As women up and down the land looked for support and consolation once the casualty lists lengthened, their priorities were not those of the church leaders who were busy trying to articulate their attitude to war, irrespective of their denomination. Patriotism or war-mongering? Pacifism or waging a 'just war'? The bishops and Nonconformist leaders alike were in heated debate for the duration, although not being patriotic enough seemed to annoy church-goers most.

However, as men streamed to the recruiting depots and women headed for the factories, many of the senior clergy in the Church of England decided that war presented an opportunity. Here was a nation ready to sacrifice, ready to unite in a righteous cause, to fight for higher things than material gain; ready for a profound Christian experience, for repentance. Some of the enthusiasts for this mission – it became the National Mission of Repentance and Hope in 1916 – wanted a moral, clean-living population, rid of sin. Others were aiming for a sense of fellowship, as expounded by the Labour MP George Lansbury:

> Since August 1914, we have lived through terrible days which have brought home to us all the futility of the mad scramble for material riches. . . . But if the futility of

> material things is being proved, there is something else which we are all able to recognise. No one hates and detests war more than I do, yet out of it come great noble deeds which fill us with admiration and love. . . . The trenches call out this spirit of brotherhood and comradeship just because each is striving to do his best for all.

Not altogether surprisingly, in a country beset with shortages, longer hours, missing relatives and a sense that sacrifice after sacrifice was being made with real lives, the National Mission failed to bring about the hoped-for 'awakening'. Years later, its effect on the exhausted men returning from the trenches of Flanders was summed up by the poet Siegfried Sassoon, who punctured it in his fictionalized autobiography. He described arriving from France as a wounded officer, and being presented with a leaflet by the Bishop of London, 'who earnestly advised me to live a clean life and attend Holy Communion'.

But the Mission had poked one hornets' nest: women were supposed to be active in it. However, it was immediately pointed out that they had no status, authority or recognition in the Anglican Church. 'It is scandal that there should be no place for women in the councils of the church,' wrote the supporters of the Mission, refraining from suggesting anything further, such as the ordination of women. Instead, they came up with the notion of 'bishops' messengers' who would participate in the outreach of the Mission and would speak and read, on occasion, in church: the equivalent, more or less, of the male lay-reader. They would conduct Morning and Evening Prayers. Twenty-two dioceses in England finally agreed, but not without a lot of shilly-shallying – and more often than not, the arrangement was sold on the principle that 'there's a shortage of men'.

To effect this work in 1916, the Church had to wriggle its way through a cat's cradle of ecclesiastical law and theological argument. Having decided that they could swallow the idea of women messengers speaking in church, there was the tricky question of where exactly they should stand. Certainly not in the pulpit – that was the vicar's preserve. At the lectern? Going a bit too far. Perhaps on the steps next to the lectern? If they're going to speak, why can't they use the church hall, for heaven's sake? For those for whom the convoluted ways of religious observance were unfamiliar, it might have seemed trivial; to those who regarded ritual as symbolic of the sacred, it was crucial. And that can be read in the present tense as well.

Various bishops modified the agreement accordingly. The Bishop of London said he would only allow women to speak in church when there was no other place, only to women and girls and only from the aisle in front of the chancel steps. It was all too much for the Bishop of Chelmsford, who declared that he would 'not sanction any woman telling her sisters of the Saviour's love in any church in the diocese'. The conditions attached represented the fear and prejudice which accompanied all mention of women obtaining a greater stake in the functioning of the Church.

This was not the first time that women had pushed for more recognition in the Anglican Church. All the arguments were well rehearsed and most were rooted in scripture, with particular reference to St Paul's oft-quoted injunction: 'Let your women keep silent in the churches, for they are not permitted to speak; but they are to be submissive, as the law also says. And if they want to learn something, let them ask their own husbands at home; for it is shameful for women to speak in church, for Adam was formed first, then Eve.' For the explanation – and the justification of this passage – you don't have to return to World War I or to biblical roots; it can be heard at any discussion of women vicars and women bishops today. Most fundamentalists and biblical literalists endorse it heartily, and many of milder faith cannot or will not relinquish the authority over women it endorses.

A member of the Mission Council watching these events closely was a remarkable woman, Maude Royden, before the war one of the star public speakers for the suffrage movement. The daughter of a baronet, she was an unusually well-educated woman for her time; after attending Cheltenham Ladies' College she persuaded her parents that she should study at Oxford and then headed to the Liverpool docklands to do welfare work at the Women's Settlement. She was a devout Anglican who possessed a very genuine sense of empathy with the poor, which caused no little trouble in a Liverpool charity at the turn of the century. When she left the Settlement she wrote to a friend: 'I believe the women drink like fiends . . . I should drink if I lived in Lancaster Street.'

Returning to Oxford, she was accepted into the ranks of the University Extension Service as a lecturer, another unlikely role for a woman: the University nervously listed her as A. Maude Royden, to downplay her gender. The post had been secured by the Reverend Hudson Shaw, with whom she began a lifelong friendship. He too was a champion of equality in the Anglican Church, and had preached a memorable sermon in which he stated that controversies about the inferiority of women 'should be relegated to Bedlam'. Maude was by then keenly interested in questions of religion, welfare, women's rights and pacifism, and came to believe that women would achieve their goals through a combination of prayer and education. She chose to join the National Union of Women's Suffrage Societies, rather than the more militant Women's Social and Political Union, eventually editing its newspaper *The Common Cause*. Her reputation was growing and she travelled to the USA to meet suffrage campaigners and lecture; by 1912 she was managing to give more than two hundred and fifty speeches a year, ran 'Speakers' Classes' for women, and had become the first chairperson of the Church League for Women's Suffrage, which she had co-founded.

When war was declared she found herself in opposition to many of her former campaign colleagues, as she joined the pacifists who were against conscription. By 1916 she was Vice-President of the Women's International League for Peace and Freedom, and still campaigning across a broad spectrum – social conditions, child protection, equal pay for equal work for women, and equal sexual standards for men and women, strongly protesting against the double standards which were applied to marriage. The treatment of prostitutes under wartime legislation had become increasingly harsh and she argued that if women had to be chaste within marriage in order to be 'good', then so should men.

She was nationally famous – though to Church traditionalists she was merely notorious. She had come to believe that the priesthood was her calling, and combined her arguments about feminism with those of religion. However, she knew what she was up against. When the Church League for Women's Suffrage had proposed they campaign for full ordination in 1915, the *Church Times* went on the attack: 'For any sane person the thing is so grotesque that he must refuse to discuss it . . . the monstrous regiment of priestesses would be a thousand fold worse [than women in politics].' (No suggestion that 'she' might discuss it, then. . . .) In 1916 Maude published a pamphlet in which she wrote that not only were women barred from the priesthood in the Church of England, they now comprised the majority in the congregations and did most of the work in the parish. She described the reality of inequality: parishes where women weren't allowed to take collection, or be a churchwarden: 'a slur on the parish', said one vicar. A woman ringing the sanctus bell had worried another, who relented with relief when he realized the bell-rope 'hung down behind a curtain so that no one could see her'.

The argument was well received by the laity, but many of the clergy nervously responded by suggesting that the ordination of women was 'premature'. With the bishop's messengers apparently gaining a foothold across the church threshold, Maude accepted the offer to preach at the Nonconformist City Temple at Holborn in London in 1917. She was rather apprehensive, as the Congregationalists were in the process of appointing their first – and clearly – controversial – woman minister. James Adie would have been alerted in Sunderland – some of the Baptists, too, were preparing to ordain women – and Maude Royden's name was frequently in the national press.

However, for Maude, as an Anglican, it wasn't exactly the done thing to stray into Nonconformist territory. Ecumenical attitudes were rather novel; even so, she preached in the City Temple several times and accepted the new post of 'pulpit assistant'. When women over thirty won the vote at the end of the war, she celebrated with a sermon which pre-dated many later feminist changes to traditional phrases, requoting from the Book of Ecclesiastes: 'Let us now praise famous women and the mothers who begat us.'

That year an invitation came from the Reverend Hudson Shaw, now rector of the Anglican church of St Botolph's in Billingsgate, to read the lesson at a service. Headlines appeared once again in the newspapers: 'A new departure has been inaugurated by the broadminded rector of St Botolph's.' The Bishop of London was not amused and told him off, sternly and publicly. Undeterred, Hudson Shaw then asked Maude to preach the sermon on Good Friday 1919, during the Three Hours' Service. The bishop expressly forbade such an act, on the grounds that it was an especially 'sacred' service. Hudson Shaw read the detail of the bishop's injunction and saw that it said that Maude Royden should not take the service in church; so he closed the church and moved the service to the parish room, where Maude duly spoke. There was a large congregation, most of them outside, some apparently hanging on to the window sills in order to hear better and also viewing the bishop's prohibition pasted up outside. Maude responded to it all by castigating the bishops for denying spiritual equality to women and the Church.

By now, the Anglicans had finally got round to giving women the right to be voting members on Church councils, but not without more anguished debate on women 'speaking' in church. One of the resolutions put forward detailed that 'No woman under the age of thirty should be permitted to address a mixed assembly in a consecrated building.' Another stipulated that 'the Bishop should require written evidence of unblemished character from three competent persons'.

A sharp reply was delivered to the Archbishop of Canterbury, who was taking soundings on these resolutions. He had asked Dr Letitia Fairfield to prepare a memorandum for him on what he termed 'certain physical aspects' of women in relation to 'new opportunities opened to them'. Perhaps the archbishop was only wanting a medical opinion and was not fully prepared for a memorandum from an active member of the women's suffrage movement. Admittedly Letitia had become chief medical officer to the newly formed Women's Royal Air Force towards the end of the war, but she was fully conversant with the obstacles women had to overcome to qualify as a doctor. She was also one of those who, when war broke out, had been brusquely told by the War Office that her services were not wanted. Her first appointment had been as medical officer for the Women's Auxiliary Army Corps, where life was a constant tussle with the military for recognition by rank – which was not forthcoming. Her sister was the author Rebecca West, by then well known for her candid arguments in favour of free love in suffrage publications.

If the archbishop was looking for some cosy

supportive statement on traditional lines regarding women and the Church he had not got the measure of Letitia, who sent him ten pages of closely typed argument blasting several holes in ancient prejudice. She took aim at the anti-feminists who urged

> that any new opportunities opened to women, whether physically damaging in themselves or not, are mischievous in that they distract women from their primary and all-important function of child-bearing. Such critics may properly be reminded that there are now more than two million more women than men in the country (even before the war it was one and a half million) and coming to the teachings of Christianity, the vital force of these women must inevitably be used for some purpose other than that of reproduction.

She then tackled the hoary old arguments which were often considered rather indelicate to debate in public: 'ceremonial uncleanliness'. These, she stated, were based on 'an aura of superstition surrounding a certain phase of women's peculiar function', and described an eyebrow-raising personal experience. 'During the war I was shown a sugar refinery in France where women are never allowed to enter in case they were in "such a state that the sugar would turn black in their presence". A few days later I met a priest who gave me this as a reason why a woman could not speak in a consecrated building "especially where the Blessed Sacrament was exposed".' 'A dangerous pagan survival' was her verdict, adding that even in twentieth-century London she found certain 'modern ordinances of religion preserving in all good faith "the customs of magic"'.

Turning to the suggestion that women, if they should be allowed to speak in church, should only address women, she lamented: 'What explanation can be advanced which does not involve that mischievous notion of women's inferiority which is at the back of so much moral wrong. Those of us who are dealing with questions of social relationship, either from the educational or health point of view, regard this suggestion with great alarm.' The archbishop was not moved to reply.

With the battle for the chance to speak in church having run into so many obstacles, the Church League for Women's Suffrage was none too impressed and resolved to campaign for full ordination. They were spurred on by the example of the Nonconformists – the Methodists had just given women the same rights as male local preachers in 1918, the same year the Congregationalists ordained their first women ministers. The Baptists, in the words of one of their historians, 'slid' into women's ordination in the early 1920s, no doubt with James Adie still harrumphing about Hellfire. During the war, the scarcity of menfolk had propelled the Nonconformists to call on the female members of their congregations to help with welfare work and the 'socials' organized for troops on leave. And they had also lost preachers to the call-up, whereas Anglican and Catholic clergy were exempt. The country was facing the appalling fact that thousands of men were gone, never to return, and that the congregations every Sunday attested to this: and still women were not wanted by the Church. Widows and bereaved mothers were facing difficult lives but were still treated as if they were second-class dependants. When one considers that every sermon preached about loss and sacrifice was by a man, it isn't surprising that the campaigners for equality within the Church felt that their arguments had become ever more urgent and relevant.

The League pressed their case after the war and Maude Royden finally preached in the church in 1921 – still causing immense controversy, not by what she said, but by the fact that she was in the pulpit at all. The Bishop of London let it be known that he had not approved her presence and was still spitting with disapproval. It had been a protracted campaign, but she had made her mark in ecclesiastical history as the first woman to preach within the church, in the Church of England. However, perhaps the words that she is remembered for – and are still quoted today – were delivered in a secular setting, in the Queen's Hall in London: 'The Church should go forward along the path of progress and be no longer satisfied to represent the Conservative Party at prayer.'

The war had highlighted the passive role of half its congregations during the absence of so many men. Women had gained the concession to 'speak' and overturned centuries of prohibition. Nevertheless, the squawks of fear that they should be on the road towards acceptance into the Anglican priesthood was a warning that the battle was far from won. A particularly loud squawk came from the Joint Committee on Ministry of Women: 'We repudiate the idea of women being ordained to the priesthood as wholly contrary to the immemorial and consistent custom of the Catholic [i.e. entire] Church.' The succeeding decades saw a kind of nibbling advance: a lady churchwarden here, a deaconess there, the possibility of female choristers, the extension of admission to church administration. All were subject to flurries of outrage and defiance and indignation in every diocese around the country. The desire of many to make religion a total exception to the law of the land, ignoring equality and representation, was helped by the all-male bishops who wielded power in the House of Lords.

Maude Royden survived to see women make many more advances in the twentieth century, herself living a varied and fulfilled life which included a lively private side, combining both love and religion. She had met the Reverend Hudson Shaw when she returned to Oxford to lecture and had been invited to live with him and his wife Effie in Rutland. Here she had her first taste of parish work, while acting as companion to Effie while Hudson Shaw was away lecturing – a three-cornered arrangement. Effie was fully aware of the love between her husband and Maude, but she was very happy to tolerate it as they both cherished her. Both Hudson and Maude were made of strong Christian stuff with regard to marriage, and never consummated their relationship. When Effie died in the 1940s, they finally married; he was eighty-four and died two months after their wedding day. Maude, always in tune with progress, became one of the pioneers of religious broadcasting on the BBC and remained there until well into her seventies. The Church of England was still refusing to ordain women, but one listener wrote in appreciation that this 'great and devout soul has however her own diocese – the English-speaking world'. Having experienced how war could illuminate and accelerate the need for change, and having seen many women preaching in Nonconformist churches, she died, aged eighty, in 1956, with the goal of Anglican women's ordination still considered to be 'premature'.

CHAPTER 17

SECRET TASKS – A LANDSHIP AND A HAY NET

'You are only writing for Mary Ann in the kitchen,' declared the army's commander in chief, Sir Douglas Haig, and many generals took the same view: journalism dealt mainly with trivia and sensation, spoke mostly to the uneducated masses and was far too inferior a craft to be trusted with war. His view has not been completely discounted. The tensions today are as great as ever between the military seeking to act without scrutiny, the politicians desiring to use the press for propaganda, and the public wanting the truth – but perhaps not the full ugliness and horror of war.

As a journalist attempting to report warfare, I was always acutely aware that only a tiny splinter of the story ever ended up on the television screen. The idea that we could take in a broad swathe of 'the action', describe in detail the violence of close combat, the extent of military operations and the consequences of anything we witnessed, never mind 'bring the war into the living room', was a fairytale. I could convey just a brief snapshot of whatever we happened upon. If I dared, I might be able to use what I'd seen as perhaps – and a big perhaps – a microcosm of the conflict. Checking facts was a perilous business where there were warring nations or factional parties. Armies, governments or anyone officious with a gun could bar access. Winners boasted. Losers lied. Censorship lurked both on the field and back at base in an editor's office. Various people tried to kill you – or the circumstances were so dire that you spent a lot of time in a ditch or a cellar.

Even so, you had to try. Since the Crimean War, which saw the stirrings of modern journalism in the 1850s, the tensions between those reporting a war and those conducting it have been constant and complex. That said, World War I is generally held to have been one of the low points in any history of journalism. This might sound curious to those who have encountered the huge amounts of literature and pictures which have flowed from those years. Diaries, recollections, memoirs, novels, histories, official records – millions of words, mountains of statistics. However, during the war vast amounts of action went unreported, and censorship and propaganda dealt with negative events – defeats, retreats, blunders – by glossing over or not mentioning them. Not that the British nation at home was stupid or indifferent. A pervasive patriotism, allied with a sincere belief that the war was in a good cause and therefore sacrifices were justified, combined over the years to dull the demand for war news in all its horror.

These days, in a world made more connected and intimate by the internet, it is hard to digest the fact that war correspondents in the early days of fighting in August and September 1914 managed not to report the deaths of three hundred thousand French soldiers and more than twelve thousand British soldiers killed or wounded. Individual reporters faced huge obstacles. Their editors were hopelessly constrained by the newly introduced Defence of the Realm Act (DORA), which specifically stated that stories 'not in the national interest' would result in their prosecution. This covered the most minute detail of any military operation, including information which was obtained from official sources. Meanwhile, the correspondents were being harried or ignored, and finally barred from France by Lord Kitchener, the Secretary of State for War, and threatened with arrest if found in the field.

Lord Kitchener's dislike of journalists went back to the Sudan war where in 1898 he faced the war correspondents with the words: 'Get out of my way, you drunken swabs', and the Boer War in South Africa did nothing to alter his views. In 1914 he thought it adequate to appoint a Royal Engineer officer, Colonel Ernest Swinton, to write reports for the press back home. They were entitled 'Eye-Witness' and thereafter labelled 'Eye-Wash' by the troops. He was later joined by a tiny handful of official war correspondents, chaperoned, censored and on the payroll of the War Office. Their treatment was summed up by General Charteris, the

Chief of Intelligence, replying to a reporter's enquiry about what he would be permitted to write: 'Say what you like, old man. But don't mention any places or people.' The inevitable result was that the 'writing chappies', permanently under supervision and virtually part of the military machine, succumbed to self-censorship. Many also witnessed the grimness of warfare at close quarters and felt unable to describe the scale of what they had seen to an audience at home which was not prepared for stark accounts of failure and mass carnage; for the war was at first highly popular and, even as the casualties mounted, there was a powerful undercurrent of support for 'sacrifice in a just cause'.

The men at the front had little tolerance of the inhibitions of the press, conscious as they were that the real conduct of the war was being concealed from the general public. Like troops today, they had no time for the 'visiting vultures' who followed the official line and failed to mention military mistakes and poor decisions. The generals regarded the reporters as a rather unpleasant, perhaps pointless, nuisance, and were either unwilling or unable to see the line between propaganda and facts. And had the war correspondents sent material which truly represented what was happening, their editors and proprietors would have squashed it.

There was a ban on all photography. A couple of army officers were appointed to 'record history', and anyone else with a camera near the front line was liable to be court-martialled. The cheap camera was becoming very popular at home, but the penalties for happy-snapping – and the fear of being thought a spy – were so great that only officially approved pictures made it past the censor. And anyway, professional cameras were unwieldy and temperamental so 'action shots' in a hazardous zone were almost out of the question. Later in the war, official artists were appointed. Their position was broadly summed up by Paul Nash: 'I am not allowed to put dead men into my pictures because apparently they do not exist. . . .'

The film camera too was taken to France, and the officially sanctioned *Battle of the Somme* was a massive hit in cinemas, with footage from the opening day of the offensive showing troops moving up to the lines. Enemy dead were shown, and there was a memorable shot of a British soldier carrying his wounded comrade from no man's land back to the trenches. Audiences in their millions were enthralled. Some sequences are known to have been staged but the greatest omission was the actual slaughter: hundreds of thousands perished. Bodies hanging on the barbed wire, drowned in mud, men in agony: the camera then – and now – only goes so far. Hellish reality was rarely given the coverage it deserved, but this was not out of a cynical desire to keep the war going for the sake of the military or the industry feeding it. The country was haemorrhaging money, sacrifice had to have a motive and 'beating the Hun' was still in most minds.

However, the nation at home was not starved of pictures: the glamorous, the patriotic and the heroic were thought fit to set before the public – and the public was avid for such news, wanting to believe in success. With the same determination which blocked detailed and realistic portrayal of the fighting abroad, serving up only endless palatable pictures of troop movements and out-going fire, the government campaigned on the Home Front.

The efforts of those at home, especially the women, were to be elevated alongside the efforts of those in the field. This would sustain morale and provide the increase in production needed to supply the war machine. The munitionettes became poster girls, attractive and patriotic; the women pasting up those posters, nipping up ladders in lengthy skirts, were photographed by the press; the tram conductresses posed on their platforms; and the coke-heavers managed a smile on their begrimed faces. However, the same restrictions which ensured military secrecy abroad could be enforced through the dreaded DORA at home. The Defence of the Realm Act, interfering with traditional pub hours, used to harass prostitutes and a general catch-all for behaviour the authorities disapproved of, was also in place to ensure secrecy of vital work. Pictures in munitions plants showing a seemingly never-ending flow of shells served to reinforce morale and engender anxiety in the enemy, but elsewhere the cameras kept away from women who were working on something new.

In the second year of the war the trenches seemed a horrendously permanent fixture. Within minutes of the whistle being blown for men to clamber out and head towards the enemy, artillery screamed through the air and machine-guns chattered lethally. Women scanning the casualty lists at home would wonder what kind of battle consumed so many men so quickly. They had died 'fighting'. 'Slaughter' was not an official description. The men in command were neither ignorant nor indifferent – a large percentage of senior officers were killed or wounded – but most had been trained in the days of cavalry and skirmishing. Though many were mechanical-minded, the army had begun the war with precisely 254 motor vehicles. But the stalemate of trenches and barbed wire had never been foreseen. It took time to realize that a different approach was needed. And eventually, in the Admiralty, Winston Churchill had his attention drawn to a new kind of ship – a 'landship' – which would cross a trench while protecting its crew and then keep firing at the enemy. It was to be a top-secret project. Colonel Ernest Swinton had popped up in London with the germ of an idea he had picked up in France while writing his 'Eye-Witness' reports. He had seen an American Holt tractor towing the heavy guns of the artillery, an idea the Americans had acquired from a Lincolnshire firm before the war but had been dismissed by the British military. Perhaps men could be carried safely in some kind of tracked machine?

A handful of designers and engineering firms began beavering away on the project, and truly Heath Robinson shapes were constructed. Most were modelled on tractors, which were powerful and proven on heavy going, though some looked like half a tractor which had mated with an iron landing-craft. Another Lincolnshire firm, William Foster and Co., experimented with all kinds of designs including the intriguingly named Heatherington's Big Wheel and the Bullock Creeping Grip Tractor. Ironically, it was a brainwave that had almost come home to roost – Foster's was only a few miles away from Hornsby's, the firm that had had the original idea. The firm's chairman, William Tritton, along with Walter Wilson, an engineer with the Naval Air Service, eventually produced a landship that was not too heavy for the Flanders mud and had a top speed over rough ground of two miles per hour. They telegraphed the Admiralty: 'New arrival by Tritton out of pressed plate STOP Light in weight but very strong STOP All doing well, thank you STOP Proud Parents.'

Little Willie had arrived, a tracked fighting vehicle. It was first seen outside the factory on a test drive by a very surprised Mrs Able, wife of the local schoolmaster. Returning from her night shift making Sopwith aircraft, she was confronted with a monstrous, squeaking, grinding – and frightening – beast crawling along a quiet street. It was soon to be followed by Mother (much bigger, naturally): the tank was born.

Mr Tritton had started the war with 350 employees, many of whom had subsequently enlisted. Trying to keep his skilled workforce together, he was faced with the problem that the tank production line was still top-secret and his men had not therefore been given the silver badge which distinguished them as being on vital war work. Some of his men had left because they had been handed white feathers in public, or been called a coward. He forced the War Badge Department to supply badges to the remaining men, and with a new production line starting up recruited hundreds of women (by the end of the war he employed over two thousand). Offered an armed guard round his factory, he refused on the grounds that it would only attract attention. No one gossiped, no one published pictures of the women at work, because the tanks were an open secret which the town of Lincoln kept to itself.

Among those making tanks was Mrs Dorothy Hare, who went into the factory at the age of fifteen to work on a drilling machine.

> I used to make the shoes that were underneath the chain of the tank track. I drilled holes in them and shaped them on a planer. They were rough cast steel, you could cut yourself on them. That's where I

> was when the siren went, I'd stacked all the shoes up and clean forgot, I switched my machine off and all the lights went out. I turned around and went straight into the pile of shoes. They had to dig me out, I got cut a bit, but it wasn't hospital treatment. I once got my overall sleeve caught in the driller, it tore everything off me!

Other workers remembered the hours – usually twelve-hour shifts, even for the girls in the office. Dorothy Hare was on the day shift:

> It was all girls, no men except the charge hands. They never left the room, they always had their eyes on us. We would finish at six at night and the night people would take over, then we would take over from them again at six in the morning, the machines were never switched off. Sometimes I was there until nine or ten at night. I started on 15 shillings a week and built up to about 25 shillings by the end. I had a good time at Fosters, it was hard work, but I put my heart into it.

Mrs Priestley, who was also fifteen when she started as a machinist, recalled her war work when she was eighty-five: 'We didn't get many holidays, it was work, work, work, not like it is now. I worked on a lathe in the machine shop making shoes for the tank tracks. We were supplied with hats and overalls, you had to wear the hats to stop your hair getting caught in the overhead belts. We had a good look around a tank one day, but I never had a ride in one.'

Even the test runs for Mother and Little Willie in front of the King and the Prime Minister took place before an audience sworn to secrecy. It included Colonel Swinton, who knew all about secrecy and censorship. When the army took delivery, the men recruited for the new landship unit were only told they were joining 'a company for carrying on an undertaking of Great Advantage but no one to know what it is'. The word 'tank' was itself a deception, intended to suggest a water-carrier for use in the campaign in the Middle East. The vehicles arrived at Bovington Camp in Dorset by rail. The road from the station at Wool was closed, pickets were posted and everyone living on the route and in nearby farms was ordered to pull down their blinds and sit in the back room. Anyone found walking on the road was made to turn their back as the 'great secret' went by. One local shepherd, name of Patience, was reported to have refused to abandon his sheep grazing in an adjacent field. Soldiers therefore built a fence of hurdles so that the secret weapon might pass unseen – presumably making an appalling amount of noise and scattering sheep everywhere. By November 1917 the huge new weapon made a public debut, with two tanks – as they were now known – shown at the Lord Mayor's Show in London to crowds astonished by what were called 'unstoppable armoured toads'.

Foster's produced its own Tank Anthem, sold on postcards to raise money for the 'Comfort Fund for the benefit of Soldiers, Sailors and Tank Boys at the Front':

> Our tanks are 'doing their bit.
> Making a famous hit
> In this Great War.'
> When this 'big job' is done
> We'll shout 'Bravo! Lincoln' –
> 'Something made to smash the Hun,'
> Which England thanks.

At the end of the war the designers, engineers and firms who manufactured the tanks got the recognition they deserved, but the women who made them had kept their secret and by then, as Mrs Priestley remembered, 'all of us girls were finished in 1918 when the men came back'. And if Lincoln could stay quiet, so could Bridport.

'Every animal should have a nose-bag and hay net. . . . No animal should be sent on duty or fatigue without a filled nose-bag and hay net.' The Official Regulations from the Veterinary Department of the War Office regarding 'Horse Management in the Field' ran to eighteen pages. The War Office paid far more attention to horses than it ever did to women. Not surprisingly, for the cavalry were the army's elite and, to the alarm of the more progressive strategists at the beginning of the war, a number of military men thought that thundering hooves would play a very significant role. They had no inkling of the trench and the tank, of machine guns and barbed wire. The hooves that *did* matter didn't thunder, but plodded, squelched and staggered though mud and gunfire. Horsepower ensured the supply of ammunition and food. Great heavy Shires and Clydesdales, strong Clevelands, British hunters, American draught horses and bloody-minded mules were an integral part of the army machine. Lorries and motor vans were initially believed to be more efficient, but soon proved unreliable, complicated to maintain and a nightmare when the battleground began to turn to a sea of mud. Horse-drawn ambulances could make their way to areas which the FANY's vehicles couldn't reach. Messengers on horseback adapted to terrain and were speedy. Only a few of the Holt tractors had been taken to France, so most of the huge artillery pieces were dragged into position by the heavy horse teams, with the larger field guns needing a dozen each. And despite terrible losses, the cavalry was still being used right to the end of the war. By 1917 it was thought that to lose a horse was worse than losing a man – you could replace a man but not a horse, such was the shortage.

There was a never-ending worldwide quest for mounts; horses were shipped – and several thousand perished as a result of enemy action at sea – from the USA, Australia, Canada, New Zealand and Argentina. At times a thousand horses a *day* were on their way to the war zones: and not just France, for campaigns in the Middle East and East Africa used mounted infantry. In Britain, from the first week of the war much-loved hunters and hacks were bought by the Remount Service from owners who believed that there was a short and decisive war ahead. Mr Henry Chaplin MP thought it all worthwhile at the time, claiming in early 1915 that 'It was no exaggeration to say our great popular national sport of foxhunting saved our country when the war began . . . in the first levy of horses after war was declared, the War Office secured 170,000 good horses suited to their regiments, which in the absence of foxhunting would have been an impossibility.' He had not mentioned that thousands of those horses were already being replaced.

Farmers unharnessed Shires from their ploughs to be bought by the government, probably without any idea of what lay ahead. They soon learned, for the War Office was initiating breeding programmes for replacements as ever more horses died. Ponies at least were not taken, due to the specific intervention of Lord Kitchener on behalf of the country's children. The numbers involved were enormous, and hundreds of thousands of animals were as much at risk of death, injury and disease as the men. Shelling and machine gun fire exacted an immediate and dreadful toll, with horses intentionally targeted. The roads of Flanders were lined with carcasses; some horses just sank and disappeared into the soft mud and the army, desperate to get the wounded back into service, worried about exhausted and hungry horses, put in place an extensive system of Veterinary Corps hospitals.

The regulations stated solemnly that 'the over-hungry horse is so impatient that he tosses food about and wastes it, and will bolt his food without chewing properly. Wind-sucking, dung-eating, and other objectionable habits are largely due to leaving animals without food or giving an insufficiency of bulk'. All this was written before anyone had realized that feeding might take place under shellfire and the animals might be tethered on ground that sank overnight so they drowned in mud.

On the other hand, great care was taken by most of the men charged with looking after them. Horses exerted a strong emotional pull on many soldiers, who might become either attached to their teams pulling guns or be immensely distressed by injured and dying animals. It mattered to have responsible attitudes to them, for troop morale could be deeply affected – even when soldiers themselves were coping with their own injuries and fatalities. Many of the letters home written by the VADs and nurses remark on the importance of animal welfare; men in hospital sometimes found it easier to worry about a horse back in their unit than to face the gnawing fears about their pals.

Looking after the horses properly was not just a humanitarian act, it was a necessity. The priority was food, with hay and oats coming across the Channel in boatloads every week. And, according to the regulations, every horse had to have its own hay net. These were made almost exclusively by women working in small rooms or in the gardens of cottages in Dorset.

Flax and hemp had been grown in the Dorset valleys for centuries, and from 1213 Bridport's name was associated with rope-making, the town growing around the lengthy rope-walks where winding took place in all weathers. The men made both sails and ropes in medieval times and supplied Sir Francis Drake's ships when the English navy sailed against the Armada; to be 'stabbed by a Bridport dagger' indicated that the hangman had used their rope.

The wives and children took the hemp twine and made nets of every kind – 'It takes a Bridport net to catch a mackerel,' it was said. This was a complicated business, with endless variations in knotting and twining which children learned from a very young age. Net machines were patented in the early 1800s, and as they produced a sheet of netting a small loom installed in an outhouse could be the basis for a small family firm responding to the lucrative fish net market. As the British Empire spread, a healthy export industry grew, with fishing communities, especially in North America, sending to Bridport for tailor-made nets for various catches – shrimp and herring and cod.

It was never a trade which brought great riches, especially to the women outworkers and those tending the machines in the modest businesses. In a poor rural county where lace-making, gloving and button-making were carried on in hundreds of cottages, with children and women earning tiny sums for large batches of work, there were no great expectations. In good weather the women worked outside, gossiping and watching their infants at play. Although townsfolk and photographers found these handicrafts picturesque, they represented hard, painstaking labour which was rewarded with supposed 'pin-money' to rural families living on the breadline. To acquire materials and then deliver their orders, the outworkers in the villages surrounding Bridport would have to walk miles in all weathers. Eyesight was one of the main casualties, for electricity was not to be found in workmen's homes until well into the twentieth century; oil lamps and candles made for poor working conditions. Not that the male rope-makers fared much better: some rope-walks had moved indoors, but only into draughty unheated sheds, rarely ornamented with glazed windows.

At the start of the twentieth century, various local firms were beginning to expand into the new sports market – tennis nets and football goal nets – and intricate billiard pockets, a speciality of many families. New, faster machines were being ordered which could cope with large fishing nets, but hand-made nets were still needed, and most of the women were outworkers with skills handed down from their grandmothers. The war changed everything: a letter in the files of one of the main firms, Joseph Gundry and Co., dated August 1914, tersely terminates complex negotiations for a speedy new net machine from an American manufacturer in Boston:

> Dear Sir,
>
> We are obliged for yours of the 4th inst.
>
> The War has upset all our plans, and in the meantime, therefore, the matter must be allowed to lie over until we have got rid of the Germans.

The War Office was pointing its big finger at Bridport, saying The Country Needs your Nets. It had a phenomenally lengthy list of specialized demands for the industry, and the numbers involved made everyone gasp. (A few miles away in Somerset, the Taunton firm of Fox Brothers, already producing military khaki serge, received an order for army puttees – the cloth strip wound round soldiers' legs. The War Office wanted 852 miles of it. They went on to manufacture over eight thousand miles of cloth.)

The orders came through for nets, not by the dozen or the gross but in millions. Every man in the army needed a rifle pull-through cord; hundreds of thousands of lanyards were necessary, and grenades demanded hundreds of thousands of whip-cord safety-pin rings. All were small, fiddly jobs at which the women were expert. The military used nets for transporting equipment and carrying stores, and potato- and pea-nets for boiling vegetables: thousands of them. The navy wanted braided hemp lanyards, plaited and twisted, which sailors wore – and put the number in six figures. As sailors still slept in hammocks, more hammock clews were anticipated, plus nets for fishing at sea.

And as the orders piled up, hundreds of Bridport men – no different from anywhere else in the country – were enlisting to fight. There was enthusiasm to join the Dorset Yeomanry, the Bridport Volunteers, the Dorset Regiment and the local Garrison Artillery: you joined up with men you knew, with your pals, and the rural areas supplied more than their fair share of volunteers. In the first few months seven hundred were gone and eventually over sixteen hundred joined up, from a town of just over six thousand people.

Unexpectedly, a potential new workforce arrived in the shape of Belgian refugees, who were being dispersed from London because of the huge numbers needing accommodation. Bridport opened its doors and the first group to arrive were clearly impoverished, clutching only a few bundles of belongings. They needed to work and the rope-sheds immediately took on men as labourers. The women were taught the rudiments of knotting and splicing and soon joined the other net-makers.

Even so, the War Office was making unheard of demands and had reached a hay net crisis. The usual local hay net production had been geared to the occasional request from farmers and local hunts; the War Office was asking for six hundred thousand, followed by eight hundred thousand and finally a million. Used to dealing with both suppliers of raw materials and exports on an international basis, the net and rope firms went to their usual sources only to realize that the war was an obstacle on the trading routes. Local hemp had not been grown in any quantity for years, so Russia and Italy had kept Bridport supplied with high-quality material. But ships could no longer safely get through from Russia because of German submarine activity. In Italy, the advance of the Austrians towards the River Po in the north had the militarily unnoticed effect of threatening the best hemp-fields in the world around Ferrara. The British Flax and Hemp Growers' Society found itself recruited to the war effort with demand growing from the army for tents, tent lines and kitbags, and from the Royal Flying Corps for nets for balloons – not to mention linen shirts for airmen. The women spinners and weavers in the linen mills of Belfast were working flat out producing army shirts, knapsacks and stretchers. What had been a gently declining industry had suddenly burst into life again.

In the search for extra supplies manila twine (a relative of the banana plant) was found to be available, strong and pliable, so manila hay nets were despatched to the picket lines in France. The soldiers on duty duly stuffed them with hay and left their horses to munch in peace. They returned the next morning to find no trace of the nets. A thorough search ended with the obvious conclusion that the horses had found the manila absolutely scrummy; no more manila nets were ordered.

Hemp- and flax-growing questions occupied a considerable amount of parliamentary time, with sources being scoured for seed and production in Ireland expanded. Meanwhile, at least fifty thousand hay nets per week were leaving Bridport and by 1917 nets were being used to camouflage guns and equipment stores; the looms were in full production and the hand workers took on more work.

There is very little evidence that the women found themselves flush with generous wages – their sister workers in the linen industry in Northern Ireland were some of the worst paid anywhere. The Dorset women were neither unionized nor could they call on any national organization to help them, and they seem to have been overlooked in many of the war's reports into women's work. However, as production increased to a point where the navy's lanyards were no longer counted (they were in millions) but weighed, the government realized that the outworkers and braiders should be recognized as being on essential war work and protected from being sent to the Land Army which was also desperate for labour.

The production figures seem extraordinary, but the old payment ledgers offer evidence of the industrious energy of individual workers who were certainly not sitting amongst the hollyhocks in the sunshine, knotting the occasional net by hand. In May 1916 twenty-two-year-old Lily Read in the village of Loders was managing an average of five dozen hay nets a week, though she was not earning a fortune at a shilling a dozen. A year later, her work rate had increased to around twelve dozen, bringing her ten shillings – half the average pay of a woman factory worker. Just along the lane was Rebecca Northover, married to a carpenter and with six children, who would hardly be living in the lap of luxury. She was making pea nets, hay nets and hammocks; a seven-foot hammock brought her fivepence, so her week's income for sixteen of them was six shillings and eightpence (33p).

The lack of pictures of these war workers – in comparison to those in munitions, engineering and transport – and the reticence of the local press to cover an industry which had consumed the energies not only of the town but of a score of outlying villages, may well be due to the other kind of net that was being made in the town. It was another secret weapon: the anti-submarine net.

The Admiralty approached the Bridport firms

after only a few months of the war to see if they could make large wire nets so that 'a submarine should be caught in the same way that a rabbit is bolted into a purse-net and then dispatched'. German submarines were operating in the Channel and the North Sea, and the cross-Channel shipping which carried everything needed for the troops in France, and the troops themselves, was under constant threat. A meeting was held with Winston Churchill at the Admiralty, in which he said that a naval officer had thought that wire nets might catch a submarine in the same way as you catch a herring. Suffice it to say, submarines have very different qualities from rabbits and herrings and months of experimentation took place – right to the end of the war. Some of the large looms in Bridport were adapted for wire ropes, huge sheets of steel netting were made, then joined together to form a curtain which was drifted across the Channel where the navy suspected a U-boat was prowling. But even when they had entangled a sub successfully below the surface, the navy couldn't tell where it was in order to deal with it. Someone finally hit upon the idea of using glass floats which disappeared from view when a U-boat was trapped, and they later carried a light for pinpointing a vessel snared at night. Some had mines attached.

There was endless trial and error, but the nets were relatively effective. Many of the smaller nets – for harbour entrances, for example – were made by the women, and it was one of the main tasks given to the Wrens, the women's branch of the navy, when they were first formed. However, the town was reticent about its activities: scan the local press for any mention of this huge industry and there is nothing. Nearly all the paperwork has disappeared with the decline of the industry itself. The war years are a somewhat peculiar blank in most of the local accounts of the town, which is situated in a county where the activities of the Women's Land Army were covered extensively. Orders for hay nets are – unsurprisingly – not among the significant documents preserved after the war, and nets and bales do not figure as museum items. Rather like the tasty manila nets set in front of hungry horses, they have disappeared. And the women who had played a significant role running the looms, knotting and twining, spending every waking moment making essential supplies, were never given their due for their contribution.

CHAPTER 18

MOWING, HOEING AND SINGLING

When I was a child, we sometimes went for a run in our little car into the dales of County Durham and north Yorkshire. There was great excitement when we approached a steep hill – would the Austin make it? It would cough and whine as we passed the threatening sign reading 'One in Four Ahead'. Would we have to drop into first gear and crawl like a snail, with me in the back fearing we would slide backwards, possibly flipping over in the process, to be rescued by a smart man in uniform leaping from his RAC motorcycle and saluting us as we lay among the Shippam's fish paste sandwiches wrapped in greaseproof paper?

That was in the 1950s, and you expect transport and picnic food to change with the times. What I most remember now is how different the dales looked: empty cottages in most hamlets, and a number of villages which boasted newspapers up against the windows – curtains being too expensive. There were numerous Nonconformist chapels, mainly Methodist, which could muster congregations – in single figures. We would visit my great-aunt's home near Barnard Castle. She had grown up in considerable comfort in a large house in Newcastle until the great economic crash of the 1930s but now lived in much-diminished grandeur, squashing her huge chestnut-coloured Victorian furniture into a tiny stone-built cottage and running the Post Office, her livelihood, from the front room.

I, a townie, was fascinated – and slightly horrified – by the uneven flagstone floor, covered with heavy rugs. She sniffed haughtily: 'Some people make do with the Lord's good earth. . . .' And, indeed, in several of the neighbouring buildings not a floorboard nor a flagstone was to be seen. You could sniff the dampness of the earth as you went through the door, ducking low and adjusting to the dim light through tiny windows. This was not a landscape of bijou holiday homes, not even comfortable renovated country dwellings. It was scatterings of huddled stone, where modern facilities had yet to make much impression. My great-aunt's loo was an outhouse with a worrying-looking enamel pail containing a dusting of pink ashes from her kitchen range. Electricity had just about made it to the hamlet, but was fitful. The range put out a warm glow – if you sat near. We never visited in winter.

The countryside itself was glorious. Miles of dry-stone walling and cream-coloured sheep (sheep nearer Sunderland tended to be industrial grey). At the head of Swaledale or Weardale you felt yourself in a magic landscape with icy burns and ghylls trickling through bright turf. What could be better than to live in this place? 'Living in a suburb, that's what,' muttered my family, who loved the weekend 'run out' but were breathlessly thankful to get back to electric fires, fitted carpet and a New World cooker.

The countryside was for expeditions. In the early fifties it was still a place which meant muddy farming, poor accommodation and probably a lot of memories of World War II army camps, Nissen huts and food rationing. Fine if you lived in the Big House – those whose inheritance conditioned them to deal with draughty rooms and perhaps a Manor Farm to provide more comfort. But many of the grand estates were having post-war trouble, and few had the manicured, golden-era appearance which attaches to today's country seats.

More than anything, the northern countryside was not a place we townies lusted to live in. Farm work still had the ring of 'horny-handed toil'. Rusted machinery littered the fields – farmers seemed to have nowhere to discard unwanted balers and tractors. And there were tales aplenty of the muck and mud encountered by my parents' generation who had spent the last war as Land Girls a few years previously. Go back *forty* years from my childhood, to 1914, and the reality of farm work was even more of a challenge: old-fashioned drudgery, poorly paid, and living up to the description 'muck and mud'.

In France, for much of World War I the battleground was a sea of mud: deep, filthy, clinging. Curiously, some soldiers were apt to say that it wasn't as bad as at home. A huge percentage of the five million men who served in the army during the war had worked on the land: whole villages went off to war, the owners of large estates actively encouraging their workforce to follow their own sons, who were enlisting as officers. The agricultural labourers swapped one field of mud for another. Back home, mud permeated daily life everywhere. A nice walk in the countryside ended with a foot of mud on the hem of a dress. Small towns and villages had streets which were only partly paved and mud squished over the stoutest boots, spattering everything. Scrape scrape. Brush brush. Even in towns, a domestic servant could expect a daily chore that everyone took for granted: hours spent brushing mud from long skirts that had swished over crowded streets where horse droppings steamed and gutters overflowed. Rarely these days is the word 'swill' used when describing housework: a century ago, swilling the step into the house, the path to it, and a tiled or stone-flagged hallway was a daily task.

If you worked on the land, mud accompanied field work, farmyards, barns, pig sties . . . and then got traipsed into the house or cottage. In humbler dwellings, the floor was hardened earth which could soften unpleasantly in prolonged rain – and you had permanent indoor mud. No wonder the Victorians declared that cleanliness was next to godliness, for it took intense devotion to hygiene to keep clean. Bathrooms and inside lavatories were for the wealthy few; farms and labourers' cottages had just a sink indoors and a long wait for water heated on the kitchen range. The farmyard stank, the sweating workers stank. And life on the land was no elegant picnic. The bucolic scenes so beloved of artists and early photographers often omitted the squalor of labourers' cottages, the cheek-by-jowl relationship of humans with poultry and pigs. Only the estates of the rich, enclosed and well tended, resembled the artists' images, and as the twentieth century approached many landowners had let their tenants' cottages decline. Agriculture generally had been in decline for almost half a century prior to the war, as domestic food production was edged out by foreign imports and cheaper goods from the colonies.

Countrywomen were not carefree apple-cheeked lasses bearing a basket of apples to market. They were second-class citizens, often living very narrow lives and worked to the bone. They had large families, but little income, and were called on to pick potatoes, make hay and feed the livestock just to keep the family going. Many of the skills which used to supplement rural incomes – making lace, making buttons, assembling jewellery, gloving – were losing the competition with industrial Britain's urban factories and mechanized production. Just ten years before the war, a report on agricultural life was published which stated that research had proved that 'more women in the country[side] go insane than in any other class in the community. This is not so much from overwork, but because of the monotony of women's work on the farm.'

Wives worked at keeping the farm going and so did children. A rural childhood was recalled by the venerable countryman Ralph Wightman, who came to represent the voice of the countryside on BBC radio in the 1940s and 1950s. Born in 1901, he had a clear-eyed view of life as a boy in the Piddle valley in Dorset, remembering that when he left the village to go and study in Newcastle it was 'an escape from monotonous toil, and from the dirt I had always disliked'. He looked back on a life where most of the children had to milk a dozen cows before they went to school. 'Many of the cottages consisted of one room downstairs and two up for a mixed family, so that there was gross overcrowding. Windows might not open, and water for washing had to be dipped from the stream or carried from the pump.'

In these days of streamlined plumbing and constant hot water, never mind cold, the preoccupation with keeping clean is all about preening and wellbeing. In Wightman's childhood, it was all about scarcity and discomfort. One bath per week and the observation that 'head-washing was less frequent than the Saturday bath – for boys; girls in good clean families would go for months without washing their heads. . . . I knew a farmer's wife who had a "skivvy" living in. Jane was never seen to take water upstairs for the traditional, female, afternoon wash before putting on her white cap and apron. So her employer asked "Jane, when do you wash?" To which the reply was "Fridays, mum."' Jane, like the farmer's wife, would probably not wash in the morning because there was nowhere private as the men got ready for work. Added to which there was the range to riddle, the floor to swill, water to boil, candles to trim and oil lamps to fill – the only lighting in the village.

Wightman's family had a smallholding and was by no means amongst the poorest, many of whom in his village were squashed into a single room with no direct access to a water pump, no drains of any kind and earth floors. Their children's clothes were sometimes cast-offs from the rich, 'which may have been cut down from garments clearly impregnated by aristocratic sweat, and had been passed down from one growing child to another.' His verdict? 'They soon gave up the unequal struggle.'

That comment conveys the desolate aspect of rural life, a constant struggle to get food on the table. Instead of being able to eat well, surrounded by good land and healthy livestock, the average family could only just survive. There was no surplus to sell. When the war came and, after a couple of years, the nation's food supply began to concern the government, Wightman noticed that 'there was a change in the whole feeling of the countryside. For the first time in memory of most people home-grown food was needed and profitable. No longer was it true that the only way to make a living was not to spend anything.'

Before the food situation began to worry the government, there had been little enthusiasm shown by women to head for the fields. In 1915 the government had thought it prudent to compile a list of women willing to go and work in industry, offices and on the land; but the countryside saw no rush to the plough and the dairy. The middle and upper classes were interested in horticulture, with poultry-keeping, gardening and hot-house cultivation considered ladylike and practical. Farm work – manual labour – wasn't seen as suitable. And in the villages there was considerable resistance to a female workforce, not least because of the conviction that they would undermine the men's pay rates.

County by county, committees were formed to find willing women and amenable farmers short of workers. Posters went up showing a soldier departing from his family with the words 'I Leave the Land to You.' The result was the Women's National Land Service Corps – bringing mainly middle-class townswomen to try milking, butter- and cheese-making and other tasks which on the whole avoided heavy labour; the result was also a lot of cartoons, comments and criticism of what quickly became known as the 'lilac sunbonnet brigade'. The Prime Minister, Lloyd George, referred to 'a lot of sluggish and bantering prejudice and opposition' and 'bucolic guffaws' and the pace of recruitment was slow. Considering that members of the Corps – who were not provided with a uniform, merely a green armband – were encouraged to head for Harrod's store in London where they could purchase the 'Harrod's Farm Outfit' for what would have been over a month's pay in most female employment, it's clear that the response was never likely to have been overwhelming.

Unsurprisingly, there were official attempts to talk up the recruitment campaign, with the *Monthly Labour Review* chirruping that two thousand women had already been trained, all of whom had had secondary education and had 'gone onto the land mostly for patriotic motives'. The *Daily News* acknowledged the problem but observed that 'No woman can be expected to enjoy milking cows at four on a winter morning, or spreading manure, or cleaning a pigsty. It is frankly admitted indeed, that much of the most necessary work is hard and unpleasant, and by no means extravagantly paid. That is why the appeal is made exclusively to the *patriotism* of women.'

Another common problem was noted in Sussex, where Miss Bradley, in charge of recruiting, announced that in the county 'there was a strong feeling against "foreigners" ' – women from beyond its borders. Rural life was still remarkably isolated; many of the men who had left the farms to go to war had never left their villages before. The bicycle was just beginning to offer a quicker way of getting about instead of the ambling horse-wagon, but was still too expensive to buy on a labourer's wages. The idea that 'foreign women' should descend on the fields, even if only from just over the county boundary, was a sticking point.

Food shortages were beginning to bite because of the German U-boat campaign, and there were dire warnings that the nation had only a few weeks' supply of wheat in reserve. Prices were rising, and efforts were made to divert soldiers into agricultural work to help with planting and the harvest. Even Queen Mary was busy with vegetables, planting potatoes at Frogmore House in the grounds of Windsor Castle: 'We again went to Frogmore to finish planting our potato plot & worked from 3 to 5. Got very hot & tired.' She was photographed with a spade digging elegantly while wearing a very large beflowered formal hat.

How to stir rural communities – particularly the women who lived in them – into action? Help was on the way from Canada, where the Women's Institutes were flourishing, revitalizing village life. The first steps to form WIs were taken tentatively in Wales in 1915, and slowly the message of co-operation and organization at the grass roots level began to spread. Not without a number of false starts, because the very idea that women should take an interest in matters beyond their own village met with apathy. At the start of the century, the Agricultural Organization Society (AOS), a rural cooperative movement, had made little headway in getting countrywomen to discuss schemes for improving education and skills. They wouldn't take part, fearing being made fun of by the men.

At a farmers' meeting in Manchester where women had been invited to attend, they said nothing and 'sat there like oysters'. When afterwards asked why, they admitted that they had disagreed with much that had been said by the men, and replied, 'If we'd spoken, you know what we'd get when we got home.' Broader horizons, ambition, improvement in their own lives – none of these thoughts prevailed.

It took the war to spur matters on. With the Welsh WIs taking root, the initiative gained ground: education, cookery lectures, egg collection and marketing, jam-making, gardening advice. The WIs began to find ways to encourage and inspire women to spread their wings – and gain some confidence. The government showed interest, and in the manner of all committee-making at the time the AOS, which was government-funded, set about finding a grandly titled lady to take the lead. This, to many people, was an essential element in women's organizations for maintaining respectability as well as clout. The inter-marriage of the grandest families – in which many of the men were active members of the House of Lords – enabled a small number of women to pull strings and exert influence in politics and public life. The war intensified these connections, as these confident women moved among politicians and men in public office. The titles resonated in the country-side as well as in smart London salons: thousands of people were employed or depended for their livelihoods on the local big estate, often the only source of work and frequently the only source of charity as well. Some were still near-feudal, and it was usual for village women to bob a curtsey as the carriages of the gentry rolled by.

The WIs needed a leader. Lady Salisbury declined; Lady Aberdeen looked suitably fitted for the post, strongly in favour of women's rights, but was immersed in other charity projects: she had been Governor-General's wife in Canada where she was familiar with the WI and in 1915 had held a demonstration of 'what women have done and can do in agriculture' in a house in Carlton House Terrace. In the centre of fashionable London she filled the garden with plough horses, a cow, some hens, chickens and goats, to a background of butter-churning and milking. The house belonged to Lady Cowdray, interested in the venture but fully occupied as treasurer for the London branch of the Scottish Women's Hospitals. The chickens belonged to her daughter, Lady Denman. She got the job.

Trudie Denman had a passion for poultry and revelled in keeping her chickens within squawking distance of Buckingham Palace. Energetic and well connected, just before the war began she had returned to Britain from Australia, where her husband had been Governor-General. She had already added a small footnote to history at a ceremony to read out the name of the country's new capital, Canberra (chosen from a list including Kangaremu, Paradise and Sydmelaperho). Officials had worried how the winner should be pronounced. 'How Lady Denman says it', was the answer.

When she took command of the WI she was already well versed in organization, having chaired a highly successful war charity which illuminated the priorities of the period: SSS – Smokes for Soldiers. Sailors and soldiers returning wounded from the front were met at ports and railways stations and provided with free cigarettes, cigars or pipes. The charity's volunteers met all hospital trains and went into military hospitals. No one thought to demur in those days: the society's patron was Queen Alexandra, herself known to light up discreetly. Huge amounts of money were raised, and in two years 265 million gifts were distributed. Trudie Denman used the ballroom of her home in Buckingham Gate as a packing station and could be said to be partly responsible for a change in the nation's smoking habits: packs of cigarettes – easier to keep dry in a uniform pocket – supplanted the pre-war rolling tobacco that working men usually bought.

Eggs supplanted cigarettes as her principal interest in 1917, especially a way to market them which would profit individual countrywomen. The WI gave her the chance to use her remarkable organizational skills, and she immediately set it on its journey to being a force to be reckoned with. Believing that women would get nowhere if government officials were in charge, she brought the Institutes together in an independent federation. Trudie Denman understood the isolation of women in farming areas, realizing that many had not been touched by the new nature of the war: fathers, husbands and sons had marched off to enlist, but they themselves – distant from the poster and leaflet campaigns of the government and rarely reading newspapers – were yet to be convinced that everyone was going to have to 'do their bit'. This was the chance to bring women together, to learn, to gain more skills, to market their goods. Jam-making was involved, to be sure, but the principles were being laid down of national cooperation and for women to be involved in effective food production rather than merely subsisting on the land. This dovetailed with the government's increasing desperation about shortages, but instead of directing countrywomen into more manual work it was accepted that the WIs should use their experience to bring produce to market – and run their own markets as well. Ralph Wightman had noted the change in his Dorset village – home-grown food being sold for a profit – and a quiet revolution was starting to take place in the lives of countrywomen.

That still left the government short of the muscle needed to work the soil. The propaganda machine duly produced enticing posters: 'God Speed the Plough and the Woman who Drives it', the sun glowing brightly on the horizon as the woman in fetching slouch hat, smock and boots grasps the plough handles lightly and walks daintily on firm furrows behind the horse. The Land Army was born, an innovation even in the name since women weren't associated with the word 'army'; it was a bold move. The words 'National Service' were in large capital letters on the posters; once again, women were being included in the war machine.

In his memoirs the Prime Minister, only too conscious of the few weeks' remaining supplies of food, remembered the advent of the Women's Land Army worker through rosy-tinted spectacles: 'Breeched, booted and cropped, she broke with startling effect upon the sleepy traditions of the English Countryside. She was drawn from a wide range of classes of society. . . . She brought with her enthusiasm, energy and unprejudiced mind that stimulated the activity of her fellow workers.' Lloyd George was perhaps forgetting that there had been no mad rush of breeched and booted women to the farm gates.

The reaction from farmers was not encouraging either, mainly because the spectacle of a government-backed 'Army' meant they were going to have to pay 18 shillings a week minimum to these women. Not a fortune and nowhere near men's pay, but painfully more than many farmers were parting with to schoolchildren and pensioners, whom they were using in considerable numbers. However, by this time the Minister of Agriculture had to state that there was only three weeks' food supply left and brought in measures to force farmers to cultivate along officially prescribed lines.

There were other organisations set up specifically to cater for the enormous demands generated by years of fighting. The Women's Forage Corps had been formed in 1915, and the Women's Forestry Corps was delivering timber for trench-building, ammunition packing cases and a host of other military needs. A Miss Bennet kept a diary which is full of delight at 'axeing at great trees'. Her words convey the sense of freedom which she had been given, living in a camp on the South Downs with other girls, miles from anywhere, and supplied with unfamiliar tools for a girl – a billhook, an axe, a saw and a cord measure:

> Life is just what I have always longed for. After dinner tonight we had some music. It was strange to see the girls dancing, breeches and jersey, in a log hut with a stove in the middle. It will be glorious here in spring. . . . We have not seen a soul since we arrived, outside camp people. A fire in the woods and such figures as we cut would frighten anyone. We dress in sou'westers and short oilskin coats and no smock. We look like Skipper Sardines.

The Land Army marched off to work, and even that caused more than a ripple in some rural areas. Conventions die hard, and the countryside proved more than resistant to the sight of female legs. The Sunderland Women's Suffrage Society tried to allay fears:

> 'A woman engaged in ordinary fieldwork and dressed in ordinary women's garb is not a sight to attract the fastidious; but that objection again is being removed, and it is to be hoped that the fashion set by the National Service girl will be followed by all women workers on the land. The uniform worn by the girls is not only practical but eminently attractive and no girl need feel their vanity hurt when she sees herself in it.

This was not the view of stoutly Victorian matrons, whose own skirts still swept the ground during the war – a lesson learned by Annie Sarah Edwards, born on a farm in Sussex and who saw a man 'posting up a great big poster thing saying Join the Land Army' when she was a teenager working as a tweenie. Anything was better than being 'the lowest of the low' as she saw it, in domestic service. She was already used to hard work: when she was a child, the pigs and cows had to be seen to before school, in her dinner break and in the evening. There were always ironing and needlework waiting to be done. In the summer she weeded the garden and stone-picked the meadows, and went 'rook-scaring' through the newly sown fields with a bit of paper on a stick. After harvest she went gleaning, picking up the little ears of corn and taking them in a sack to the nearby windmill. At sixteen she went into service, where life was 'all work and bed'.

The Land Army demanded references, so Annie approached the elderly wife of the canon who lived in her village, to be told: 'Do you know what it involves? You'll be dressed as a man, and I object to that – it's a disgrace to show your ankles.' Annie recalled the interview sixty years later, and was still not wholly convinced that the canon's wife was wrong, adding, 'And it was [a disgrace]. *I* had my skirts to the ground.'

The munitions workers had already established *their* image in tunics and trousers, but were mainly centred in industrial towns and worked indoors. The Women's Defence Relief Corps had introduced the idea of longish smock and gaiters and boots, but not as a compulsory uniform. Now the Land Army girl was officially clad in twill breeches, pullover and short mackintosh, also a light smock for summer, with smart laced gaiters and boots – and was seen in villages and remote hamlets, where women's clothes had not changed much for a century or so: bonnet, long skirts and apron. The Land Girl was met with the remark: 'Neither a man nor a woman!' Shifts in fashion in any age provoke shrieks of 'outrageous', but in 1914 only a tiny handful of women would ever show their legs in public: actresses, dancers and very daring lady cyclists, usually in divided skirts, were just about acceptable. But the countryside was conservative and the Land Girls were a shock. Nor did the uniform eradicate traditional habits: Annie toiled in the fields in summer and had a searing memory of being 'wet through with sweat, and my corset and its steel bones were wet through and rusting; I took them off and threw them in the lavatory in the barn!'

There are also numerous photographs of women working the land during the war, wearing ancient poke bonnets to keep the sun off their faces while they wield hoes as they trail their thick long skirts through the mud. For many, the gaiters and boots 'belonged to the war' and were to be tolerated just as long as it lasted. However, there had been signs that mere practicality was not the only attraction. A busybody county field labour committee had early noted that some Land Girls were wearing their 'trousers' when they were off-duty. 'Ordinary feminine dress' should be worn at such times, they declared, only to be roundly defeated by yet another agricultural committee. Even then, there were ructions on Sundays as Land Girls were shepherded to the local church: appalled congregations objected to trousers in the pews.

Annie recalled, 'No days off, no holidays. Sundays I had to feed and water and bed the horses, then Church or write a letter or read.' She described her upbringing as 'strict' and had imbibed the mantra that 'You should be seen and not heard – we never dared ask questions. You knew your place, and never interrupted your parents when talking.' Coming from such a home and then going into service, Annie, like hundreds more, found the Land Army, despite its rules and expectation of obedience, gave her a taste of freedom. The middle-class women found the open-air life a contrast to their sheltered rounds of tea parties and charity work – Annie remembered some of her colleagues moaning about thistle-pulling, mud and dung-spreading. Even so, they saw the experience as temporary, and assumed they would return to 'normal life' at the end of the war. On the other hand, working-class girls found the hard work very similar to that they had already experienced. For all the publicity which was extracted from the girls' presence on the land, is wasn't a passport to a different life. Their counterparts in industry had often experienced the novelty of canteens, regular meals, washing facilities and better pay. Their country-based cousins got fresh air and no great welcome.

There was still scepticism: in Northumberland, out of over three hundred women who had come before the selection committee only seventy-three had passed, and of these '*several* had been considered to be really taking the place of a man'. In County Durham, at a public meeting in East Herrington, there was the kind of 'pat on the head' encouragement which inevitably accompanied any praise of the female workforce: if only farmers would *try* the women . . . the farmers would see they were far more useful than they *seemed* to be . . . women had already shown how well they could support the troops and look after the wounded, 'showing all the good qualities men suspected them of having, but were not quite sure about. . . .' This last phrase was reported as having been received with 'much laughter'. Part of the reluctance to embrace the concept was nervousness in the general public, particularly in older women, about 'loss of womanly attributes'. Annie Edwards had been told in her village that they hoped 'my trousers wouldn't alter my life'.

The ancient poke bonnets were worn to keep the skin pale – a tanned face was the sign of the rural working class, and as townswomen joined the Land Army advertising hammered home the dangers of work in the open air. For example, a jar of Oatine was essential if 'exposed to in-decent weather or bad atmosphere which soon has its effect on the complexion and, if help is not given, good looks soon fade and hands become hard . . .'

To boost confidence in their abilities there was a burst of 'farm competitions', where the Land Army assembled to display their skills. Bishop's Stortford saw 340 women from Hertfordshire and Essex competing for 'silver cups' in 'ditch and hedge-trimming, milling and hoeing – the latter being done on an uncommonly nice piece of mangolds'. The Midland counties were testing over a hundred women in 'pulling, cleaning and piling roots, mowing by hand, hoeing and singling'. The competitions highlighted the physical effort needed in most tasks – just three girls entered for 'motor tractor driving', though by the end of the war women were recognized as having done this 'at least as well as men', with over three hundred behind the wheel.

However, regardless of the successes, *Punch* magazine and its ilk had endless fun with farming and females, much of it related to dairying, with pop-eyed maidens pouring a jug over cows which they had been told 'needed watering' and asking which horn to pull 'for cream or milk'. Fear of change and the suspicion that 'women were taking over' lay behind the pictures.

Punch was probably not the preferred reading of Miss (later Dame) Meriel Talbot, who had been appointed director of the Land Army and was another formidable organizer with a strong sense of moral values. She was forever caught between recruiting a girl who was likely to make a bad impression – 'who would not or could not stick it' – and giving reassurance that those who persevered would retain the right kind of 'character'. The Land Army handbook pressed the point: 'You are doing a man's work, so are dressed rather like a man; but remember that just because you wear a smock and breeches you should take care to behave like an English girl who expects chivalry and respect from everyone she meets.' Even so, of the first forty-eight thousand women who applied fewer than a quarter were accepted, and the official figure at the end of the war was of just over twelve thousand remaining of thirty-eight thousand recruited. Much higher figures were often used in newspaper reports at the time, however, and for the critical last year of fighting the 'Army' at work on the land was supplemented by tens of thousands of men from the regular army and thousand of prisoners of war.

The impact of the Land Army probably far outweighed their contribution to agricultural output. An enraptured *Dorchester Chronicle* witnessed two hundred and fifty women marching through the town in 1918. It was still unable to avoid commenting that they had 'doffed the conventional skirt so long associated with their sex' but then warmed to the sight: 'Many of them wore their breeches and gaiters, picturesque smocks and jaunty hats with a delightful touch of piquancy and the chic so valued by the fair.' The *Chronicle* then rose to new heights: 'Gazing at their robust yet supple figures and observing the sparkle of their eyes and the bloom of their well-moulded cheeks one would have no shadow of doubt that the open-air life and healthy labour has done them a world of good. . . . Here is dawning a new era for womanhood and therefore the human race!'

A slightly less breathless view might see the propaganda about sturdy and capable women, the extraordinary countryside sight of breeches and gaiters, along with the increasing involvement of countrywomen encouraged to improve their own lives, as a remarkable contribution to change.

The women could do it – and many who cared about country life were convinced they should. The poster of a girl behind the plough had lasting resonance.

CHAPTER 19

MARCHING, NOT FIGHTING

At the start of the war, there was much banter about the women who appeared in a variety of uniforms for the voluntary organizations. 'Aping the men' was derided and disapproved of. Fair enough if Vesta Tilley marched up and down, as long as it was only in the music hall. Shouldering a rifle was part of her act – and that was the limit of women's proximity to the image of a fighting soldier. When anyone foolishly ventured to suggest anything more, shouts of 'Amazon' and 'Boadicea' would set the men chortling and leave the women wide-eyed at the idea of female combatants.

Two years into the war there had been a slight shift in opinion, as nurses and volunteers came back from France on leave with eyewitness reports of front-line action. Families had had to adjust to daughters who had seen death and violence, yet who retained a strong conviction that they had a job to do in the war zone. However, they did not demand to take the place of the casualty and fight on the front line. Women had proved they could endure warfare at the front, but there was no expectation that they should conduct it.

One famous exception was known: amid the carnage of the Balkan front a vicar's daughter from Poppleton in Yorkshire put down her bandages, took the Red Cross insignia off her arm and asked the Serbian officer next to her if she might take up a rifle and join the battle. He agreed at once, and Flora Sandes became Private Sandes, 2nd Infantry Regiment, 1st Serbian Army.

A volunteer with some St John Ambulance training, she had travelled to the Balkans in 1914 at the age of thirty-eight. She believed that nursing was 'surely the most womanly occupation on earth' and later said she had absolutely no intention of becoming a soldier. So began a highly successful military career, giving her the added distinction of being the only British woman to fight officially in World War I. She was outgoing and charming, practical and tenacious, having no illusions that what she was doing was considered acceptable at home. She valued nursing, but as the Serbs came under heavy attack she decided that she could better help them by using her shooting skills, learned in her country upbringing.

Flora found herself welcomed by her new comrades – 'for an Englishwoman to be fighting side by side with them seemed to please the soldiers immensely, and I soon became well known, the men always calling me "Nashi Engleskinja", *our* Englishwoman'. For two and a half years she endured the hardships and dangers of front-line war, writing letters to her family and friends at home with a splendid matter-of-factness:

> I have often been meaning to write to you, and just now 'time' is the one – and only – thing I have plenty of. I am sitting in a hole about 7 feet by 4 feet, and 3 feet deep, with two officers of my company. We can't stir out of it from dawn to dark, and even after dark it is not healthy, as there are always stray bullets, which though not aimed at you, may prove just as annoying. We had a man killed last night by one of these chance shots, while eating his supper, and another wounded. If anyone at home begins asking me to describe the War, I shall tell them to go into their back garden, dig a hole and sit there for anything from three days and nights to a month, in November, without a thing to read or do, and they can judge for themselves – minus the chance of being killed, of course.

Private Sandes wasn't in the tradition of women trying to pass themselves off as men in order to fight. She was adept at dealing with innuendo and unwanted approaches, and was accepted as a competent and reliable soldier, cutting a smart figure in uniform, breeches, high-laced boots and army cap. Her bravery was unquestionable, having been awarded Serbia's most prestigious medal while attacking the Bulgarians. Her letter home was typical:

> I dare say you've heard that I got knocked out by a Bulgar hand-bomb, so I never got to Monastir after all; but I've had a very good run for my money all the same, as I had three months' incessant fighting without a scratch. . . . The Serbs are fine comrades. We thought once we should all get taken, but they wouldn't leave me! I've had ever so many cards from them asking when I'm coming back, but as I have twenty-four wounds and a broken arm the doctors seem to think I'll have to wait a bit.

On her lengthy journey through the mountains to hospital she passed through the hands of Mrs Harley's Transport Unit – yet another British volunteer ambulance group, run by the sister of Sir John French, commander-in-chief of the British Expeditionary Force to France in 1914. News of her exploits began to spread. After another stint with her regiment Flora was injured again. She headed back to Britain for convalescence, but trying to obtain passage on naval transports proved impossible: although by now a sergeant-major, she was still a woman. Eventually she reached London, intending to raise funds for a charity for elderly Serbs she had started with Evelina Haverfield, whom she had met in Serbia with the Scottish Women's Hospitals.

At home she soon understood that she was the odd woman out – 'at first it was rather uncomfortable being stared at because in uniform, but everyone was so nice to me I got used to it'. The War Office wanted her to brief them on Serbian operations, which initially puzzled her. 'I was unaware that they knew of my existence. Even policemen and taxi-drivers would now and then stop me and ask how little Serbia was getting on.' She launched an appeal via a letter in the *Morning Post*, and as subscriptions and clothing began to arrive was asked to give a public lecture. By now she had realized that she was spending half her time 'trying to dodge reporters' and getting into a complete dither about speaking in public. Evelina Haverfield, an aristocratic old-hand at lectures, was doing the rounds of schools and colleges and public halls. Flora, a mild-mannered daughter of the vicarage, and much happier on the battlefield than the platform, was now aware that the war was pushing middle-class women into a public life inconceivable before she had left. She found the stage at the Alhambra in London

> rather a big place to make one's debut – but when I found myself standing alone, in uniform, in the middle of that vast expanse of stage, feeling about the size of a peanut, and facing a packed house which looked,

> to my dazzled eyes, as though it stretched away for several kilometres, a voice, which did not sound at all like my own made some kind of speech. I have never had the slightest idea what I did say, but I knew some of the audience were crying.

Further talks followed, and she not only collected enough donations to help the elderly horse-transport drivers of her unit but also managed to clothe an entire division of the Serbian army with British shirts and pants and great quantities of Australian knitted socks. By this time she was in great demand and was invited to talk to British soldiers in France; even so, she was hesitant about appearing in front of the military: 'I felt very nervous at first as to how they would take such an innovation as a woman lecturer, and in uniform, for most men hate to see women trying to be masculine, but they did not seem to take it that way at all, and the first friendly round of applause that greeted me was reassuring and told me we were going to be friends.' She fascinated them with tales of the life of ordinary soldiers in the Balkans, told funny stories and didn't avoid the realities of the bad times. And she raised considerable funds for her charity.

Even so, time after time she was conscious that, although she was celebrated, the idea of a uniformed woman soldier was still very suspect. In Calais, she met 'three dejected British Tommies' who had just had their leave cancelled: 'I told them I was a soldier too, and they listened politely, but evidently believed not a word of it. As there was nothing to stop me I went off to get something to eat, and a bright idea struck me to bring them back a bottle of beer each. "*Now* we know you are a soldier," they exclaimed gratefully. This thin story invariably made a hit, and the men used to laugh and cheer till the place sounded like a football match.'

After serving in the army until 1922 and marrying a Russian émigré officer, she finally returned to Suffolk with her sword and her medals and died peacefully in 1952. Having been in army uniform for seven years, she recalled the frustrations of returning to civilian life: 'I cannot attempt to describe what it now felt like, trying to get accustomed to a woman's life and a woman's clothes again; and also to society after having lived entirely with men for so many years. Turning from a woman into a private soldier was nothing compared with turning back from a soldier to ordinary woman.'

In late 1916, while she was in the thick of the fighting in Serbia, the War Office was wading into waters which she knew much better than they did. How was it going to replenish the thin lines at the front, even though conscription was in force and every last fit man was being 'combed out' of civilian occupations and turned into a soldier? Not that the example of Flora Sandes would have given them any ideas: the last reservoir of human energy was female – but only to substitute, to replace, to be

> The girl
> behind the man
> behind the gun.

And there was no ambiguity in the recruiting posters the next year. 'Women urgently wanted for the Women's Army Auxiliary Corps [WAAC]: Cooks, Clerks, Waitresses, Driver-mechanics, All Kinds of Domestic Workers'.

The civil service, the politicians and the military had spent months agonizing over every aspect of a female military outfit. Confronted on a daily basis by the appalling casualty lists, they desperately needed to release men from the chores which every army relies on and send them forward into the trenches. Aware of automatic hostility in many quarters to the very idea of 'militarized' women, but also prodded by the myriad women's voluntary organizations with their own agenda, they were trying to form an army that wasn't quite an army. It might look like one, sound like one, but wouldn't fight like one.

For months the ladies who headed the large volunteer groups had bombarded the War Office with suggestions and demands, foremost among which was the insistence that women should be commanded by women. Meanwhile the military tried their best to ensure that no one would ever mistake a member of this new Corps for a 'real' soldier (the wrangling over whether a girl should ever be allowed to salute went on for more than a year). It was a struggle that went on, even when the Corps was up and running, and at stake was the traditional exclusivity of manliness allied with soldiering and womanliness allied with, in this case, not being like a soldier at all. Memos discussing army rank went the rounds, with a cautious note from one of the contenders to lead the new force: 'I believe (from what one hears from men with whom one has discussed the question) that it would be wise to avoid ordinary military terms of rank.' There were to be no colonels or sergeants or privates, just officials, forewomen and workers.

Army discipline was a thorny problem, with the repeated reservation that it 'should be strict, but not include saluting or other pseudo-men touches'. Army pay produced a new twist to the argument about equal pay, with General Sir Douglas Haig not against it, but insisting that it would need a ratio of 200 women to replace 134 men; he didn't seem to notice that the guiding factor in the workplace was that women were cheaper to employ. Army Regulations were complicated by, as General Haig put it, 'the likelihood of sex difficulties'. Here, he was beaten to the answer with advice from the commandant of the VADs, Katherine Furse, who had already foreseen the likelihood of pregnancies: 'Unmarried mothers, or those about to become so, must be discharged. They should not, however, be lost sight of, but their names and home addresses should be given to some competent organisation.' Furse was experienced and understood what might lie ahead, and she was not going to have the military sending its disciplinary tank grinding over young women in a new environment. There was noticeable tension between those who had organized and led large numbers of female volunteers for some years and the rigid approach of the military top brass. The former were immensely exercised already that all the new Corps' appointments were going to be made by the latter.

Such appointments during the war reflected not only the outstanding abilities of women who ran huge administrations to great effect, but also their relations with the country's elite – literally. Mrs Mona Chalmers Watson was appointed to be in charge of the WAAC. She was the sister of the First Lord of the Admiralty, Sir Eric Geddes; cousin of the controller of the Admiralty, Sir Alan Garrett Anderson, and also of Dr Louisa Garrett Anderson who was in charge of the Endell Street Women's Hospital – whose aunt was the suffragist leader Millicent Fawcett, coincidentally intensifying the campaign for the vote; another brother, Sir Auckland Geddes, was Minister in Charge of National Service and Chief Recruiter of the Army. This was in no way unusual. The inter-connectedness of the establishment was powered by marriage: the increased prominence of women in public life merely demonstrated that they were now not merely wives or sisters but using their confidence, education and connections to great effect in real jobs. No one shouted Nepotism! The class system and habit of deference were strong enough to cause few raised eyebrows and the women themselves had real qualifications – Chalmers Watson was the first woman medical graduate of Edinburgh University (her mother Helen Geddes Anderson, was a pioneering supporter of women's Medical studies), and had worked with Dr Elsie Inglis. Even so, she nearly fell at the last hurdle in the appointment race: despite being an authoritative and experienced administrator, it had bothered Lord Derby, the Secretary of State for War, that, despite her connections, she was not a 'titled lady'. This time, professionalism won the day – a small but significant step forward for women in the complicated undergrowth of elite family trees.

She took charge as controller (not General) of the WAAC, this curious hybrid which was under the War Office but had women in charge; women who were enrolled, but not enlisted, military-ish in look, but unmilitary in objective. To entice recruits already in other jobs the work had to have a touch of glamour, or at least a sprinkling of patriotic duty. The uniform was unlikely to deliver that – long gabardine 'coat-dresses' and (after experimenting with a cap with a crêpe de chine veil at the back) brown felt hats, prototype of the girls' school hat for many a decade. However, the skirts were considered progressive as they were 12 inches off the ground and the colour was khaki – a hard-won concession from the military males.

A major advertising campaign ensued, with meetings and exhibitions emphasizing patriotic service and good wages, and posters with groups of smiling girls 'looking to you to join our circle'. An immense amount of time and effort went into recruiting for all the women's services, which suggests that by no means every fit and able female was by now longing to do her bit. Three years into the war, weariness and not a little misery were beginning to sap patriotic enthusiasm. There were some scathing comments in the press about 'thousands of idle women and girls who think it sufficient to do a few hours every week in voluntary work'. Nearer the general truth would be the thousands of bereaved and hard-pressed women trying to keep families together as the economic winds grew chillier and the cost of living climbed. More cleaning, cooking and serving meals didn't have great allure. The Land Army was recruiting too, and finding it tough going. The munitions factories were simply unable to hold on to many of their workers year after year – the work was physically exhausting and the poisonous fumes, noise and accidents were taking their toll.

The best place to reach likely recruits was now the cinema, with audiences lapping up Charlie Chaplin and Mary Pickford. So the War Office produced a short film showing a sweet girl who stared up at Nelson's Column in Trafalgar Square and looked thoughtful before tripping off to the recruiting office. There was drill and a few gentle outstretched arms for PT, then life in camp – peeling potatoes, cooking and waitressing. There were also clean and spacious huts, and shots of folk dancing, tennis and a little gardening and some girls larking around imitating Chaplin with moustache and cane, then a smart march-past through Folkestone.

Today it would be unlikely to cause a stampede to the colours, but this was aimed at young working-class girls who might be attracted by the provision of meals, accommodation and clothing – it was very soon noticed that many arrived without much underwear since to them it was an unaffordable luxury. The war had not erased poverty and the military offered girls a chance to leave home and gain some independence, still a rarity for those in poor areas. Supervisors in munitions factories had already noticed that providing free food, even if it wasn't particularly appetizing, helped with production. And the opportunity to gain some status, to be recognized as part of an army, wearing khaki, was not to be underestimated. In a hierarchical society, if you were female and not born with advantages the routes to a better life were only gradually opening up, and this might be one of them. A decade earlier, the members of the suffrage movement had begun to parade past the public with their placards; most had been educated and mainly middle-class. Munitionettes had gained fame by appearing in public in their tunics and daring trousers, holding their heads high and 'keeping the army fighting'. Now here was the chance to march in style past the crowd and be seen as serving the country, in official uniform. Many of the girls were immensely proud to be a WAAC.

Not everyone was impressed. There had been dislike of the 'militaristic' uniforms of some of the early volunteer organizations, and the very sight of the new Corps frequently provoked hostile reaction. The war had elevated the male fighting soldier to an admired, if not heroic, figure; however, the very term 'soldier' was traditionally a fairly tarnished word. Wellington's 'scum of the earth' resonated through Victorian times, garrison towns were seen as sinks of iniquity, and joining the army was for many a last resort in a hard world. Make that soldier a woman, and there's no doubting the misgivings about the innovation. And having taken the big decision to don uniform, the pride derived from it was often dented by public scorn. Olive Taylor, who had come from munitions work, remembered an outing from her army camp near Woolwich:

> Some of us looked forward to going into Woolwich and perhaps enjoying egg and chips, but we were subject to such insults

> in Woolwich that we never tried again. Here we learned for the first time that we were regarded as the scum and that we had been enlisted for the sexual satisfaction of the soldiers. This, after the way we had worked ever so hard, and put up with so much deprivation for our country's sake, was absolutely terrible. We were broken hearted about it and never went into town again. What a treat it would have been to be able to enjoy egg and chips, something some of us had never even tasted.

Rumours were swirling around the Corps because several thousand members would be stationed in France very soon. The press had a field day with innuendo and a fit of moral panic: on behalf not of the women, but of the men. Luckily, the newly appointed Chief Controller (Overseas) was a fount of common sense and independence. As stories began to appear about couples 'walking out' together, followed by tales of a soldier being posted as a guard outside the 'WAAC Maternity Home', Mrs Helen Gwynne-Vaughan confronted the army top brass who were quick to complain that women's sexual shenanigans were damaging the morale of their men. This was a military organization that had no objection whatsoever to French brothels, having agreed that they constituted 'local customs' and were therefore not out of bounds to British soldiers. For the record, the army was also particularly convinced that married men had 'greater carnal needs' and many soldiers still believed that sex improved one's strength. One hundred and fifty thousand servicemen were treated for VD during the war.

Such matters were difficult to air in public: it was so much easier to take the conventional route and pin the blame on Eve. Mrs Gwynne-Vaughan was having none of it. Well before the deployment of the corps she had already confronted one nervous army officer who remarked, 'If these women are coming, we shall have to wire [off] all the woods on the Lines of Communication,' with the reply, 'If you do, sir, you will have a number of enterprising couples climbing over.'

The military senior ranks, she realized, were completely inexperienced when it came to dealing with women. They had fixed, conventional views, and neither knew about nor wanted to have dealings with the employment of the opposite sex, something that had arisen with many managers in engineering firms in the early days of the war. And other than servants, they hadn't actually *met* many working-class women. She also saw that the deployment of the Corps bothered the public at home far more than it caused any trouble in the war zone. There would inevitably be some association between the troops and Corps members, she knew, and difficulties would sometimes arise; but she had no intention of letting this destroy the whole enterprise. Although the attitude of the times regarded an unwanted pregnancy as only the woman's fault, whatever the circumstances, she insisted that women who found themselves pregnant should be treated sympathetically and discharged on compassionate grounds. (Many maids in domestic service on the Home Front might have benefitted from her views.)

However, the newspapers went on running teasing tales of 'dastardly rumours and furtive falsehoods' and, despite Gwynne-Vaughan's efforts, the Ministry of Labour sent a committee of five ladies to France to investigate 'immorality'. They returned with a report which said the WAAC were 'a healthy, cheerful, self-respecting body of hard-working women, conscious of their position as links in the great chain of the nation's purpose, and zealous in its service'.

They were working hard and in conditions which certainly had not been shown in the recruiting campaign, with long hours and basic rations; their tasks were mundane, and the hierarchical nature of the organization, despite the lack of traditional ranks, meant that class differences were reinforced. Dr Flora Murray of the Endell Street Military Hospital had looked at them and wasn't surprised to find that there were some 'really healthy and robust girls, but these were usually found to be girls of a higher class, while the average of those from the villages and towns bore signs of bad housing and under-feeding'. She pointed out that better pay was the obvious answer, to get 'proper food at good prices' rather than exercise and advice. Yet again, it had to be pointed out that it was taken for granted that the country's poorer women were proportionately less well fed than the men in their families.

The Corps had now acquired royal patronage. Queen Mary had agreed to become their honorary Commander-in-Chief; much more than a gracious formality, it was an endorsement which conveyed respectability and acceptance. Queen Mary's Army Auxiliary Corps sounded slightly more soldierly; a month later, its members had the chance to prove they were, when their camp at Etaples in northern France took a direct hit. A huge bomb destroyed their huts, though the women themselves had taken cover in trenches. Eight days later an aerial torpedo exploded in one of the trenches, killing nine WAACs. This incident grimly confirmed that they were in the line of fire, taking the same risks as the men, with Mrs Gwynne-Vaughan telling a posse of pressmen bent on portraying helpless women as victims that the enemy was entitled to try to kill them – they were doing soldiers' work.

The other two women's services were much smaller, but followed the same pattern as the WAAC in needing cooks and cleaners, storekeepers and clerks, along with some technical jobs. The Royal Navy, as in so many cultures across the world, had a fund of sailors' tales and superstitions about women going anywhere near ships, having apparently forgotten the sterling work done on board by powder-mistresses and bosuns' wives during Nelson's wars. And the press were enjoying the prospect of more fun with 'sailorettes': 'Some thousands of bright young girls are busy today cultivating a nautical roll in their walk, with the object of qualifying for the newly formed Women's Navy, the jolly Jill Tars. Will they be needed to do Jack's washing or darn his socks?' In charge of the service was Dame Katherine Furse, who had been supervising VAD work; efficient and smart enough to have imported most of her directing staff from the VAD, she knew the navy had the advantage of style and made sure that her service would not be mistaken for any other. The first obstacle she managed to swerve round was the suggested title of Women's Auxiliary Naval Corps, thankfully winning the day with the Women's Royal Naval Service (WRNS), neatly abbreviated to Wrens. There was one major drawback to their recruiting. Most people associate the navy with going to sea, which was precisely what the Women's Royal Naval Service was *not* going to do.

Its members were divided into those who opted to served in their own home towns, 'Immobiles', and those 'Mobiles' who could be based anywhere in the country – and presumably hoped to 'see the world'. This was picked up quickly by the press:

> Wrens are energetic, resourceful little birds – though there was much fluttering in the

> nest when the Wren regulations became known. Some fair idealists, who had hoped that Wren work was like yachting in the Solent, resented rigid rules. Others were disgusted to learn that their official service and useful presence would never be accepted on a man-of-war. In fact, our Wrens were not to vie with men in action, but to keep the home beacon burning in their stead.

With deft publicity, the Wrens managed to avoid much of the ancient prejudice which met women soldiers in the WAAC – for a start they had an air about them, as the *Daily Sketch* trilled: 'Peer's Daughter for the Wrens – Titles are still rather scarce in the women's branches of the three Services, but I notice among the principals of the Wrens the elder of the two daughters of Lord Waleran, the former Unionist Whip. Her sister is Viscountess Southwell.' Their air was somewhat reinforced in the memoirs of Vera Laughton Matthews, later the Wrens' Director in World War II, who had joined as a young officer on the first training course at the end of 1917. Her first memory was of another girl refusing porridge at breakfast, only to be told, 'This is not porridge, it's kedgeree.'

The uniform conferred large felt tricorne hats on its officers – and if you could afford it, a rather well-cut navy blue jacket and longish skirt nine inches from the floor, with a double row of gold buttons. This was something which pleased their families, many of whom could trace their connection to the navy back to galleons in full sail. There were fetching caps for the ratings, with yet again long frock-coats which 'did not ape the men'. Thus attired, they underwent training and set off for the ports and naval bases to undertake what Laughton Matthews frankly described as extremely routine duties, as shown in the illustrated magazines – 'Wrens at work hanging carcases of mutton and at work with the potato-masher at the Royal Naval College, Greenwich, where over 2,000 meals are prepared daily.' Hardly a life on the ocean wave.

She also dismissed the idea that the women she trained had joined because of patriotic fervour. They were young working-class girls with little education looking for a job. However, over seven thousand served and they caught the imagination of the public. As they were nowhere near sailors at sea, there was less resentment at their military role – and they seemed to get into less trouble than the WAAC, leaving their Director, Katherine Furse, quite happy that they were known as the Perfect Ladies – and more often the Prigs and Prudes. Vera Laughton Matthews was proud to have joined them: 'To see women garbed in the uniform of that most conservative of institutions, the British Navy, to see them going about the naval ports on their lawful occasions, following the official routine as to the manner born, and most completely at home, gave one quite a lump in one's throat, it was so splendid and unexpected.'

To the Wrens and WAACs (there had been great discussion as to whether something pronounced 'Wacks' was the proper nickname until the women themselves said they approved) were added the Penguins. How this came about is unclear and whether it ever stuck is doubtful, but it vied with WRAF for the Women's Royal Air Force, which was formed in the last year of the war. However, the Royal Air Force itself was such a novelty that no one was yet used to the airmen, let alone the airwomen. The women's branch had a somewhat chaotic start with staffing difficulties among its senior officers and no great traditions to either build on – or overcome. There was the advantage of the thrill and glamour of flight: aeroplanes were still a rare sight for most, and only a tiny number of people had ever flown in one. They still evoked wonder even when they were piloted by the enemy, and raids over English towns had sometimes resulted in amazed spectators staring skywards rather than running for cover.

Recruitment in early 1918 was eased by two thousand WAACs and Wrens being transferred, followed by Katherine Furse in charge. Though clerical and domestic work was inevitably dominant, the WRAF was more eager to give technical training, something that the *Lady* magazine, even after more than three years of war, found unspeakably exciting:

> Until I saw the official list of potentialities I had not quite realised the catholic comprehensiveness of them. The list opens quietly and restfully: duty's path is here a beaten track in which walk clerks and storewomen and women for household works. More or less beaten, too (by this fourth year of war) is the track of the motor transport girl. These and their doings I can understand; also the doings of such as are draughtswomen, photographers, upholsterers and painters. But being myself a highly technical person, what does fill me with awe and wonder is the idea of women as aero-engine fitters, riggers, acetylene welders, magneto repairers, and so on. Truly 'the women are splendid.'

Towards the end of the war, rumours arose that women might even more splendidly take to the air, with a suggestion that the Royal Flying Corps (as the Royal Air Force was originally known) was considering training women pilots. Gertrude Bacon believed herself to have been the first Englishwoman to take to the air when she accompanied a French pilot in 1909. She talked of the rapture of flight, the thrill of sitting on a perch – no seat available – behind the French flier Monsieur Sommer, and the 'upside down sensation of looping the loop'. As one of only a handful of women aviators, she mulled over the desire of women to help the war effort in this way:

> Women must not fly in wartime, for women must not fight. This is the last ditch of convention to which our males firmly cling. Many a female heart beat high with eager longing, when rumour said that women pilots were to be trained for the Royal Flying Corps; and bitter was the disappointment when the veto was placed on this promising scheme. 'May we not even fly the machine in England, over the Channel to the men in France?' pleaded the girls.
>
> 'No,' said their fathers, husbands, brothers, (even their sons). 'Because you might meet a Hun on the way and then you would have to fight.'
>
> And that settled it, though the women murmured to themselves 'Yes, and we could do that, too – if necessary.'

No one had dreamed of the women's services before the war; even those who had thought of a role for women in an emergency had confined themselves to nursing and ambulance work. The very idea of women imitating the military was frowned upon, and those who put on military-style uniforms for the voluntary organizations were frequently criticized. Nor did the three women's branches come about as an inspired idea or by popular demand. Sheer desperate necessity produced them. The war was a man-eating machine. Thousands upon thousands were already back home, terribly maimed or otherwise unfit to fight again. Volunteers had been superseded by conscripts – and they were not enough. Now the War Office was 'combing out' men: going to all the groups of workers who had hitherto been exempt, because they were either engaged on essential work or had initially been rejected, and sending them very quickly towards the front line. The work which was needed to keep the army going was far from actual soldiering: food, paperwork, cleaning. So there was little novel employment for the women – and they would be paid less than the men for doing the same work.

Some were lucky enough to be trained in technical tasks in communication, or were taught to drive, and hoped that when the war ended they might benefit with a better job. There was no indication that the armed services would keep them on – and at the end they quickly dwindled, loud harrumphing in the corridors of power indicating that there would be no need whatsoever for a female force brought about by the particular circumstances of the Great War.

CHAPTER 20

V FOR VOTE

Saddam Hussein's statue in Baghdad was brought crashing down in 2003, live on television, with a small crowd of cheering Iraqis watching the US army pulling and heaving. It soon came to represent the end of a regime, the literal toppling of a dictator. It was a useful symbol and carried a message, but didn't usher in all that had been hoped for. Symbolic gestures – especially on battlegrounds – are popular, though they don't always lead immediately to a new dawn. And more than a century ago, the women in the suffrage movement understood such gestures.

In June 1917 a curious and low-key exchange in the House of Commons presaged a symbolic victory for women, signalling that their efforts in the war might well gain them in the near future the bigger victory of the vote and perhaps more rights. Pre-war suffrage activists, now spread right across the Home Front in every kind of women's organization where they were using their unique experience and knowledge of public life, paused from their efforts to read a small note in the official parliamentary record, *Hansard*.

Mr Cory asked the First Commissioner of Works what procedure he proposes to adopt to enable the House to express its views on the subject of the removal of the grille in front of the Ladies' Gallery; and when such an opportunity will be afforded?

The First Commissioner of Works (Sir Alfred Mond)

It is proposed to ascertain the views of the House on this question, and probably the most convenient method will be by the introduction of a supplementary Estimate of the probable cost of such removal.

There was absolutely no reaction recorded from the MPs: no cheers, no 'Hear, Hear's. Not surprising, as the all-male chamber had repeatedly snorted with laughter and jeered in derision every time the pesky 'grille' had been discussed – a metal lattice across the window of the Ladies' Gallery above the House of Commons. It is almost possible to believe that on this occasion some MPs were either gritting their teeth or feigning a short snooze, for the dry parliamentary procedure concealed a long-running set of skirmishes over a much-despised feature of the Houses of Parliament. And a symbolic victory was in sight. But from all those who had campaigned for women's suffrage there was a resounding cheer.

In the decade preceding World War I the more militant of them had defied convention by using their small army of activists in violent and shocking tactics against the much bigger forces of government and public opinion. Having found that persuasion, petitions and demonstrations brought no change, they embarked on guerrilla tactics, with mixed results. They grabbed the headlines and they also alienated those who were opposed to violence and law-breaking. Some saw them as freedom fighters, others as dangerous rebels using terror tactics. They saw themselves as a militia force.

They were lampooned by cartoonists – 'the shrieking sisterhood', drawn as snaggle-toothed crones and ugly spinsters; sneered at by politicians – 'Women are well represented by their fathers, brothers, and husbands', said Winston Churchill smugly; jeered at by crowds and attacked by mobs. The militant suffragettes were like a guerrilla force who ignored the law, only to retort that they were refused any part in making that law.

For the lawmakers, the politicians, laughter was the common response to years of pressure. Most of the members of the House of Commons had no problem in guffawing happily, even when listening to complaints about the treatment of women prisoners being force-fed. There were no female MPs or officials in the building. Women members of the public could only sit, segregated from men, in the Ladies' Gallery, above the Press Gallery. It was small, hot and stuffy – and symbolic, as the Honourable Members themselves knew, when chaffingly discussing its problems in May 1912. *Hansard* records:

Mr Sands
asked the Hon. Member for St George's-in-the-East, as representing the First Commissioner of Works, whether his attention has been called to the unsatisfactory system of ventilation in the Ladies' Gallery; and whether any improvement can be effected?
Mr Wedgwood Benn (Lord of the Treasury)
No complaint of the ventilation of the Ladies' Gallery has for some time reached the First Commissioner. An independent system for that part of the House was constructed in 1907, and upon this it is difficult to effect any improvement.
Mr Keir Hardie
Would not an improvement be effected by removing the grille?
Mr Wedgwood Benn
I do not think the removal of the grille would affect the ventilation.
Mr Keir Hardie
Could the grille be removed?
Mr Wedgwood Benn
I do not think that arises out of the question.
Mr MacCallum Scott
May I ask whether the Hon. Gentleman, as a Minister, is responsible for putting ladies in that cage?'

Hansard probably didn't need to record the subsequent ho-hos and boys' club jollity.

The 'cage' was a heavy, ornate metal lattice in the stone window arches of the Gallery which obscured the view intentionally – the view *from* the Members up to the ladies. That it should cause the ladies some inconvenience wasn't in the mind of the architect who designed it in the 1830s so that the gentlemen in the chamber wouldn't be 'distracted' by ladies watching them at work. It had been a bone of contention on many occasions, its similarity to the restrictive practices of the Muslim harem frequently acknowledged, but stirring no MPs into getting rid of it. Arguments for its removal were met with the indisputable fact that the Palace of Westminster was a male workplace, as one of the suffrage posters declared:

> This is 'The House' that man built.
> And this is the Minister weary and worn
> Who treated the suffragette with scorn,
> Who wanted a Vote, and (a saying to quote),
> Dared him to tread on the tail of the coat
> Of the bold Suffragette determined to get
> Into 'The House' that man built.'

And determined they were, heading in 1908 for a particularly worthy target.

Not that all would have agreed with the methods to be used: there were various strands and groups in the suffrage movement, swirling with debate and argument about campaign priorities and tactics. Some disagreements were intellectual, some political, others personal, and in the first decade of the twentieth century the issue of militant action divided many. Taking to the streets and merely demonstrating with marching and banners was a major step for many women. It counted as shocking – especially for 'respectable' people. The very idea of doing something unconventional in a public place was frightening – in the main, women lived private lives. So deeply entrenched were these views that it was hard to imagine what might happen if women physically invaded what was seen as male territory. That suffrage demonstrators were frequently assailed by aggressive young men and also manhandled by the police was completely outside the experience of middle-class families, many of whom couldn't believe that this could be allowed to happen. If the opponents of women's suffrage rested their case on the very frailty of women and their inability to cope with public life, then why attack them physically? When some groups of suffragettes upped their game and opted for attacks on commercial and private property, there was more debate and angst on all sides: such behaviour was new territory, only associated with a mob. That well-dressed women should be carrying hammers in their handbags in order to smash windows was a disquieting novelty. These were Edwardians in long skirts, corsets and hats; dignity and propriety ruled their lives. Even a fishwife – the epitome of rough manners – didn't go around breaking windows and setting fire to buildings. Public opinion wrestled not only with the sight of ugly confrontations and arrests, but with the disturbing notion that women, the upholders of morality, were at the heart of it all.

The Women's Social and Political Union (WSPU) under mother and daughter Emmeline and Christabel Pankhurst was committed to militancy, unlike the National Union of Women's Suffrage Societies (NUWSS), led for many years by Millicent Fawcett who believed in campaigning through meetings and political pressure. They had split in 1903, and the terms 'suffragettes' and 'suffragists' emerged, to describe respectively women committed to militant and non-militant action.

The symbolic parliamentary grille was despised by all, but action came in 1908 from the Women's Freedom League (WFL), which rather deftly defined itself as 'militant but non-violent'. Led by the imposing figure of Charlotte Despard, they specifically targeted government property, rather than private houses or commercial premises, and made the American-style commitment not to pay tax: no taxation without representation. Its members were frequently arrested after protests in all-male courts, demonstrations and assaults on buildings, with Despard – well into her sixties – leading the fray. The *Manchester Guardian* newspaper later recalled that

> It used to be said that the London police always disliked having to intervene at demonstrations in which she took part because she always took all the risks there were, and they were always afraid that she would break. Tall, straight as a lance, and with the air of a great lady, she used to be an astonishing figure as she stood on the plinth of the Nelson monument or marched at the head of a defiant procession in her plain long frock and lace mantilla, but the appearance of physical fragility was combined with one of spiritual force.

The WFL was an eclectic organization with nationwide adherents, and, although attracting writers and the well connected, it had broad aims which saw members supporting trades union activity and women on strike and putting forward the idea that housework should be classified alongside all other 'work'. On 28 October 1908, the WFL demonstrated outside the House of Commons while three of its members, Violet Tillard, Helen Fox and Muriel Mathers, headed for the Ladies' Gallery. All were seasoned protesters, and would not have been in the least surprised to see their subsequent behaviour described a short while later by the Speaker of the House as 'disorderly and discreditable'. The next day, the *Times* condemned them for 'childish demonstrations which silly women think clever'. Other newspapers decided it was a thrilling diversion from the plodding debate on the Licensing Bill: 'A young, smartly gowned but dishevelled woman of unusual prettiness was struggling with attendants wearing faultless evening dress and badges of authority. . . . Mr Speaker, shrieked the pretty lady, resisting with all her strength the efforts of the sergeant-at-arms to put his hand over her mouth, "we have listened too long to the illogical utterances of men who know not what they say. Attend to the women!"' Unfortunately, efforts to hustle Helen Fox, 'that ornament of the Women's Freedom League', out of the Gallery were hampered by the padlock and chain which secured her to the brass grille. Ten minutes of concentrated wrestling followed, with the occasional burst of speech from the suffragette, while a large banner was manoeuvred through the grille on the end of a rope by Violet Tillard. Next to her, Muriel Mathers, also chained to the grille and busy jabbing Commons staff with her hatpin, was shouting: 'For forty years we have listened behind this grille. We, the women of England; we, your wives, sisters and sweethearts . . .', until she was interrupted by the unmistakable screech of metal being heaved bodily out of stone by a dozen men, with suffragettes attached. Totally unmoved, MPs continued with the debate and the grille, minus suffragettes, was reinserted a short time later.

To many, these were stunts and served to intensify hostility to the suffrage movement. On the other hand, as hundreds of women – many of them well known or with impressive pedigrees – kept being imprisoned and subjected to brutal treatment it was difficult to pretend that they were a deranged minority indulging in 'mindless violence'. They knew how to argue their case, producing heavyweight literature and displaying forceful oratorical powers at serious meetings and sharply argued debates throughout the country. Their campaign was hard to ignore. Apart from anything else, it was in modern terms 'empowering' women to undertake new roles: leaders, protestors, public speakers, organizers, planners. They became familiar with the workings of the law, got a personal taste of how women were treated in court and prison, learned to deal with the press, started up their own publications; even if they were still without status in public life, they experienced what it *might* be like – which only increased their determination to achieve it.

The year before the war began, all sections of the movement were affronted by yet another refusal by Parliament to consider giving women the vote. The militants were in full cry – the tea pavilion at Kew Gardens went up in flames, numerous golf courses had holes dug in them, racecourse grandstands were set on fire, pictures in Manchester Art Gallery defaced, railways stations vandalized, post boxes set ablaze, empty houses torched, telephone wires cut, fuse boxes blown up, and, as Sylvia Pankhurst proudly recalled, 'old ladies applied for gun licences to terrify the authorities'. Politicians were having to consider that perhaps something should be done – though there was no party political consensus as to what. Emily Davison, an experienced militant who had endured nine prison terms, stepped in front of the King's horse on Derby Day. Her death is one of the best-remembered incidents of the whole suffrage campaign, yet at the time her action was seen more as an outrage than a tragedy, and she was not a heroine to the general public.

Much more than arm's length away from the violent acts, the non-militants, especially the NUWSS, were able to rouse tens of thousands to demonstrate peacefully. But even their dignified marches were frequently still the object of cat-calls and abusive language. No one was quite sure what would happen next. It turned out to be the declaration of war with Germany.

Ready and waiting were thousands of women who were battle-hardened in their own way. All were realists, and the most prominent knew immediately that they couldn't continue their own fight while the country needed defending. They had to rein in their frustration and channel their energies elsewhere. They had reason to worry about a halt to their campaign – momentum might be lost. They were also divided amongst themselves, both suffragists and suffragettes, because of a strong streak of pacifism in their ranks. However, the majority were in no way different from their fellow citizens in terms of patriotism and fervour for national unity. Realignment was breathtakingly swift, leaving diehard campaigners quite bruised, but the government was to be left in no doubt that their allegiance was first and foremost to the cause of victory.

Within days of war being declared, Christabel Pankhurst was addressing audiences on 'The German Peril'. No stranger to making demands of government, she now held out for women to be able to use all their abilities to push for victory. As the society ladies mobilized, committees proliferated and charities and welfare groups sprang into being, the names of suffrage campaigners were woven into almost every group of volunteers. They knew how to network, to publicize, to organize. Those who had seen how government and authority worked were not unaware that the war might give them the opportunity they had been looking for. There was consternation among many that they would have to throw in their lot and work alongside men in the war effort, without any concession to dearly held principles, but there was also a feeling that this might give them the chance to work *within* society for change, rather than batter on the door from outside. The non-militant NUWSS took one day less than Christabel to show its colours, with Millicent Fawcett voicing a similar hope that her members would be able to help, then getting into her stride a week later with the clarion call: 'Let us show ourselves to be worthy of citizenship whether our claim to it be recognised or not.'

The word 'citizenship' was perceptive. Who knew what lay ahead in the way of proving what women could do? Mrs Fawcett very quickly grasped that her army of supporters was about to be tested in many new ways, and had broadened its objective from the vote to embrace full citizenship.

Even with the old tactics put on hold, a good deal of work was still carried on towards the hoped-for franchise. Those who had rooted objections to military activity continued to be equally energetic in the cause of peace. In the context of international peace conferences, support for conscientious objectors and protest against conscription into the forces the pacifist suffragettes were prominent. Others concentrated on social welfare, as war tore apart families, orphaned children and created more difficulties for the very poor.

In total opposition to her mother, Emmeline Pankhurst's younger daughter Sylvia established the Workers' Suffrage Federation and immersed herself in London's East End. One week into the war, Sylvia was organizing free daily milk to be distributed to nursing mothers in Bow and Canning Town. She started 'cost price restaurants', where meals cost just a penny for children and twopence for mothers. A successful toy factory was set up to provide an income for scores of needy out-workers who found that, at a time of self-imposed war austerity, no one was buying artificial flowers, fancy brushes, trinkets for the dressing table and sweets. While the middle and upper classes were free to make themselves useful and live in the public limelight, Sylvia felt strongly that poorer women had no choice but to earn what they could while their husbands were away. Her Federation opened a Cooperative Boot Factory, dividing the profits among the workforce: a necessary product, for boots were standard wear for all, with most families putting aside a tiny sum every week for a precious new pair. The war had brought the added problem that the husband, who had to extend the life of the family's boots with constant repair, was probably now away in the army.

It took someone who worked and lived among the poor to see how differently their lives were affected by the war. Housing conditions were appalling by modern standards, with whole families squashed into one or two rooms – slums were commonplace features of most towns. Health was precarious, and instead of today's worry, obesity, causing problems, vast numbers of children and adults could only be described as skinny. Hundreds of thousands of women lived harsh lives, knowing that only charity would enable them to make ends meet; the welfare state was decades away. Sylvia spent the war years in an unceasing struggle against poverty and just about every social injustice, railing against the hardships inflicted by war.

With most suffrage groups immersed in mobilizing women into the war machine, the first two years of the war saw little tangible progress towards gaining the vote. The entire country seemed to be embroiled defending the nation, and the thought of an extra skirmish in hitherto intractable territory was difficult to entertain. Nevertheless, with organizations such as the NUWSS prominently organizing hospitals, supplying ambulances and supervising employment vacancies for women, pressure was discreetly maintained in the right quarters. Many of the former campaigners came into regular contact with officials, MPs and members of the establishment. They kept their finger on the political pulse and sniffed the air for opportunity. And in 1916, discussions about men in the trenches – and their vote – made the suffrage noses twitch. The war was playing havoc with the qualifications needed to register to vote: you had to be resident in the UK for twelve months prior to an election. Many men in the forces had already been overseas for much longer, and no one could say when they would be returning home. This war was like no other, its duration unknowable, and thousands of male voters were likely to be disenfranchised. Talk of changing the rules spurred the women into action – if change was proposed, why shouldn't it include votes for women?

Yet another committee was born, the Consultative Committee of Constitutional Suffrage Societies. The strategists dusted off their arguments and set to work, this time in a very different atmosphere from that in 1913. Women were now working throughout industry, often doing the job of a man with the vote;

others were risking their lives in France and other war zones, next to enfranchised men; and on the Home Front, the housewife was as vulnerable to the shells and bombs of enemy aircraft and ships as the registered male elector next door.

Initially the committee, despite its impressive name, was rebuffed by the government, but at the end of the year there was a new Prime Minister in No. 10 – and Lloyd George was relatively more sympathetic than his predecessor, Mr Asquith. The NUWSS gingered up its huge network of regional and local affiliated organizations, rustling up letters and petitions signed by teachers, clergymen, Poor Law guardians, mayors, trades unionists, postmasters, factory inspectors and just about anyone in public life. The Manchester and District Federation was especially proud of the fact that it could list 'all Trade Unions representing Women Munition Workers, and the most important of the Trade Unions in this area which are affected by Female labour'. It was democratic, non-militant and impressive work. Mrs Fawcett headed for Downing Street with a very large delegation, mostly war workers. And Mrs Pankhurst of the WSPU wasn't far behind, this time without a hammer in her handbag, to charm – perhaps wheedle – Lloyd George 'into speeding the legislation: "Whatever you think can be passed in the war circumstances we are ready to accept."'

The all-important Bill started on its way through Parliament and the House of Commons was more than usually well attended for the debate, though it cannot be said that MPs stood up to cheer the idea to the finishing line. Centuries-old views don't shift in a trice. The Victorian image of a fragile female having a fit of the vapours when faced with a ballot slip clearly flitted through some Members' minds: the Hon Member for the City, Sir Frederick Banbury, opined that 'Women are likely to be affected by gusts and waves of sentiment. Their emotional temperament makes them so liable to it'. He added a helpful illustration from America: 'The only woman – Miss Rankin, I think her name was – who had taken a seat in Congress in the United States, when a short time ago the question of whether there should be peace or war came up, became hysterical and could not give her vote.'

Nevertheless a considerable amount of the debate concerned women's contribution to the war effort, and there was much praise. But there were still dissenting views, especially from Mr Burdett-Coutts, who remained convinced that women should operate only in the domestic sphere where they exercised their 'moral superiority', as opposed to men's physical force exercised in warfare. Ramsay McDonald was ready to point out that such antiquated arguments appeared to be more relevant to fighting the battle of Waterloo than the war in progress:

> 'What is happening today is that the whole of the nations of Europe engaged in this war – men, women, and children; factory,

> workshop, and Army –are organised in one complete unity of social resistance, to defend themselves both by offence and by ordinary defence. When my Hon. Friend talks about the force that is being exercised in Flanders now, what is that force? The force made by women in British factories hundreds of miles away from the scene of battle.

Listening with suppressed excitement were the ladies in the Gallery, squashed in, hot, and still stuck behind that large brass grille. A month earlier they had scented that victory might be on its way. The dry exchange in July between Sir Alfred Mond and Mr Cory about the removal of the grille had passed almost without comment in the chamber. An assiduous MP had queried the cost, only to be told that as the war was costing £7 million a day 'the cost may not be important'. A symbolic moment, and here now was the real thing: legislation to vote.

The war forgotten for a moment, Rae Strachey of the NUWSS sat squeezed between her fellow campaigners:

> For all their certainty, the women . . . were desperately excited. Often, as some of them had sat there before, to hear their cause mocked at, or obstructed, or outvoted in the Chamber below, the scene was painfully impressive. Through the bars of the absurd

> little cage in which they were penned, they saw chiefly the tops of the heads of the legislators, but the atmosphere of excitement which pervaded the House was noticeable even so. . . . The tide had really turned, and when the time for the division came there were found to be but 55 opponents in the whole House, while 385, seven times their number, went into the other Lobby. This vote was larger than even the most optimistic had expected. It was victory without reserve.

It took another month to shift the dratted grille: 'the door of the cage is open', announced the Home Service Corps' publication *The Review*, which felt it necessary to burst into verse:

> Oh Had it but a tongue – what tales it might
> unfold,
> Of haughty looks, of lovely smiles, of manners
> bold,
> Victorian scenes and beauty frail, bonnet,
> fichu and farthingale.
>
> Outbursts of rhetoric have thrilled its heavy
> mass;
> And dreary arguments have chilled its
> lacquered brass.
> Words of wisdom deigned to woo it, beauty's
> eyes have glinted through it.

And Militants have chained their limbs against its side
Regardless of a scoffing world, who jeer or chide.
The storms of strife, the wordy wars no more will beat against its bars.

Its passing is inaugural of better things,
The clouds of superstition lift and daylight springs.
The barriers gone, our eyes – more bright – gaze, unimpeded, at the light.

It cost £5 to remove the grille. The Representation of the People Bill passed into law on 6 February 1918. The vote was granted to women over thirty who were householders; women over thirty who were the wives of householders; and women over thirty-five who were graduates. Limitations – but even so, in my home town the largest number of women in any single constituency in the country were now entitled to vote: in the December election over twenty-nine thousand women could now join forty-four thousand men at the Polling Stations in Sunderland. The NUWSS appealed to them to use their vote: 'You are now responsible for the good government of the Town and of the Nation.'

The MPs put women's contribution to the war effort at the forefront of their arguments for the Bill. Many felt that this enabled them to side-step the fact that they had denied the vote to women as ordinary citizens for so many years in peacetime. They were treating it as a prize rather than a right, or, as the writer Dorothy Peel put it a decade later, 'rather as a biscuit is given to a performing dog who has just done its tricks particularly well'.

Additionally, those who had worked in the munitions plants, in transport and in the engineering factories were mainly under thirty – the age at which they would qualify to vote. This was an immense irony – or else pointed to the success of the suffrage campaigners, regardless of wartime circumstances. More likely it was a complex combination of both: women's contribution to the war, the earlier campaigns both peaceful and militant – and a changing society.

For most it was a triumph that the vote had been won, even if partially and not on equal terms of qualification with men. But with fighting still raging on the front line, the Home Front could at least call one victory its own.

CHAPTER 21

VICTORY – WHAT NOW?

The vote was won, and so was the war. Victory and celebration went hand in hand with exhaustion and grief. The country was changed.

Unceremoniously, women were tipped out of their wartime jobs to make way for the returning men: their work had always been 'for the duration'. If life were to be returned to 'normal', the women would have to return to the home. Protest was brushed aside – those women who tried to keep their jobs were even met with cries of 'parasites', 'blacklegs' and 'limpets'.

In too many households there was no breadwinner coming back from the battlefield. Nor, for a generation of women, was there the traditional prospect of marriage and security. Was it some consolation that they knew they had shouldered responsibility and demonstrated skills as never before? That they had proved they could keep the country going, feed the voracious war machine and show courage in the face of danger? Only up to a point. They *could* do it – but it wasn't enough to shift the traditional shape of society – and for so many it was scant consolation in the face of bereavement and insecurity.

In late 1918, after the Armistice, there was no sign of equal pay, and only older women had gained the vote – thus excluding the majority of those who had worked in munitions, engineering, transport and the Land Army. Just a few professions were being opened up to women, but medical schools were about to exclude them again. And it was still possible for arguments about their 'mental, moral and physical inferiority' to be aired in public. Women still lacked political and economic clout.

Few realized how much they had done for future generations. They had become citizens. Even if the law, prejudice and convention were still obstacles to full recognition, they had taken great strides towards equality, leaving footprints all over traditional male-only territory. Not as queens, saints, martyrs or odd-balls but as ordinary women.

They had entered public life, been on the public stage, and in a century which was to see the rise of mass communications they had been pictured and filmed, put on cigarette cards, on posters and postcards, interviewed and written about for the first time in great numbers, whatever their background. They had left an indelible image as they went about their daily work. They had also written letters, kept diaries, taken photographs and begun to publish memoirs. Their personal lives had become entwined with national events, showing that the war couldn't have been won without them.

They also looked different. Skirts had risen considerably for the first time (though Queen Mary was to remain reassuringly swathed in Edwardian skirts for another decade until just her ankles appeared), and shorter skirts meant greater freedom. Wartime shortages had led to simpler fashions. The diversion of steel into ammunition had crumpled the corset industry. Wartime wages had stretched to cheap cosmetics: they were worn by the stars on the cinema screen, so why not by the girls on the High Street? And the fistful of hairpins needed to control a cottage-loaf hairstyle was tossed away in favour of the 'bob'. This was not ephemeral fashion, but a wholesale refiguring of the female image, especially for the millions of women who had decided that comfort and serviceability trumped wasp-waists and flapping petticoats. Not everyone threw off their old clothes immediately, but so great had been the numbers of female workers that they now represented a force for change, when formerly style and fashion had been the prerogative of royalty and the rich. Coco Chanel, the little black dress and trousers were waiting in the wings.

A 'total war' had brought about a partial victory for women, though many may have wondered if their efforts were going to be remembered. The difficulties in the bleak landscape of the immediate post-war years were not conducive to day-dreaming about an easy ride to greater opportunities and fairer rewards. Rules and regulations could be easily brushed aside in war, but attitudes and prejudices took time to change and remove. It wouldn't have cheered the members of Blyth Spartan Ladies – cup-winners – to learn how long it would take to get any kind of level playing field.

They would have liked to go on playing, but everything conspired against them. The munitions factories shed their workers in peacetime. The men's professional game resumed and few of the returning servicemen were ready for the change in their favourite game. Yet again, 'only for the duration' had progress been allowed. However, the Dick, Kerr's ladies were made of sterner stuff. In the next couple of years they had a highly successful set of matches including internationals. Playing in front of tens of thousands all over the country, they raised huge sums of money for ex-servicemen and also for the unemployed. Many disliked their success and their ability to pull in more spectators than the men's games. Hoary old arguments were trotted out about the unsuitability of a woman's body for such activity, and finally the Football Association banned women from using League pitches. St James's Park, scene of many of the successful charity games, was reclaimed by Newcastle's all-male management in 1921. Mr Frank Walt opined 'The game is not a woman's game and though it was permitted on professional grounds as a novelty arising out of women's participation in war work and as a novelty with charitable motives, the time has come when the novelty has worn off. . . .' The 'novelty' retired to playing fields and patches of grass for the next half century, kept in its place with regular defensive play by the male football world:

Daily Herald, 2 June 1950: Durham Football Association has refused the request of Mrs Joan Tizard, 30, a teacher at Moor Secondary School, Sunderland, to take an examination for a referee's certificate. Mr J.B. Blenkinsop, Secretary of the County Association, replied: 'I do not think we want women controlling men on the football field.'

Daily Herald 11 February 1963: Eleven year old Marlene Garner barred from her school football team (Slade Green Primary School). An officer for Bexley, Kent, School Sports Council said: 'We imposed the ban after complaints from schoolboy footballers who did not like being beaten by a team with a girl in it.' Former teammates said 'We did not like having a girl in our team because it made us feel cissies.'

Guardian, 28 December 1965: Britain's worst football team suffered yesterday the most humiliating defeat since it laid claim to the title by losing to the holders at the end of last season. The eleven men of Hillingdon Tyre and Battery Works from Poole in Dorset went down to the Shaftesbury

> Ladies F.C. by 5 goals to 7. Gallantry played no part in the outcome of the match at Bournemouth. Only a goal by a sympathetic referee, Mr John Lyttle, made the margin less hurtful to male feelings. The women, showing a brave disdain for shin-guards, were spurred on to victory by supporters shouting: 'Kiss him – that will slow him down.'

Where you may play, who you may play, how you play – all subject to decades of argument, with no one recalling the success of the munitionettes. The women's game is only now approaching the level of recognition it enjoyed almost a century ago.

The suffragettes and the munitionettes and the train cleaners and the postwomen would have smiled wryly, for football wasn't central to their lives. However, they would have shown a range of reactions to the result of their efforts in shaping today's lives. In 1918 there would have been incomprehension in the shipyards and steelworks that jobs for women wouldn't be an issue in the future: no one foresaw the disappearance of heavy industry, and with it a whole working-class culture. Equally, the women squawking for their maids to come back into service would never have dreamt that their children and grandchildren were going to have to open their own front doors. If any single item might symbolize the end of an era, it would be the frilly mob-cap now making a once-a-year appearance on the head of a pantomime dame.

In the postal service, the banking industry, office work and administration you cannot advertise for a specific gender these days. How that would have horrified the managers during the war, who carefully shepherded their workforce into segregated entrances, offices and canteens. And though shorthand and typing became the bane of many women in mid-century, the advent of the computer has resulted in both sexes pounding the keyboard.

The pioneers in the professions probably expected to face an uphill journey, gradually pushing down the boundaries. The court room saw the first female barrister four years after the war ended, with juries already including women, though it was another forty years before women would preside over county and high court.

It took seventy-five years for a woman to attain the post of professor of surgery, something for which Elsie Inglis and Louisa Garrett Anderson would have been ably qualified. The appearance of male nurses would have raised wartime eyebrows. A century on, the argument about who does what on the wards resembles the exchanges between the wartime VADs and the professionals. The Endell Street Hospital in Covent Garden has had a twenty-first-century makeover as a fashionable private club known as the Hospital.

The wartime women police had a narrow remit – confined to dealing with females. And so it remained for decades, as reported in the press in November 1949: 'A "Women's Scotland Yard" came into being yesterday when four Chief Inspectors began their duties in the Metropolitan Police Force.' The reason? 'Women have turned so much to crime in the past few years.' The moral panic about munitionettes' behaviour resurfaced time and again in various guises, with the only parts of the country without WPCs in 1950, Cumberland and Westmorland, fretting about the 'underlife of Kendal – which springs from the unmaidenly behaviour and irresponsibility of young girls and the presence in the town of a large number of long-distance lorry-drivers'. The problem was left unsolved, due to the conclusion that women police 'would be of no earthly use . . .'. Thirty-three more years to go until the first assistant chief constable took up her position in Merseyside.

In 1918 the royal family was perhaps more aware of possible change than any other family in the land. Most of their relatives had been tipped off their thrones and the revolution in Russia was spreading ideas about equality, though whatever the Members of the new House of Windsor felt they wouldn't be talking in public about it, even if they were now anxious to find a way of being less remote from their subjects. The job remained the same and continues so today: ceremonial, public appearances, polite conversation, smile and wave. A reigning monarch has the formidable role models of Elizabeth, Anne and Victoria to follow; a royal wife's role is still one of charm and charity, though now in an international glare of publicity – and skirt lengths are also still a matter of public discussion.

The formidable society hostesses who chaired hundreds of meetings and committees throughout the war would recognize many of the voluntary organizations today – and probably feel a bond with the spirit of public service and concern which still characterizes unpaid work, much of it done by women. They would be surprised to be asked whether they wished to be addressed as 'chair'. On the other hand, the Land Girls would find that the word 'farmer' still hasn't quite embraced females, though they would cheer with joy at the machines which deal with mud and mangel-wurzels. The WI is still going strong and Sir Hubert Parry's setting of Blake's poem 'Jerusalem' can be heard sung sweetly at their meetings: an echo of the wartime campaign for votes, for at a 1918 Suffrage Demonstration Concert, Millicent Fawcett had asked the composer if it could be the Women Voters' Hymn. He replied 'I wish it indeed might become the Women Voters' Hymn, as you suggest. People seem to enjoy singing it. And having the vote ought to diffuse a good deal of joy. So they should combine happily.'

The Anglican Church a century on would look familiar to Maude Royden. It's a battleground, with women having had to make their case for equality in a fog of ancient and mystical argument – which has at its heart much in common with the Football Association's worries about a female ref.

At least in politics a woman has been in charge as Prime Minister, making an unforgettable impact. However, the suffragettes would most likely be amazed that, the battle having been fought so hard, the chance to sit in the heart of Parliament is still not fully exploited by women today, nearly a hundred years after the first woman took her seat.

The entertainment world would look familiar to those who stared longingly at film stars in the early cinema and loved the popular music of the music halls. Film, television, theatre and rock concerts still feature female stars who live lives very different from those of their audiences and deliver dreams of glamour and success. And many today also follow in the tradition of entertaining the troops, heading for the theatres of war and linking the services with their families back home. One fundamental shift happened in World War II – Vera Lynn, 'The Forces' Sweetheart', told me adamantly that recruitment wasn't on the bill: 'My singing was nothing to do with the war – there were no war songs. I was taking a bit of home to them. Not like the First World War which was often "Go out there and fight, boys!" Nothing like that. They were just ordinary songs they were used to hearing when they were home.'

Curiously, the munitionettes, whose work seemed

most symbolic of the war effort, would possibly gasp at the sight of today's munitions employees working in the Primary Cartridge System and Igniter Assembly Rooms at Glascoed near Monmouth. And they would gasp in recognition. All women, all paying meticulous attention to the task in hand, all working with dangerous materials. The only ammunition plant in the country, it relies on women's nimble fingers to fill cotton bags with TNT, then sew them carefully, needle and thread carefully avoiding any grain of the explosive. They would also marvel at the safety systems, the welfare provisions and the wages – equal pay for equal work.

The memory of shunting around the heavy shells would be revived in the British Aerospace factory near Washington in the North-east, except that robots whirl and twirl the shells today. The munitionettes knew they could do the job, and thought they should. Among the 81mm shells, Tracey Burlinson from Sunderland is their heir: 'My mam wanted me to get a nice girlie job like a hairdresser, but this is the real thing. And I've got a passion for the job – it serves a purpose. Pack it here, send it further down the production line, then off it goes to the front line.'

Education has fuelled the achievements which the women of World War I could only dream about, backed by the law. Attitudes have been changed, prejudice challenged. Time and again, in the years since those on the Home Front went out to prove what they could do, women have been able to argue: 'If they could do it then, we can and we shall do it now.'

On the battlefield itself, there are women soldiers. Even the most progressive of the suffrage campaigners and social reformers wouldn't have expected this. They never advocated a woman taking up arms, and Flora Sandes was unique in her experience. Today, the British army still restricts areas which involve close combat, but this doesn't mean that women aren't in the thick of fighting. Helicopter pilots, women soldiers, RAF fast jet pilots, medics, transport and naval personnel can all find themselves under fire – and returning it. This, perhaps above all, shows the distance travelled in a century: women officially fighting on the front line, having proved themselves in battle on the Home Front.

CHAPTER 22

WE REMEMBER

Many vivid memoirs were published which chronicled the exploits of women who worked under fire and in terrible circumstances, only to be overtaken, inevitably, by the avalanche of military histories. The tactics and the strategy, the weaponry and the fighting: military history and generals' memoirs naturally concentrate on the battlefield. The contribution of women, on the Home Front and in support behind the front line, was either ignored or marginalised.

However, women's achievements resonated extraordinarily in family minds and memories, rather than in official records. In families, parents pass on social history – and women are central to the stories about the morning the Zeppelin came over the town or the day the letter arrived and the children watched as all the blinds were pulled down in the house. Diaries and letters still surface today which give a family yet another vignette of a world turned upside down. As the years pass, people recall 'My Granny made shells.' 'My aunt was in the VAD and went to France.' 'We've got a photograph of Dad's great-auntie in her pudding-basin hat and long skirt – in the Army!'

The names of those whose exploits caught the public imagination during the war have largely faded. Vesta Tilley, Elsie Inglis, Mabel Stobart, the Women of Pervyse, Flora Sandes and many more were nationally famous – but they failed to be included in the official record. Of Elsie Inglis it was said by Winston Churchill that she and her medical staff 'would shine forever in history' . . . she had an Edinburgh Hospital named in her memory – which is now no longer. Flora Sandes is still famous in Serbia but not in Britain; and Mrs Katherine Harley's grave in the Salonika Military Cemetery bears the inscription: 'The Generous English Lady and Great Benefactress of the Serbian people: A great lady. On your tomb instead of flowers the gratitude of the Serbs shall blossom there for your wonderful acts. Your name shall be known from generation to generation . . .' but not in her home country. Mabel Stobart and the Women of Pervyse achieved heroic wartime status and then gradually slipped from view, and Maude Royden lived a long and stimulating life with her name just echoing faintly today.

Two names have survived in popular memory, which point to the acceptable and traditional roles played by women: Mata Hari, the traditional image of an untrustworthy and seductive foreign female, embroiled in the murky world of espionage. And

Edith Cavell: a staunch and upright woman of great courage, whose efforts to help smuggle British soldiers out of occupied Belgium led to the Germans executing her. It is not to detract from her dignity and bravery to note that she fitted the traditional role for a woman in war: a nurse and a martyr – and after her death at the hands of a firing squad became a potent element of British propaganda. However, she stands alone on her handsome plinth in London, with no other women from that war alongside.

No one in 1914 would have had the slightest idea that a century later thousands and thousands of British people would be gathered at ceremonies the length and breadth of the country to remember. These islands have a long history of warfare, but apart from formal records and family tales passed down the years, there was no tradition then of remembering those who had died in war. Society's formalities knew neither poppies nor the words . . . at the going down of the sun we will remember them. Even as the men volunteered and the women headed for the munitions factories, there would have been incomprehension that a hundred years on, they would be the subject of a nationwide silent tribute.

That war shattered individual lives, changed society, and altered the way we think about conflict. Its details and its statistics still resonate. And the commemoration today still reflects many of the changes which that war brought.

My home town is a now a northern industrial giant in severe decline. The shipyards which worked flat-out in the war years are long gone, the pits only recalled by the odd winding-wheel as public ornament, and the myriad trades and skills which flowed from all this heavy, dirty work are merely family tales. For a century, though, the armed services, especially the army, have been a popular escape from a declining job market. And they still are today. The area's recruitment figures are exceptionally high. Even so, this does not quite explain why the Remembrance Commemoration is one of the largest in the country. This is not a 'military town', there is no large base nearby and the nearest it comes to a place in military history is a lively folk memory that it declared for Cromwell and the Parliamentarians, giving it yet another reason to keep its distance (twelve miles and a gulf of feeling) from that place called Newcastle, which was Royalist.

Yet every Remembrance Day sees a huge gathering at the local War memorial, one of the largest in the country. And in 2012 the stone column was added to with an entirely locally-funded memorial wall to those who have died in conflicts since WWII.

The ceremony has a sprinkling of establishment representatives, but it is very much an ordinary citizens' occasion, with a long list of local organisations determined to play a part.

And the march-past is testimony, not only to the

desire to remember, but to the changes which WWI initiated or accelerated in society:

The military bands leading the way are no longer all-male. The khaki of the artillery regiment includes khaki skirts of the women soldiers.

The local M.P.s – three of them – are women. The Mayor is a woman.

The majority of the scouts are women. The Fire Brigade, the Police, the Lifeboat crews, even the Colliery Band all have women marching.

The service has a woman in a cassock holding high the local St Cuthbert Cross. The Anglican Choir from the Minster is female. The Canon is called Sheila. And the two jets which roar across the sky right on time – come from a Training Squadron with women pilots.

We remember the men who died – and the women who fought on the Home Front.